HAIRDRESSING MANAGEMENT

Leo Palladino

and

John Perry

Stanley Thornes (Publishers) Ltd

First published in 1982 by Stanley Thornes (Publishers) Ltd
Educa House, Old Station Drive, off Leckhampton Road,
Cheltenham, Glos, GL53 0DN

British Library Cataloguing in Publication Data

Palladino, Leo
   Hairdressing management.
   1. Hairdressing — Management
   I. Title   II. Perry, John
   646.7'24'068   TT957

   ISBN 0–85950–338–0

Text typeset by Tech-Set, 3 Brewery Lane, Felling, Tyne & Wear.
Printed and bound in Great Britain by Ebenezer Baylis & Son Ltd,
Worcester and London.

Contents

Preface   vi

Chapter I
    Introduction to Hairdressing Management   1

Chapter II
    Opening a Salon   6

Chapter III
    The Salon Layout   24

Chapter IV
    Personnel Management and Social Relationships   33

Chapter V
    Work Study in the Salon   53

Chapter VI
    Procurement and Control of Salon Materials and Equipment 71

Chapter VII
    General Salon Administration   87

Chapter VIII
    Financial Accounting   99

Chapter IX
    Cost Accounting in the Salon   129

Chapter X
    Budgetary Control in the Salon   154

Appendix
    Specimen Hairdressing Apprenticeship Indenture   193

Index   199

Throughout this book a hairdressing salon has been used as an example of a business and the word 'salon' may be used interchangeably with 'clinic', 'shop', 'business', 'beauty salon', 'barber's', 'beauty parlour', 'hairdresser's', etc.

Preface

Hairdressing Management has been written for all students, and those interested in the subject of management. A careful study of the contents will show that at every level of management there is something to be applied in everyday working. The book covers all existing hairdressing and beauty therapy syllabuses and can be used to prepare for examinations in the subject.

Throughout the book the 'hairdressing salon' has been the example used but the subject matter also applies to the beauty salon and other business ventures. It should prove helpful to all those contemplating starting up a business.

Those wishing to make a special study should find sufficient to meet their requirements. Those who wish to 'dip into' the contents and use a part, or parts, for their daily needs are more than adequately catered for.

It is to be hoped that the book will encourage subject stimulation and further understanding and that study at higher levels might be initiated.

Our sincere thanks are extended to all those who helped to make this volume possible, and particularly for the continued encouragement of our publishers.

LEO PALLADINO
JOHN PERRY

CHAPTER I

Introduction to Hairdressing Management

The successful owner/manager of a modern hairdressing salon needs to have acquired skills additional to those possessed by a good professional hairdresser. The precise composition of these additional skills varies with each individual business but they are often grouped together under the general heading of management skills. The intention of this book is to outline, for both students and practising hairdressing managers, the commercial, administrative and managerial skills that are required for the effective and efficient operation of a modern hairdressing venture.

One of the many definitions of management is: 'the process by which people seek to achieve a desired objective despite the limitations imposed upon them'. It is, therefore, important that both the objectives of a salon and the limitations to the achievement of these objectives are identified by the salon management. The main objective is to satisfy the client but at the same time the business must be profitable so that owner(s) and employees may enjoy a standard of living compatible with that of the community they serve.

Although through the ages technical advances have been made in respect of the tools used by hairdressers, hairdressing is still a 'craft' and, given the technical facilities, the performance of a salon still depends on the expertise or otherwise of the staff. Before the beginning of the nineteenth century this limitation on technical ability was the major cause of hairdresser failure but one effect of the Industrial Revolution was to establish the hairdresser as a businessman and entrepreneurial manager rather than a village general factotum. In the last 200 years the majority of retail-oriented trades have developed into diversified multi-branch organisations that have either absorbed or proved too competitive for the small corner-shop enterprise. Hairdressing salons have, with a few exceptions, remained privately owned, although the initial investment needed and subsequent managerial expertise required has resulted in some salons being proprietorised as partnerships or private limited companies, rather than sole traders.

Many of the failures of hairdressing salons since 1960 are attributable to the inability of managers to keep up with the commercial and social changes resulting from the 'Social Revolution' that started at the end of the nineteenth century, but gained momentum particularly in the second half of this century. The majority of the changes are backed by statutory laws and, while identified as limitations within the context of our definition of management (paragraph 2 above), are frequently factors with which good owner/managers should have been able to cope.

1

The major changes that have come about as a result of this social revolution, and their impact upon the management of hairdressing salons, may be summarised under the following headings:

1. Clients' Requirements

The modern hairdresser is required by clients to be able to 'dress' hair to a variety of styles and, indeed, frequently to advise on the suitability of a particular style. Owner/managers must, therefore, not only acquaint themselves with the current styles but also ensure that their employees are familiar with them. New hair styles frequently require new methods and possibly new equipment or tools; thus management has to review continually the methods and equipment employed and make sure that employees are familiar with their operation.

With the ease of transportation available to present-day clients, many more hairdressing establishments are readily accessible to them to 'service' their requirements. Hairdressing managers consequently face increased competition and, therefore, in addition to possessing technical competence, must pay attention to employee/client relationships, competitive pricing, salon environment and work-planning to ensure that appointments are commenced and completed on time and to the clients' satisfaction. Statutory legislation, such as the Trade Description Act, Health and Safety at Work Act and Employers' Liability Act, make it possible for a client to obtain redress through the Courts when a hairdresser fails to fulfil what were previously only moral obligations.

2. Employees' Rights

The main effect of the social revolution previously referred to has been the change in the relationship between employer and employee. In hairdressing, owing to the high proportion of owner hairdressers compared with those employed by others, the change from 'dictatorial employer' to (almost) 'dictatorial employee' has not, at least on the surface, been traumatic. By the late 1970s when trade unions possessed negotiating rights for over 50 per cent of the nation's employees, there was no union representation on the Hairdressing Undertakings Wages Council which had statutorially evolved from the National Joint Industrial Council for Hairdressing established under the Trade Boards Act 1909. Thus, the statutory minimum wages and conditions of employment for hairdressing employees, who at this time numbered over 160 000, were set by representatives of the Employers' Association and non-union hairdressing employees appointed by the Department of Employment.

The changes in employer/employee relationships within the hairdressing industry have resulted from the indirect effects of the social revolution rather than from radical changes within the structure and organisation of the industry itself. Such changes have been slow to evolve and their impact upon an individual salon has not always been recognised by the responsible owner/manager, with the result that remedial management decisions and actions have often been both late and ineffective. The loss of male hairdressers in the 1950s and 1960s was largely to industries offering high wages to unskilled employees, as well as fringe benefits, such as pension schemes, generous sick-pay and allowances, etc., which were not offered by hairdressing employers. The loss of skilled employees frequently caused considerable deterioration in the service provided if the salon management had not, through staff development or employment of part-timers, provided adequate cover for such eventualities.

With attractive alternative employment being readily available it is up to the management to foster a contented staff. This may be achieved by developing friendly personal relationships, both between management and employee, and also among employees. Given opportunities to develop and use initiative, employees may find that more highly paid employment will become less attractive, provided their earnings are adequate.

Much attention was given by successive governments in the 1960s and 1970s to the relationship between employers and employees. Legislation was passed to end the situation whereby an employer could dismiss or lay off staff without providing adequate compensation. The following are the principal Acts that came into force during this period:

Contracts of Employment Act 1963 and 1972
Redundancy Payments Act 1969
Equal Pay Act 1970
Sex Discrimination Act 1975
Employment Protection Act 1975

This legislation has resulted in the need for the managements of small businesses to think twice before engaging staff because of the high cost of redundancy payments to employees that may have to be dispensed with because of adverse future trading conditions. By the late 1970s, in addition to the National Insurance contribution which an employer had paid in increasing proportion since 1944 for each employee, a further contribution had to be paid to the State Pension Scheme. Managements were, therefore, increasingly made aware of the importance of efficient staff use and the high costs associated with over-manning. This factor has, however, to be balanced against the loss of clientele which can result from under-staffing.

3. Environmental Controls

The formalisation of the local government structure at the end of the nineteenth century not only produced an authority for public health administration and town and country planning but also provided a means of enforcing central government legislation intended to improve the environment for the entire community. A mass of legislation has followed, both national and local, which compels hairdressing managements to seek the approval of local authorities before proceeding with other than minor developments, and which provides for inspection to ensure adherence to the statutory requirements. The majority of inspections arise from complaints from clients and other interested third parties and may, therefore, be regarded as an indication of inadequate or unsympathetic management.

4. Administrative Responsibilities

Nineteenth-century hairdressers, in common with their predecessors, were generally able to regard their receipts from clients as profit or personal wages, such expenses or overheads as were incurred being regular and easily identified, for example, rent and staff wages. Provision for these could be made by simple budgeting, i.e. by keeping separate cash floats for specific purposes. The effectiveness of such simple control has been eroded during the last hundred years by a number of factors:

(a) Developments in hairdressing equipment and hairdressing service. The equipment now used in hairdressing, e.g. dryers, furniture and fitments, requires both maintenance and eventual replacement. Materials are used in many of the services provided, e.g. shampoos, conditioners, bleaches and setting lotions. There is, therefore, a need to develop control systems which include provisioning, purchasing, stock-keeping, issuing and usage procedures. The modern hairdresser also has to control overhead expenditure in respect of other services employed, e.g. electricity, gas and telephones. Staff have to receive training, and the competition from other hairdressing establishments has to be combated by continual advertising.

(b) Diversification. The hairdressing salon has often gradually developed as a retail outlet for products associated with hairdressing. With the increase in the range and quantity of such products, retailing has become an important subsidiary activity, but frequently hairdressers have not appreciated the problems associated with retailing. For example, the capital needed to maintain stock levels may be excessive if the turnover is slow.

(c) Statutory requirements
(i) *Rates.* The services provided by Local Authorities are largely funded by rates which are effectively a taxation of occupied premises. The amount paid is dependent upon the size and location of the premises.
(ii) *PAYE (Pay As You Earn).* Since 1944 an employer has been required to deduct the income tax from employees' wages. The deductions have to be recorded on specified records and forwarded on a monthly basis to the Inland Revenue.
(iii) *National Insurance and State Pensions.* Employers are required to deduct National Insurance and State Pensions contributions from employees' wages and also to contribute to such funds. These deductions have also to be recorded and sent to the Inland Revenue monthly.
(iv) *VAT (Value Added Tax).* With the introduction of Value Added Tax in the early 1970s it became mandatory for all traders to maintain records of both purchases and sales upon which VAT was charged, such records forming the basis of the quarterly return to H.M. Customs and Excise who were the designated VAT collectors. It was also the job of H.M. Customs and Excise to check the VAT returns with the original records and this effectively compelled all traders to maintain up-to-date records of transactions, i.e. books of accounts.

(v) *Owner's Income Tax.*   For the purpose of the assessment of the owner's personal income tax liability by the Inland Revenue it is necessary for the previous year's accounts to be acceptable to that authority. This requirement may be met by employing a suitably qualified person (an accountant) to prepare the final accounts. In all but the smallest concerns however it is necessary to maintain ongoing records of all financial transactions to both substantiate and aid the preparation of final returns.

The following chapters identify the business issues to which a salon's management should address itself if it is to be successful. The impact of each of these issues varies with each salon and the trading environment at any particular time; consequently the suggested procedures and controls outlined can only be of a general nature. It should be noted that many of the topics dealt with in a single chapter have been the subject of numerous specialised books on that particular discipline. In such cases, this book should only be regarded as a practical salon manager's guide and not a comprehensive textbook on that subject.

To aid understanding of the suggested control procedures, worked examples are included which refer to a hypothetical salon called 'Histyles'. It is emphasised that Histyles is entirely fictional and is the authors' 'model' of the average salon of the future with a fully developed control system.

CHAPTER II

Opening a Salon

The ownership of one's own business is a natural aim to be cherished by every employed person, particularly when the principal business function is performed in its entirety by that employed person. Many employees in the industry find themselves in such a situation and at first sight the transition to ownership appears to be an easy and attractive proposition. The decision to terminate one's employment and open one's own salon is often prompted by such events as a disagreement with colleagues, supervisor or manager, or by the misguided ideas expressed in the sentence, 'I am earning X pounds of takings of which I am receiving less than half; if I were working for myself it would all be mine.'

The realistic approach to opening a business involves a careful assessment of all the relevant factors, whether they are commercial, professional, environmental or the personal preferences of the prospective owner. Such an assessment will distinguish practical propositions from impractical ideals and also highlight the advantages and disadvantages to each of the many alternatives available.

The first consideration is the siting of the salon since this often determines the type of salon, its clientele, its layout and the staffing requirements. Salons may be classified as follows:

1. The City Salon

A salon located in a shopping centre, where prospective clients are constantly passing, is usually a busy one, and can expect both passing and regular local trade. Salons situated at or near rail, bus or air terminals generally have passing or casual trade, but demands from locally residing clients for the excellent but often expensive services are not excluded. It must be remembered that with terminal-sited salons demand often fluctuates with the peaks and troughs of travel periods; thus the salon systems and organisation have to be aligned with this environment. Salons situated away from the central points of city conurbations, i.e. those on the outskirts of large cities and towns or in the centre of smaller suburban towns, depend less on attracting passing clients and pay greater attention to satisfying the specific individual needs of regular clients who often reside in the locality. In recent years, due to the large increase in city-centre installation costs, there has been a general divergence of salons outwards towards the suburban or country areas, but it is still a popular concept that the best salons are only to be found in the costliest areas of cities. Although many of the most prestigious salons are still situated in the big city centres it is doubtful whether these salons have a complete monopoly of the avant-garde, high fashion or highly skilled workmanship.

2. The Country Salon

Even in times of escalating overheads, the country salon usually maintains a more leisurely pace of work than its city counterpart, with the result that the client/hairdresser relationship is often more informal and friendly. As well as this, there is traditionally a lower staff turnover than in the city salons, which enables the hairdresser to give individual attention to the specific require-ments of each client, particularly those who regularly utilise the salon.

3. Seaside or Holiday Resort Salons

Salons of this type are subjected to a greatly varying range of customer numbers. The high season of many resorts produces a busy and sometimes rushed period of business. If business is not conducted satisfactorily through-out the peak times then the turnover for the year may be considerably reduced. A clientele largely composed of local residents, who may be attracted by seasonally adjusted charges, will often produce more consistent demand, and a better standard of hairdressing and working environment.

Salons of holiday camps and camping sites offer a fluctuation of business, from good to nothing at all at different times of the year. Often, city or town hairdressers take working vacations in these resorts or camps where demand grows at peak periods. The services of such trained hairdressers coupled with the retention of ex-employees on a part-time basis can help overcome the staffing problems that large fluctuations in demand create. Some resort salons open for peak periods only and close at the end of the season. In reality it is not always economical or practical to operate a single business in such a manner as many overheads are incurred whether the business is open or not and employed hairdressers may be reluctant to accept temporary employment only.

4. The Store Salon

This offers another variation in trading. The main feature of this type of salon is that it relies on its potential clientele being attracted to the store by other departments. It would be unfair to suggest that this is its sole source of custom. As with all other types of salon, the manner of conducting business and the standards of service offered will determine how many clients will return on a regular basis. The goodwill and good name of the salon are valuable assets, no matter where it is sited, but it is especially important for the store salon since an unsatisfactory salon will reflect on the store as a whole. In such circum-stances, it would be unlikely that the store would extend the salon's franchise or privilege.

5. The Hotel Salon

The hotel salon is designed to cater specifically for its guests. Its popularity may encourage a larger following from outside the hotel if this is desired or encouraged. There are many advantages for those running such a salon. They may be part of a larger group, with the support this may offer; they may be specially featured in all hotel publicity; and they are usually sited in areas where high turnover can be expected. These salons often benefit from a high standard of salon layout and equipment, to fit the hotel décor and image. The spread of business outside normal working hours may additionally be conducive to the employment of part-time staff.

6. The Hospital Salon

Like other institutional-type salons, the hospital salon usually caters for the 'resident' clientele for which it is designed. This type of salon offers good business prospects almost from the beginning. How well it prospers is again dependent on the quality of service and the numbers that are encouraged to return. Once established a steady income may be relied on, even though in some salons of this type the variety of work may be restricted.

7. The Mobile Salon

This has been one of the most abused types of business since it can be conducted without authority and, to the unscrupulous, it may offer an opportunity to provide a poor standard of workmanship to a continual series of new clients from different areas. It has also allowed safety, hygiene and, frequently, taxation regulations and laws to be ignored. Many mobile salons do conduct their affairs in an ethical and professional manner and as such are reputable and acceptable business ventures. For the aged and sick they offer a service in the homes of clients, something which is often very difficult for the sited salons to do on an economical basis. It is important for those contemplating starting this type of business not to underestimate the cost of running the vehicle and assessing the time in moving from one house to another. If a 'round' can be planned then a saving in time, money and effort can be made.

8. Home Hairdressing

Home hairdressing is widely practised on a limited scale both by ex-salon hairdressers and on a part-time basis by employed hairdressers. The conducting of such ventures is illegal in most countries, including Great Britain, since planning authorities will not usually authorise the conversion of residential premises to comply with the minimum statutory standards of hygiene and safety. The home hairdresser, if able to obtain such authority, has an initial advantage since premises have been established at little cost and a drain on profits in rent and other overheads has been avoided. For practical purposes such home salons which are authorised should be considered as 'Country Salons'.

An important secondary consideration is the market potential for a salon in a particular siting since, with the exception of the mobile salon, all are dependent upon attracting clients to the business premises. In modern times it is possible to employ a market research organisation to conduct a survey, but this course of action is expensive and it is doubtful whether such organisations are experienced in assessing the potential for a service industry which depends very much on the individual ability of the employees as well as on the requirements of the intended clients. Perhaps the best way to assess the viability of a salon in a particular area is to address the issue from the point of view of the clients, with particular reference to their main requirements and how these needs are being catered for. In general, clients are influenced by the following factors:

1. The accessibility of a suitable salon, whether this is:
   (a) in close proximity to the client's residence or place of work, or in a location where they have time to enjoy the service.
   (b) easily reached, both in terms of time and expense, i.e. affords adequate car-parking or is regularly served by public transport.
2. The standard of professional service sought, as compared with the standard of service being provided by existing hairdressers.
3. The price charged for the service.
4. The ability to obtain the services of a hairdresser without either a long wait in the salon or having to make an appointment in advance.

If these requirements are not being provided then a further salon is likely to be a practical proposition. However, whether the requirements can be met by the prospective new owner is dependent upon the resources available to that person. Initially, the principal resource required is the finance to obtain premises, equip the salon, purchase stock, pay staff, advertise, etc. The next consideration is, therefore, the finance or capital available to the potential owner or owners of new business ventures.

FINANCE AND PURCHASE

Traditionally, hairdressing salons have been capitalised by *Sole Traders,* i.e. individuals providing from their own resources the complete amount of finance to commence and maintain a business. All profits made by the concern are the property of the individual owner and, equally, all losses made by the business are the responsibility of the owner. Personal finance to capitalise a business can be obtained from:

1. The accumulated savings from earnings in past employment.
2. Personal loans and bequests received by the prospective owner.
3. Loans or mortgages – which involve the payment of interest, thus reducing the profitability of the enterprise.

In practice, the individual hairdresser who aspires to proprietorship suffers from a shortage of capital and is restricted to opening a salon which involves little initial capital outlay. It is probable that both the premises and much of the equipment would have to be rented or, alternatively, that the new owner would enter into a franchise agreement with a store (a right conferred by an organisation to an individual trader to provide a particular service to the exclusion of other similar traders), hotel or public authority. In the latter case, it is likely that the franchise agreement would place such restrictions on the hairdresser that he or she would be effectively a manager and not an owner or sole trader enjoying the advantages of that position. These are as follows:

1. Independence of action.
2. Self-accountability and privacy of the financial status of the business from all except the tax authorities.
3. Expansion need only be pressed to the point where the market is adequately supplied.

No formal procedures are required to set up in business, except:

1. If non-relatives are employed the business must be registered with the Local Authorities.
2. Planning permission must be obtained if the premises have not previously been used as a salon or if an external expansion of the salon area is contemplated.
3. The business has to be registered under the Registration of Business Names Act if the name of the business is other than the true name of the proprietor.

In addition to the disadvantage of having limited capital which restricts the initial scope of the business, sole traders often suffer from the following:

1. Long working hours and little time off for holidays.
2. Difficulties in maintaining the business in the event of personal sickness.
3. A slow growth rate since expansion has to be financed from profits.
4. Specialisation may be limited to the field of the proprietor's experience and expertise.

To overcome these disadvantages, many new ventures are financed and owned by more than one person. The most common is a *Partnership*. This can be established without any formal agreement between the partners, in which case, if a dispute arises between the partners or the death or retirement of one of the partners occurs, the provisions of the Partnership Act 1890 apply.

Many of the provisions of this Act, whilst being fair and reasonable to the surviving partners or executors of a deceased partner, are frequently detrimental to the continuance of the business. It is, therefore, advisable for individuals entering into a partnership to draw up, or have drawn up by a solicitor, a Partnership Agreement, the provisions of which should include:

1. The rights and duties of each partner.
2. The amount of each partner's initial contribution to the capital of the business.
3. The division of profits and losses.
4. The limit of each partner's drawings in anticipation of profits.
5. The salaries (if any) to be paid to the partners.

6. The rate of interest (if any) to be allowed on capital.

7. The rate of interest (if any) to be charged on partners' withdrawals.

8. The location and availability to partners of the financial records relating to the business.

9. The basis of valuing 'goodwill' on the death or retirement of a partner.

10. The circumstances which shall dissolve the partnership and the period of notice to be given by a retiring partner.

11. The right of one or more partners to introduce a new partner without the consent of all the partners.

12. An arbitration clause which provides for the submission of any dispute to an arbitrator.

The advantages of a partnership are:

1. Increased initial capital offers a greater choice of the type of salon to be opened or acquired as a going concern.

2. With greater capital available, the salon can be developed and expanded more quickly.

3. The partners between them may possess both the professional hairdressing expertise and the commercial and managerial skills required to develop and maintain a successful business.

4. Work and responsibility can be shared.

5. Provision for sickness and holidays can be made and with expansion to include ownership of other salons, managers will be available from within the parent organisation.

6. In the case of smaller concerns no additional staff need initially be employed.

7. The affairs of the business are private except to the partners and tax authorities.

Partnerships do, however have the following disadvantages:

1. The partners have unlimited liability for the debts of the business except if one or more of the partners are limited partners, in which case the extent of their liability is limited to the stated amount of capital shown in the registration with the Register of Companies under the Limited Partnership Act 1907. In practice, since the limited partner may not, during the existence of the partnership, draw out or receive back any part of his initial contribution or enter into management of the concern, very few limited partnerships have been formed.

2. Profits as well as duties have to be shared.

3. Each and every partner is equally responsible for every decision made and, consequently, if disagreements are to be avoided which may prejudice the continuance of the partnership, the decision-making process is often protracted.

4. A partnership may be adversely affected by the death of a partner whose share may be withdrawn to pay beneficiaries. The impact of such an occurrence may be reduced by the taking out of life assurance policies on each other by the original partners.

In modern times there has been a tendency to form *Limited Companies,* normally *Private Limited Companies,* rather than partnerships, principally to obtain limited liability for the owners and to ensure a continuance of the business upon the withdrawal of one of the founders. On balance, the Private Limited Company is the capital structure most appropriate to the hairdressing industry; its restriction on the number of members or shareholders (from 2 to 50 persons including employees and ex-employees), coupled with the restriction on the right to transfer shares, enables the founders to retain control of the company, even in times of capital expansion by ensuring that new capital is balanced by an equal capitalisation of retained profits. In such circumstances, the controlling capital is the original investment made by the founder members whose combined vote can guarantee the positions of the elected executive directors, normally themselves. In theory, the expansion to a *Public Limited Company,* where shares can be made available to the general public, should only occur when a large capital injection is required. In such instances, the possibility exists that control of the company may pass to the new shareholders, whose objectives may not be in accordance with those of the founder members. For this reason, together with the fact that hairdressing is a personal industry whose success is strongly dependent upon a good client/ hairdresser relationship, with direct recourse to upper management in the case of discord or dispute, very few hairdressing concerns are public companies.

The advantages of the Limited Company over partnerships are:

1. Each member or shareholder has limited liability for debts incurred by the salon(s).
2. A larger number of members can produce a larger initial capital.
3. Executive responsibility can be designated to elected members, thus eliminating the delays associated with collective decision-making.
4. The company has a separate legal identity from its individual members and, therefore, members may contract with the company or sue it. In practice this allows members to receive fringe benefits enjoyed by employees in addition to a salary as an executive of the company.
5. The company continues to exist regardless of changes in its membership.
6. The statutory regulations which require books of accounts to be kept and returns of capital investment and trading results to be made make the concealment of irregularities more difficult.

The disadvantages of a Limited Company are:

1. The costs of formal registration and preparation of the statutory documentation i.e.

    (a) The Memorandum of Association.

    (b) The Articles of Association.

    (c) Statutory Declaration that the Company Acts have been complied with.

    (d) Payment of Registration fees based on the nominal capital value of the proposed Company.

    (e) Obtaining from the Registrar of Companies a Certificate of Trading.

2.   The field of activity is restricted to the areas described in the Memorandum of Association.

3.   The content of year-end financial accounts must be in accordance with statutory requirements.

4.   The accounts submitted to the Registrar of Companies are available upon payment of a small fee to the public at large.

5.   Members are not entitled to a share in the management of the salon unless they have been elected as directors by their fellow members.

It is arguable that the capital available to the prospective owner or owners is the most important factor in determining what type of salon is initially obtained. It is also important that there is a demand for the services of such a hairdressing establishment within the selected area. A mobile salon which requires comparatively little initial capital, is unlikely to be successful if the proprietor restricts operations to areas which are already served by efficient local salons. The blend of capital available and market potential may be called the strategic factors. There are, in addition, many tactical factors which are dependent not only on the strategic decisions but also upon the interaction of other tactical factors. This interaction of both strategic and tactical factors is discussed below.

Whether to purchase an existing salon or to open an additional salon is probably one of the first decisions to be made. The former alternative is dependent upon a salon being available for takeover at a price within the capital available to the prospective buyer. The latter is dependent upon the availability of suitable premises and the potential client-demand being able to justify another salon. A compromise is often made by taking over a going concern which for some reason or other has been allowed to run down or is not meeting the market requirement. This type of business often attracts the first-time buyer.

Taking over an existing business which has run down involves payment for the fixtures, fittings, lease and, perhaps, 'goodwill'. A sum is usually asked which covers most of these points. The business may be advertised privately in the trade press or it may be dealt with by a business agent. If on viewing the salon it is considered to be in an area requiring an enterprising salon, that there are no serious problems which cannot be overcome, and that the type of work that may be required in that particular area can be supplied, then an approach may be made to the vendors or agent, with a view to making an offer for the business.

Making an offer for a business should not be done until a fair assessment of its worth has been made. This involves careful consideration and examination of the business. When the facts are gathered they may then be explored to ascertain whether the business is what is required by the potential buyer, or if it could be adapted to meet his requirements.

A number of questions need to be asked when considering buying an existing business. First, just what is being purchased? What does the sum of money being paid actually buy? Is it for freehold or leasehold premises, fixtures, fittings and stock, goodwill or the living accommodation that might go with the business? It is usually necessary and advisable for a solicitor to act on behalf of the buyer who, in turn, usually deals with the vendor's solicitor.

The solicitor does the following on behalf of his client:

1. Ascertains that the premises are, in the case of a sale, the vendor's to sell as freehold, or if the premises are to be leased or rented that all aspects of any lease or rental agreement are acceptable to his client.

2. Obtains a complete list or inventory of the fixtures, fittings and equipment which are included as part of the sales transaction.

3. Agrees a method of evaluating stock-in-hand as at the date of transfer.

4. Ensures the exclusion of the purchaser from responsibilities for any debts or charges incurred by the business prior to the date of transfer of ownership.

In addition, the majority of solicitors advise the prospective buyers, particularly first-time owners, on the commercial viability of the proposed venture. Even in instances where the solicitor can see no obvious detrimental features from the facts presented to him, he may advise:

1. The obtaining of an independent valuation of the assets offered for sale.

2. The means to validate the accuracy of the trading data supplied by the vendor or their agents.

As a result of these reviews, the physical status of the assets offered for sale, whether these are premises, fixtures and fittings or salon equipment can be established. Additionally, information relating to the current business or trading position of the salon will also be available to the prospective buyer, i.e. the volume and regularity of present trade, the hairdressing services requested, the total turnover and the cost of maintaining and operating the salon etc. Analytical investigations will not, however, identify the reaction of current employees to the takeover or the impact upon the salon's client relationships which may result from staff changes.

If it is the new owner's intention to employ staff it is usually prudent to retain the existing employees. In such cases provision must be made for both the employee and employer to assess their compatibility. An opportunity can usually be made for the new owner to interview each member of the staff whose continued employment is contemplated, in order to establish mutual agreement on future conditions of employment, the employee's personal development within the salon and acceptance of any envisaged changes in working methods, salon layout etc. By pursuing such a course of action a large amount of uncertainty is removed from all parties affected by the transfer with the result that the impact upon the clientele is minimised. It is important for the new owners to appreciate that many of the clients who patronise the salon do so because they have a particularly good rapport with an individual hairdresser. If that hairdresser terminates their employment with the salon it is probable that the client will either follow the hairdresser to the next place of employment or transfer their custom to another salon as an expression of disagreement with the new management that caused the rapport to be broken. New salon methods and techniques, changed salon layouts and certainly price increases which may result from a change in ownership will also tend to alienate longstanding salon patrons from the new owners; but these factors may not deter the clients from patronising 'their' hairdresser who is in complete concurrence with the changes.

The circumstances may be such that the new owners have such a large personal following that they do not require the patronage of more than a small proportion of the present clientele or they do not require the services of more hairdressers, particularly if they are not professionally competent to provide all the services to be offered by the newly structured salon.

In instances where the new owner does not intend to employ the current staff, it is necessary for the vendor to terminate the employees' contracts. This involves:

1. In the case of apprentices, a transfer of indentures to a new employer if one can be found.

2. The payment of separation or redundancy money to staff with more than two years' continuous full-time service.

In such circumstances the current turnover shown by the vendor's records has little significance for the new owners and any amount paid for 'goodwill' to the vendor would be purely gratuitous. It is appropriate, therefore, for the nature and significance of 'goodwill' to be clearly understood by all prospective owners.

In accountancy terms, goodwill is considered to be an intangible asset and is the difference in the capital outlay required to purchase a business compared to the sum of the values of the tangible assets obtained, e.g. land, buildings, fixtures and fittings, equipment, stock-in-trade etc. Vendors frequently claim with some justification that considerable time and money has been spent in building up the clientele and a good name within the community. It is also claimed that the cost of engaging and training a competent staff that has been incurred by the vendor should be recovered from the purchaser. The goodwill charge is, however, often inflated in view of the market conditions prevailing; e.g. if the salon is situated in a busy shopping-centre where no other business premises are available for sale, or planning permission is not likely to be given for another salon, a number of potential purchasers are likely to be competing for ownership of the business.

In practical terms, goodwill can be regarded as a negotiable factor which is variable in value, not only between the vendor and a particular purchaser but also between purchasers. Each purchaser should consider the following when evaluating goodwill:

1. The volume of 'passing trade' that is attracted to the salon, due to the salon's siting, compared to the volume of trade which is principally of a personal nature between the clients and the present owners or staff. If the latter condition prevails, and the staff are to be retained, it is a positive factor but if the former, it is a negative factor.

2. The business style and methodology employed by the present owners is similar to that of the prospective purchaser.

3. An assessment of the amount of additional business which may be attracted to the salon by the new ownership, whether this is of a personal or general nature.

The value of goodwill included in the price charged for an operating salon is usually beyond the capital available to the newcomers to proprietorship. It is also extremely unlikely that a newcomer would have the opportunity or capital to create a purpose-built salon and, therefore, it is usually necessary to convert existing premises. If the premises are rented, concurrence to the alterations will be required from the owners of the building and also the Local Planning Authority. In general, this type of acquirement can be achieved with a lower capital outlay than the purchase of a going concern, the cost of refitment being more than balanced by the saving achieved through not having to pay for goodwill.

PUBLICITY

It is apparent from the above paragraphs that any change of ownership will affect the volume of business conducted, and in the case of new salons it may be weeks or months before the full potential volume of business will be reached. During this period of time most of the overhead expenses, e.g. rent and rates, will be incurred to the same extent as when the salon is fully occupied. In addition, expenditure will be necessary on an above average level to advertise the salon. Once new clients have attended the salon they must be encouraged to return. This will depend in part upon the standard of service being offered, the type of staff and their abilities, and the prices charged. Aesthetic, hygienic and comfortable surroundings will also feature high on a list of factors that impress clients. The presentation of services forms an important part of the establishment of a changed business as well as the continuation of an existing one, since the recommendation of existing clients is one of the best advertisements for a salon and also the cheapest.

A regular, satisfied clientele who recommend the salon to their friends can often maintain the required level of business without any advertising being necessary to attract the general public. Even when this happy state exists, the presence of a salon should be indicated by well-placed signs in prominent positions and aesthetic arrangements of the salon window-displays and reception areas made in order to attract passing trade.

When a new salon commences business it is usually necessary to advertise formally the complete range of services available within the salon. Often it is within the capabilities of the hairdressing staff to display services. Alternatively, commercial firms may be contracted to deal with presentation. Advertising through newspapers, magazines, television, cinema and local radio is a useful means of presentation of salon services to large numbers of people. Letterheads, appointment cards, shows, talks, demonstrations and competitions are other means of presentation. Direct canvassing in the locality affords a means of communicating information, particularly when supported with neat well-designed brochures. Whatever means are used to advertise the salon's name and services, many people require a personal recommendation before they will give it their patronage.

EXPANSION

With the establishment of one successful salon the ambitious owner will be encouraged to extend and expand his business to other sites when space becomes a critical factor. Care must be taken, however, not to assume that the subsequent salons will produce similar results. Indeed, it is likely that the initial trading results will compare unfavourably with those obtained by the first salon, unless it is possible to employ hairdressers with a large personal following. For the same reason, if experienced employees are transferred to the second salon from the first, it is likely that the latter will suffer a downturn in business until additional clients can be attracted to replace those who have transferred their patronage, with their favourite hairdresser, to the second salon. In this respect, it is disadvantageous if the salons are only a short distance apart. It is, however, an advantage to be within easy reach of a sister-salon when demand, coupled with staff absence, necessitates an immediate source of replacement hairdressers.

The development of one or more salons into a chain of salons is more likely to be successful when there are close links between the salons. When they are sited near to each other the goodwill of one salon may be passed on to the next. It is also easier for one salon to help another. Each salon in the chain develops its own identity within the set-up, yet derives much of its stability from the others.

Other advantages of multi-salon or chain-type businesses are: an established pool of staff from which others may be trained; the benefits of bulk purchases of materials and equipment; the ability to deal with problems and difficulties which for the single salon unit could be serious; the blanket effect of covering a wider area and becoming better known, perhaps more quickly; and better career prospects for all concerned.

The disadvantages involved are: the initial expense of starting each salon; possible overstretching of resources; a thinning-out of skilled staff; becoming more anonymous and losing the individual approach required by many clients, and allowing the chain to become too large to manage.

The single salon has its advantages in that it becomes a personal, individual unit; it can cater specifically for a specialised clientele, perhaps more easily; it can be small enough to be overseen and managed comfortably. Often the owner or manager becomes the central key figure. Anything happening to that

FIG. 2.1   Business Plan — Histyles Dec. 19-6 to Nov. 19-7 (All values £)

Income/Expenditure	Dec. 19-6	Jan. 19-7	Feb. 19-7	March 19-7	April 19-7	May 19-7	June 19-7	July 19-7	Aug. 19-7	Sept. 19-7	Oct. 19-7	Nov. 19-7	Cash Totals
1. *Initial Capital* Capital Input 4000													
Less: Fixed Assets 1800 Stock 1400													
Cash at Bank 800													800
Planned Cash Balance from Previous Month	800	1590	750	400	290	760	1090	990	1620	1485	85	465	
2. *Plus Receipts* Salon Services Retail Sales	4000 2540	1500 200	2000 250	3500 600	4000 600	3500 600	4000 600	3000 750	3500 250	3500 600	4000 1000	5000 2010	41 500 10 000

3. Less Expenditure

	1	2	3	4	5	6	7	8	9	10	11	12	
Stock Purchases	1200	180	200	400	500	500	500	500	600	1200	1800	1400	8 980
Employment Costs	2000	1600	1600	1700	2100	2000	2000	2000	2000	2000	2200	2500	23 700
Drawings	500	400	400	400	400	800	400	400	400	400	400	600	5 500
Rent	1500	—	—	1500	—	—	1500	—	—	1500	—	—	6 000
Insurance	200	—	—	—	900	—	—	—	—	—	—	—	1 100
Rates	—	220	—	—	—	—	—	—	280	—	—	—	500
Electricity	—	—	150	—	—	150	—	—	150	—	—	150	600
Gas	—	—	100	—	—	100	—	—	50	—	—	100	350
Telephones	—	—	—	50	—	—	80	—	—	80	—	—	210
Laundry	50	30	35	40	60	50	50	50	35	50	50	60	560
Stationery	100	—	—	—	—	—	—	—	—	100	—	—	200
Meals & Refreshments	50	10	15	20	20	20	20	20	20	20	20	20	255
Salon Cleaning & Maintenance	150	100	100	100	150	150	150	150	350	150	150	150	1 850
Free Working Capital (Cash)	1590	750	400	290	760	1090	990	1620	1485	85	465	2495	2 495

Capital Adjustment

		1	2	3	4	5	6	7	8	9	10	11	12	
Capital Reserve (Private)	1500	1100												1500
Less: Withdrawal for Private Use	400													(400)
Plus: Repayment							400							400
Reserve Balance		1100	1100	1100	1100	1100	1500	1500	1500	1500	1500	1500	1500	1500

individual can affect the whole salon adversely. Chain salons produce their own personalities in each unit, yet benefit from central management. Once the first and second salons are established, systems of operating are found to be satisfactory and staff training levels are meeting demand, then further expansion can be contemplated.

It can be seen from the above that whether the intention is to start a new business, take over a business or to expand an existing concern, the factors requiring consideration are both numerous and varied.

The intuitive balancing of all these factors and the subsequent decision to select a particular venture which will be both professionally and financially successful is a gift which few people possess. In the majority of cases, the successful enterprise has been initiated and developed as a result of careful and methodical planning coupled with the measurement of performance against a plan and, where necessary, the taking of immediate corrective action. Business plans can be developed to cover every facet of a proposed or existing enterprise, the one common feature is that all plans are evaluated and expressed in monetary terms.

For illustration purposes we have shown in Fig. 2.1 a business plan prepared at the time of the formation of our hypothetical salon, 'Histyles'. The layout is in the form of a cash flow statement or budget which, if realistically compiled, will show:

1. The achievement or otherwise of the ambitions of the owners.
2. A means of comparing the viability of several opportunities available to the prospective owners.
3. The critical periods of time in the development phase of the new venture.
4. A means of assessing the impact of actual trading results upon the business as a whole.
5. The facets which require management control and decisions on an on-going basis.
6. Information on the basis of which the future can be planned.

Many of the aspects of the plan, and therefore the evaluations, are based upon the subjective judgement of the compiler. Consequently, it is prudent to either prepare two plans, one of which is based on optimistic assumptions and the other on the most pessimistic, or for the plan to be prepared by two people. The business plan can be divided into the following sections:

1. Initial Expenditure

This is, in general terms, of a capital nature and is frequently represented by the value of the 'fixed assets' of the business. These include the cost of freehold land, freehold buildings, lease premiums, fixtures and fittings, furniture, salon and office equipment and motor vehicles. Also included in initial capital expenditure is any sum paid for goodwill which may be inflated for planning purposes to cover expenses incurred by the purchaser which will not reoccur in the course of normal trading, e.g. solicitors' fees etc. These costs will considerably reduce the financial resources available to new owners to meet initial trading expenses. The sum remaining, in accountancy terms, is 'working capital' some of which will have to be expended before a cash return is received from a client. Into this category of initial expenditure fall such items as rent for premises or equipment, purchase of stock, cost of advertisements, costs of engagement of staff and the proprietor's living expenses.

The initial expenses are generally fixed in nature and the amounts are known to the planner. Consequently, very little opportunity exists for subsequent savings, although some may be achieved in respect of the working capital expense items.

2. Receipts from Clients

These may be in respect of remuneration for the hairdressing service received or for the retail sale of associated products. In general, the latter is obtained as a result of the former attracting customers to the salon. The critical factor that has to be assessed for planning purposes is, therefore, the volume of clients likely to use the salon. For the new proprietor of a new salon there is no historical data of past performance on which assumptions can be based. An idea of the volume of business to be expected may be obtained from the performance of other salons which have commenced similar operations in the same environment within recent years. In the probable absence of information as to the time-scale of the trade build-up it may be expedient to assume that it will be an even increase over the total period until the optimum level of business is achieved.

Other factors may affect the volume of trade to be expected by the new business in the same way that they may influence the established salons, whether under new ownership or not. The most important of these factors are reviewed below:

(a) The volume of passing trade is unlikely to be affected by a change in ownership, but it is important to establish whether the trend is an increase or decrease in volume of trade. Care should be taken in the case of the former trend, that it is an increase in volume and not an increase in sales revenue as a result of increased charges. If the trend shows a decrease then management action is needed to redress this trend which may be reflected in the later stages of the planned activity.

(b) The client/hairdresser relationship may have both a negative and positive impact upon the volume of trade — negative with the loss of clients whose regular hairdressers have left the salon, and positive with new clients to the salon who follow the replacement hairdressers. For planning purposes it is advisable to assume that less than half of the anticipated personal followings will either be lost or gained.

(c) The introduction of new techniques, new services, new facilities etc., should result in an increase in the volume of trade at various stages during the planning period. There is also likely to have been an associated increase in expenditure, both prior and subsequent to the introduction of the changes.

(d) For planning purposes the seasonal variations in trade should be carefully allocated to the segments (normally a month) of the plan to avoid the possible cash flow crisis which can result from poor phasing of projects which involve heavy expenditure and are not compensated for by an immediate increase in income.

(e) Changes in the environment of the community as a whole should be considered when anticipating the volume of trade to be expected. An increase in the population due to the development of new industries, commercial organisations, housing estates etc., offers the salon an opportunity to expand its clientele. Likewise, a salon in an area whose principal industries and occupations are in decline can anticipate a reduction in business, particularly for the more expensive services.

Unless a system of standard costing is in operation it is inappropriate to increase the estimate of planned clients' receipts by an inflation factor since such an adjustment not only presumes that the inflation rate is predictable, but that a price increase will have no impact upon the volume of trade. In addition, it will be necessary to apply the same inflation factor to expenditure to maintain the balance of the plan. The result will be that any comparison between plan and actual performance will contain a variance attributable to the difference between actual and predicted inflation, rather than performance differences only.

3. Expenditure

From the accountancy point of view, this is divided into:

(a) Revenue expenditure which represents the expenses incurred in the day-to-day running of the business and includes:

(i) Employment costs, i.e. wages etc., paid to employees.

(ii) The cost of materials purchased for use in provision of the hairdressing service or for resale to clients.

(iii) The overhead expenses such as stationery, laundry etc.

(iv) The establishment charges, e.g. rent, rates and interest on loans.

(v) The cost of using the permanent assets of the business and of maintaining the efficiency by means of repair, renewal and replacement.

(b) Capital expenditure which is expenditure that results in the acquisition tion of a permanent asset, or in the permanent improvement of, addition to or extension of an existing asset which will then earn further revenue.

For business planning purposes it is more appropriate to consider expenditure under headings of:

(a) Fixed costs which are costs that will be incurred whatever the volume of business conducted, e.g. rent of the premises, rates payable to the Local Authority and capital expenditure. In the case of the last item, it may be expedient to defer any planned capital spending that would not improve the volume of trade.

(b) Variable costs are those which are directly proportional to the level of business activity being conducted, e.g. the cost of materials used in hairdressing, the cost of stock purchased for resale and the cost of employing temporary staff.

Careful consideration of each anticipated item of expenditure will identify that the number of items that can be completely classified as either fixed or variable is strictly limited. It is no coincidence that these items are the ones that require careful planning and ongoing management control. The planning process, therefore, involves the development of related management strategies to cope with the problems shown in the business plan. The extent of this activity is dependent upon the sums of money involved and usually relates to employment costs. The preparation of the business plan may, for example, have identified the need to increase the number of staff to meet the demand at certain periods of the year while in other periods the demand is such that the staff will be underemployed. Management has in this instance the opportunity to:

(i)   Attempt to arrange maximum availability of staff at peak periods and minimum attendance at slack periods by controlling employees' holiday periods.

(ii) Obtain the agreement of staff to work overtime at specific periods in the future.

(iii) Seek temporary staff.

(iv) Identify the optimum number of permanent staff to be employed, i.e. the number required to support the lowest level of activity whilst working under normal conditions.

4. Capital Adjustments

The development of the first three sections of the business plan will provide an 'end of line' statement of the 'free' working capital available to the salon management at each stage of the planned period. The amount of this working capital will be reduced if additional fixed assets are purchased or if the owners withdraw a portion in the form of interest on their original investment or a portion of the original investment itself. (It should be noted that for planning purposes the normal drawings of owners for personal living expenses are regarded as expenditure – see Section 3 above.) Conversely, the first three sections of the business plan may identify a negative working capital at a particular stage if current trends and policies are continued. Management has the opportunity to take immediate corrective action or, if expedient, to plan a short-term injection of capital in the form of a loan which will usually involve the payment of interest.

The capital adjustment section of the business plan is of little significance if the previous sections of the plan show an increment in working capital throughout the planning period and its preparation can, therefore, be eliminated. For reference purposes it is, however, included in the business plan example shown in Fig. 2.1.

CHAPTER III

The Salon Layout

It is unusual for a salon to occupy premises that are purpose-built, and even more unusual for an existing layout to conform to the new owners' ideas as to the size and proportions of working areas most suitable to provide the desired salon environment. Consequently, the requirements of each new owner will be different. Apart from the personal preferences of individuals there are several principles of salon design, décor, layout, and choices of equipment that must be followed to ensure that the salon is safe to operate and conforms to all legal requirements or statutory regulations.

STATUTORY REGULATIONS

These are originated by national and local government and are intended to ensure minimum standards of safety, health and hygiene for clients, staff and the general public. The principal aspects of this legislation are as follows:

1. Salons have to be registered with local authorities and be open to inspection by them.
2. Planning permission has to be obtained for all external structural changes.
3. Minimum standards of cleanliness, safety, facilities and fire precautions, applicable to both private and public areas of the business premises, are laid down in the Offices Shops and Railways Premises Act 1963 and the Health and Safety at Work Act 1974.

It is important that the salon layout meets all the requirements of these regulations.

When planning a new salon, or changing or refurbishing an existing one, the following factors should be taken into consideration:

1. The number of clients expected will help to determine the numbers of hairdressers to be employed. This is, of course, restricted by the available salon working space or floor area.
2. The type of clientele to be catered for is largely dependent on the social environment locally prevailing. The successful salon not only provides a hairdressing service of the required standard of professional expertise, but creates a salon environment compatible with a significant proportion of the potential clients.

   If the available clients are of the type requiring a luxurious, 'exclusive' salon with a high degree of personal service, and they are prepared to pay the higher charges associated with such requirements, then the salon layout will be completely different to that found in salons that cater for a fast turnover of larger numbers of clients. The exclusive salon is likely to provide a private area in which the complete range of services available may be performed by one highly qualified and experienced hairdresser without the client leaving the chair. The faster turnover salon is likely to be a more open one, where the clients move to the various service areas. This might involve a separate shampoo section manned by a junior member of staff, possibly using a shampoo machine, separate chairs manned by the stylists, and a communal drying area.

3. The range of hairdressing services to be offered determines the degree of hairdressing expertise required from the staff. This in turn will determine the fixtures, fittings, equipment and utilities – water, gas and electricity – that are needed.

4. The availability of well-qualified, professional and suitable staff is another important consideration. It is pointless planning to cater for large numbers of clients when there are few or no staff available. 'Importing' staff to an isolated or remote area involves extra cost and/or the provision of suitable accommodation.

5. The salon environment must conform to the minimum standards of heating, lighting, cleanliness, safety, hygiene and fire precautions stipulated in the various Acts.

In addition to the main salon hairdressing areas, facilities are required to perform the ancillary functions of a modern salon. In order that a high degree of continuity and privacy is afforded both to the clients and staff, the ancillary tasks which usually require special equipment and fittings should be performed in separate rooms or areas. Suggestions for these are as follows:

1. The Reception Area

The reception area should be immediately inside the salon entrance. This should be designed to ensure that the main salon area is not open to view by passers-by or all those entering the salon. The receptionist should be able to greet each client and to view the whole of the reception area, preferably including the area where coats, bags and packages are left. The reception area should be comfortably furnished for the benefit of waiting clients. If the reception area is also used for retail sales then adequate space for display materials should be allowed.

Reception of the client precedes any practical operation and sets the tone between client and operator in the provision of services that may follow. It will include a pleasant greeting, the making of appointments, answering questions, possibly giving advice, and generally offering information to meet clients' needs. Details of methods of work used, type of products in vogue and the prices of different services may all be required.

The building of a clientele will, to some extent, be dependent on the appearance of the reception area. This will strongly influence the first impressions gained by the clients. If the layout and design are tastefully arranged, and maintained in a tidy and hygienic condition, clients will be encouraged to return for further attention.

The reception desk should house, in an uncluttered way, the appointment book, diary, telephones and the individual client record system. This is usually a card index system which is maintained by the receptionist, or another member of staff, and records the services and products used for each client on each visit to the salon. The cash register is also usually located in the reception area and the desk is often designed to fit the variety of shapes that cash registers may take. Provision should also be made for a drawer or cupboard for the receptionist's personal use. Private records of the staff should not be kept in this area.

2. The Manager's Office

This should ideally be situated near the entrance and lead off the reception area. Staff, clients, and other callers may be interviewed without entering the main work area. The Manager's office should be a 'secure area' where cash and other valuables may be kept for short periods. Private staff records, filing systems and other office facilities may be usefully housed here. The Manager's office must be a suitable area for private discussions to be conducted.

3. The Stockroom and Dispensary

These are two areas which have traditionally been combined, with access readily available to all staff but not to clients or the public. With the increase in the range of proprietary preparations, little dispensing is now performed on a routine basis by hairdressers, and in the interest of stock security and control it is prudent to limit access to the main stores. In such instances, provision must be made for hairdressers to 'hold' a limited amount of stock in a suitable position in the working areas.

4. Staff Room

It is desirable and, in the case of large salons, mandatory that a separate area is provided as a staff room. This should be inaccessible to clients, and, ideally, have a separate entrance. It should provide facilities for the preparation of refreshments and wash and cloak facilities. Communication between the staff room, the main salon and the reception areas must be possible at all times. Ideally, an internal telephone system should be used, but often a system of buzzers and/or bells is adequate. Shouting through the salon to the reception is not an acceptable means of communicating.

SUITABLE PREMISES

When assessing the suitability of available premises, prospective new owners who have defined their requirements will have to identify alterations that may be required to adapt the premises to their purposes. Clearly, too, the costs involved will require further consideration. It may, in the end, be necessary to reject what was thought to be suitable on the grounds of alteration costs.

It should be established from the vendors as soon as possible whether there are any known restraints placed on development by local authorities and, in the case of leased or rented premises, any limitations imposed by the landlord on structural alterations.

Unless the approved alterations are of a minor nature, i.e. a change of colour scheme or décor, it is advisable to employ professional shopfitters or constructional tradesmen, who will be able to provide detailed plans and estimates for the installation of variations to building structures and related facilities. The use of such agencies, as well as determining the practicality of effecting the alterations, will also ensure compliance with statutory and local regulations in respect of fire precautions, provision of entrances and exits, security of wiring, etc.

It is, however, with the opening of the salon that the management's prime responsibilities commence in maintaining at all times the minimum standards laid down in statutory regulations. The majority of managers and staff who study the regulations, which by law have to be displayed in the salon, will appreciate that the statutory standards are often below those which would be expected in a good professional salon. In practice, it is often the case that due to a lack of financial resources, only the minimum requirements are initially adhered to. This results in the introduction of salon operations and expediency-prompted habits in both staff and clients which produce an undesirable environment. The principal matters requiring continual management attention are:

1.   Access

(a)   To and from the salon.   The safety section of the Offices Shops and Railway Premises Act specifies the requirement for exits in the event of an emergency such as a fire. The number and type of exits are dependent on the number of people located in the premises, the nature of the material contents stored on the premises and the siting of the salon in the building. In general terms, the requirement is for two independent exits which are safely negotiable. For instance a good ground-floor salon may have as a secondary exit a window which allows a person to effect an easy exit. A third-floor salon would require a secondary exit with an independent staircase or fire-escape located on another side or face of the building to that which contains the normal entrance/exit. It is the duty of management to ensure that emergency exits are clearly marked and accessible at all times. Doors should not be locked in a manner which precludes immediate opening from inside the salon or be concealed and obstructed by fixtures and equipment.

(b)   Freedom of movement in the salon.   In addition to complying with the statutory requirements, it is good management practice to allow ample space for the movement of both staff and clients. Mention has already been made of the importance of removing the commercial and administrative functions from the main salon area. This will allow more space and reduce the amount of movement in the busy operational area. It is suggested that, where possible, gangways be provided preferably carpeted or covered in a different floor-material so that they are readily recognised. This may help to channel movement away from overworked areas and prevent obstruction. It is important that all movement areas, especially stairways, are safe, i.e. well lit, with handrails provided, and walking surfaces conducive to firm footholds. All gangways or walkways should not be adjacent to work-surfaces to prevent possible accidents occurring or materials being spilt.

2. Environment

The three major environmental considerations are:

(a) Heating.   The Offices Shops and Railway Premises Act specifies a minimum temperature of 16°C or 60.8°F after the first hour of normal working. Whilst such a temperature may be adequate for people performing active tasks it may be considered unsuitable for employees and clients who are stationary. Management must give careful attention to the type and cost of heating the entire salon. The Act states that heating systems should be free from injurious or offensive fumes. Apart from specifying that a thermometer is placed in a conspicuous place on each floor, no further restrictions are stated. It is obvious that an excessively high temperature – above 24°C or 75°F – can be just as detrimental as a low temperature. As well as being uncomfortable for clients it is tiring for staff. This is wasteful on fuel and therefore costly. Heating systems should be adjustable to accommodate changes in climatic temperatures and to vary heat levels between the various rooms and areas according to the activities taking place.

It is important that storage areas are kept at a constant moderate temperature to prevent loss of stock. Heat retention, i.e. reducing heat-loss by roof lagging, double glazing for doors and windows, cavity wall insulation etc., should also be considered in order to reduce running costs and conserve fuel.

(b) Ventilation.   The Act states that there must be effective ventilation in every room where employees are required to work and that provision must be made for securing adequate supplies of fresh air or artificially purified air. Devices intended to provide fresh air are often detrimental to maintaining the required temperature unless carefully and expertly installed. For artificial air purification systems to be effective, installation and maintenance can be expensive. The problem of achieving a good, balanced ventilation flow is probably one of the most difficult facing management and this should receive careful consideration when selecting premises and establishing layout in the salon. In this connection, premises with high ceilings and ease of access to outside walls may be advantageous. The siting of steam-producing activities, e.g. shampooing, near to ventilation points, can also be helpful in maintaining balanced ventilation. Regrettably, the effectiveness of an artificial ventilation system is restricted to supporting or supplementing a natural system.

(c) Lighting.   Although the Act states that adequate lighting, whether natural or artificial, must be provided, no standards are laid down except that windows and artificial lighting fitments must be kept clean and in good repair. Lighting in a good salon should be adequate and suitable for all the activities performed: gentle light that blends with the decor of the reception area; strong, bright light for emphasising display items; and natural light without glare or reflection in styling areas.

3. Cleanliness

Great emphasis is placed in the Act on the maintenance of clean premises, fixtures and appliances. The standards laid down are probably well below those to be expected in a first-class salon where cleanliness and hygiene are maintained at all times. Sterilising units must be in good repair and in operation throughout the working day. Tools once used must be cleansed and sterilised ready for use again. No linen must ever be used on a client after having been used on another. Disinfectant dishes or bowls must be washed regularly, with sufficient changes of their contents for the material to be fully effective. No self-respecting, professional operator should be other than clean, tidy and fully conversant with the rules of hygiene generally. Cleanliness is the concern of all members of staff in the interests of health and safety. Those who try to dupe the public by having sterlising units on show without even the means of having them connected, going through the pretence of cleaning linen and other measures designed to save expense, are not only doing a disservice to their own clients, but a disservice to the profession of which they purport to be members. It is the duty of all in such a personal service to safeguard and maintain the highest of standards. Those detailed in the Act should be the very minimum.

4. Personal Facilities

An important statutory stipulation of the Act is that adequate personal facilities should be provided for the use of staff and clients. These include drinking water, toilets, washing, cloak, rest and refreshment equipment, to be readily available. It is sound policy to consider the needs of staff and clients separately. Ideally, the staff room facilities should be adjacent to the main salon, with client access restricted or prohibited. The client facilities should be provided near the reception area.

5. Equipment

For ease of reference, the range of equipment is divided into the following groups:

(a) **Fitments** including basins, work surfaces, chairs etc., are required to be kept in good repair. Chipped, cracked or broken basins are likely to be dangerous and unhygienic. Damaged chairs are likely to cause accidents. It is usually uneconomic to retain damaged or broken fitments. It might cost far more in damage to clients' and staff property than it would to have them repaired or replaced. Injury to clients or staff can be caused as a result of collision with sharp edges and protruding equipment parts. Dangerous obstructions or features should be eliminated, or at least, guarded. Unsuitable or inappropriate equipment may damage staff and clients directly or cause materials to be spilt, thereby causing further indirect damage. Sensible use of makeshift equipment is one thing. Blatant disregard for staff and client safety is another.

(b) Electrical equipment.   Much of the apparatus used in the modern salon is electrical. Since many salon processes utilise water and water containers, it is important to ensure that all electrical gadgets are safe to use. Leads should not be frayed; plugs and sockets should be correctly fitted; leads should not trail over walkways or gangways.

Many electrical faults are not readily seen and it is prudent to have all electrical apparatus examined, tested and serviced by reputable, qualified electrical engineers at least every six months. In the busy salon it is advisable to have a system whereby appliances found to be unsafe, not working or suspect, should be labelled or at least placed where they are not readily accessible to other operators, until the damage is repaired. So often, a damaged piece of equipment is discarded, only for another equally busy operator to pick it up, use it, and possibly cause further damage. If equipment is seen to need connections made fast or to have leads coming loose etc., make sure it is placed safely away.

(c) Protective clothing.   It is now a legal requirement for clean protective clothing to be worn when dealing with clients in the salon. It should be removed when leaving the salon and put on when entering. Whilst there are a variety of disposable garments available, much reliance is still placed on launderable items. Ideally, disposable garments can be used over launderable clothing particularly when services involving dyes etc. are being used, to protect the appearance of the clothing. Nothing is more likely to offend than soiled, stained garments, even though they may have been recently laundered. The same may be applied to towels and other linen items. Unsightly, soiled items can be thought unclean, and dissatisfaction or offence can easily be caused if this is disregarded. All clients and staff should wear freshly-laundered or disposable garments, used once, and then discarded or sent for laundering. Garments which are in direct contact with the skin, e.g. towels, should be freshly laundered for each client for hygienic reasons. With the rapid turnover of dirty gowns, towels etc., it is important that they are removed from the salon as soon as possible, or kept in suitable covered receptacles until they can be removed.

6.   Safety Facilities

Even in the best-run salon, accidents are bound to occur from time to time. Hopefully, the majority of these accidents will be minor in nature. The Offices Shops and Railway Premises Act and the Health and Safety at Work Act require both fire-fighting equipment and first-aid equipment to be provided and readily available. Management must ensure that such facilities are present, fully stocked and readily accessible, and that the staff know how to use them. In the case of fire, it may be appropriate to hold fire drills as part of the salon training programme. These exercises should include the immediate termination of power supplies, both electrical and gas. Knowledge of where the main water stopcocks or taps are housed can be advantageous. It may be prudent to arrange for at least one member of staff to have first-aid training so that a qualified first-aid practitioner is in attendance. Such a person may receive a supplementary wage or allowance, and could be responsible for the first-aid equipment and materials.

7. Negligence

To lack attention or care is to be negligent. In recent years, the law has increasingly deemed that the managements of business concerns are responsible for all incidents occurring on their premises or involving members of the staff during working hours. It is, after all, good business to maintain good client–staff relationships at all times. This particularly applies in the event of an accident, where a sympathetic attitude on the part of management can be most helpful. Apart from the need for client care, the threat of legal action compels management to take every precaution to eliminate accidents, and this should not be overlooked in the interests of commercial expediency. The following factors are important:

(a) Hairdressing skills and competence. Members of staff should not be asked to perform hairdressing operations without having received, and assimilated, the relevant training. Attendance at a technical college; maintaining the apprenticeship training schedule; proof of attainment of the required satisfactory completion of training periods; and gaining of associated certificates – these all contribute to a recognisable skill. This, however, needs to be maintained. Completion of training often indicates only that one is qualified to *start* to practise. Quality of craftsmanship is determined by application of the basic principles, practice and constant striving to become better. This is an ongoing process. The professional, skilled operator will look for ways in which to update, be fashionable, to improve and take pride in doing so. It is important to display evidence of attained skills and qualifications. Members of the public like to see this and follow the career successes of their favourite operators. No matter how busy the salon is, or how willing the inexperienced operator is to try a technique, clients must not be taken advantage of and be used as guinea pigs. Practice can take place on models who know and understand that practice is being carried out for the benefit of the learner, but never on unsuspecting, paying clients. New materials, new products and new equipment must be understood before being used, and staff must prove their competence in its application.

(b) Testing processes, techniques or systems. New techniques, processes or systems should be tried out, preferably on models, before being used on clients – particularly new ones – before becoming part of the salon's repertoire. It is important to safeguard models by carefully following the manufacturer's instructions. It is both careless and unsafe to deviate from the manufacturer's explicit instructions for the use of products when, invariably, only they fully know the chemicals contained in them.

(c) Testing of products and materials.   Apart from the checking of systems and processes, chemical preparations must be tested on the individual client. This should be done to ensure that the product causes no general side-effects and that no adverse effects are produced. Prior to the application of a permanent hair-colourant, a skin test should be made 24–48 hours before the application. If the reaction is negative, i.e. there is no sign of inflammation or reaction, then the application can be made. If the application proves to be positive, i.e. a reaction is to be seen, then no application should be made. To disregard a positive reaction to the skin test would be to be guilty of negligence. Tests should be made wherever possible to ensure that the client is safely treated with the minimum of chance or risk taken with their well-being.

(d) Use of non-standard salon products.   From time to time a client may request, or produce for use, a particular product. In such cases, even if the operator knows that it is safe to use, a note of indemnity should be obtained from the client prior to the application, thereby safeguarding the operator and management. If it is known that the product is likely to cause reactions or adverse effects then permission for its use must be refused.

In the best-managed salons, even with dedicated and professional staff, accidents are bound to occur from time to time. The cost in respect of damages payable to the injured party, whether settled in or out of court, can be financially crippling to a business, not to mention the damage it may do to the reputation and consequent amount of business conducted. It is therefore important that adequate insurance is taken out against all eventualities, particularly third-party (clients') claims, either against the management or individual employees. The advice of a solicitor and insurance broker should be sought so that complete coverage and protection for all can be obtained.

CHAPTER IV

Personnel Management and Social Relationships

Management has been defined as a social process involving responsibility for the activities of groups of individuals in the employment of inanimate items in a prescribed manner to achieve a desired objective. This definition identifies that the prime responsibility of all levels of management is the direction and control of people. The establishment of a formal personnel department within a business does not relieve the other managerial staff of this responsibility. In general, personnel departments provide a service to other managers by:

1. Developing a single policy as regards the conditions of employment, i.e. remuneration, holidays, sickness benefits etc.
2. Administering the personnel selection, development and termination procedures.
3. Co-ordinating the staff training programme.
4. Arbitrating in instances of strained interstaff relationships.
5. Assisting when invited in personal problems encountered by the staff.

The responsibility for the day-to-day direction and control of personnel still rests with their immediate superiors who are required to develop satisfactory social relationships not only with, and between their subordinates, but also with other managerial staff. In the hairdressing industry, where the majority of businesses are small, the establishment of a formal personnel department, or even a personnel officer is uneconomic and the entire personnel function rests on the salon manager.

In addition, since hairdressing is a service to people and it is normal for every employee to have direct dealings with clients, it is important for the hair-dressing manager to ensure that the correct social relationships are developed and maintained between staff and clients. It is generally on the performance and personality of the individual hairdresser that the clients base their assessment of the salon as a whole, but this assessment is also influenced by the interactions amongst the staff, whether this is between the manager and the staff or between the staff themselves. Poor relationships must inevitably lead individual hairdressers to become discontented with the profession of hairdressing and will manifest themselves in poor hairdressing which will further reduce the possibility of maintaining, let alone increasing, the clientele.

In the past, the management of personnel and the development of accept-able social relationships were frequently ignored or left to instinctive reaction, but in modern society where alternative facilities are readily available to clients and the rights of the employee are increasingly being protected by statutory laws, these matters become of fundamental importance to hairdressing managers. The number of variations of behaviour and human reactions is often said to be dependent upon the number of people involved, since it is rare to find even two people who are in complete accord on all matters. Accordingly, it is impossible to establish detailed formal practices and procedures which are certain to result in a satisfactory social environment for employees, management and clients. The following are, however, general principles that form the basis of any sound personnel policy.

1. Personnel Planning

One of the prime causes of discontentment amongst employees in modern society is the lack of opportunity for continual personal advancement within their chosen careers or professions. In hairdressing, following the completion of the period of apprenticeship, there are few establishments that offer the ambitious employee the chance to advance into management. Such employees are compelled either to seek the limited managerial opportunities which may arise in other salons or to open their own establishments. Frequently, this ambition degenerates into 'job chases' which, if successful, may initially provide the employee with improved remuneration for their services but in the long term produce the same frustrations. Many employees do not have such ambitions and are content to practise their profession within the original salon, provided the remuneration is adequate and the social environment is satisfactory, only terminating due to changes in personal circumstances which often involve leaving hairdressing.

These 'stay put' employees provide management with as many problems as the ambitious employee for the following reasons:

(a) Unless the salon expands there will be no opportunity to engage further apprentices.

(b) The unskilled and semi-skilled tasks normally performed by a junior employee will have to be performed by a senior person. This may cause discontent amongst the senior employees as well as being uneconomic.

(c) An employee will develop a 'personal clientele' which may be lost to the salon when the hairdresser leaves.

(d) On the termination of an established hairdressing employee, either a skilled hairdresser has to be recruited, which may produce a personality clash amongst the current staff, or a redistribution of the work will be necessary to incorporate trainee staff. This latter action can have a direct effect on the clientele.

To attempt to overcome these problems, management needs continually to relate the recruitment and selection of staff policies to the complete business plan. For example, if a salon is intent upon a plan of expansion into a chain of salons, it would be prudent to select a few applicants for apprenticeships who, in addition to showing potential as hairdressers, also have the potential and ambition to be supervisors and managers. If, however, the business plan is to retain a salon in its present form, recruitment should be directed to replacing anticipated terminations and providing a short-term solution by engaging part-time hairdressers and/or temporary unskilled or semi-skilled personnel.

2. Economic Staffing

The statutory requirement that employees must be paid for their presence during normal working hours irrespective of whether work is available, coupled with the fact that employees cannot be laid off and re-engaged without compensation, although socially just, has presented management with considerable problems. Failures by management to both identify and address these problems may produce one of two conditions within the salon:

(a) Overstaffing, which means that the business is, to an extent, uneconomic. This condition is usually characterised by all or some of the following undesirable features:

(i)   High prices that aggravate the problem by further reducing the clientele.

(ii)   Low individual remuneration to the staff, which results in a high staff turnover and, in time, a lowering of the standard of hairdressing service provided.

(iii) Lack of funds available to maintain and update the equipment, fixtures and fittings.

(iv)   A reluctance to adopt new methods and techniques which may be expensive to introduce but saving in labour.

(v)   Low return on investment to the owners.

(vi)   The absence of a staff-training and development scheme.

(b) Understaffing, from the point of view of many managements is considered to be preferable to overstaffing. However, the long-term effects are often just as damaging. Understaffing results in:

(i)   An inability to accommodate all the potential clients.

(ii)   Delays and deterioration in the standard of hairdressing provided.

(iii) Increasing staff fatigue which will manifest itself in temperamental outbursts and possibly in physical breakdowns.

(iv)   An inability to absorb the effects of the absence of staff due to holidays and sickness.

(v)   Lack of supervision of the hairdressing work performed.

(vi)   'Ad hoc' provision of the administration and support functions, i.e. stock-keeping, dispensing, reception, appointments, cleaning, accounts and wages preparation.

(vii) No staff-training in new methods and techniques for experienced hairdressers and little time for the guidance of new entrants and apprentices.

(viii) Neglect of safety, health and hygiene regulations.

Prior to the engagement of additional staff it is important that management identify:

(i)   The exact duties or tasks to be performed by the newcomers.

(ii)   Whether these tasks can, as a result of reallocation of duties, be performed by the current staff.

(iii) Identify the qualities required by the newcomers to perform the tasks.

(iv)   Ensure that the managers responsible for the selection are themselves qualified in the professional skills required and also in the techniques of personnel selection.

The identification of tasks and the development of job specifications, which are the basic management tools employed in meeting these requirements, are detailed in Chapter V of this book under the heading of 'Work Study in the Salon'.

3.   Selection of Staff – Importance to the Business

The complete process of selection of staff is expensive to the business and takes the form of:

(a) Cost of advertisements.

(b) Costs of management time spent in reviewing applications, conducting interviews and the decision process leading to final selection.

(c) Expenses incurred by applicants in attending interviews.

(d) Costs of training the new employee. It should also be appreciated that even an experienced hairdresser requires training in the administrative methods employed within the salon.

(e) The disturbance to the current staff and possibly clients.

(f) Additional administration costs in fulfilling the statutory requirements of contract of employment regulations and employee-related pay deductions.

(g) Adverse publicity which may originate from employees who terminate shortly after commencement of employment due to incompatibility between the newcomer and the salon environment.

Managers as well as intended employees, have much to lose if the selection process is anything less than satisfactory. The effectiveness of the complete selection process is reflected in the staff turnover rate, i.e. the number of terminations divided by the number of staff employed during a given period. An increase in the turnover rate should be investigated as a matter of urgency by management to establish whether terminations are caused by:

(a) True external personal factors experienced by individual employees.

(b) Employment conditions in society as a whole having an adverse effect on the hairdressing industry.

(c) Deterioration in the working environment of their own salon – normally indicated by the unexplained termination of long-service employees.

(d) Unexplained terminations by employees with less than one year's service.

In the case of (d) above, a careful and critical review of the selection procedure should be undertaken immediately.

4. Selection of Staff – the Employment Market

Following the identification of a requirement for additional staff, it is necessary to identify possible candidates for the vacancy. These may be obtained from the following sources:

(a) Previous unsolicited approaches by people interested in obtaining employment in the salon.

(b) As a result of recommendation by current staff.

(c) By an approach to the local college of further education, if hairdressing is part of its curriculum.

(d) Through employment agencies, both public and private.

(e) Replies to advertisements placed in the local press and in trade journals.

The use of (e) above as compared with the other sources involves:

(i)   The public declaration of a vacancy which may not be completely privatised by the use of a Box Number.

(ii) The complete selection process is a matter for direct negotiation between the candiate and the employer and is not influenced by the opinion of a third party.

With the identification of possible candidates, a decision has to be made by the employing management as to the interview policy to be employed. This may be influenced by the number of applicants, but two general methods may be used:

(a) Sort the applications into an order of likely acceptability and interview in that order, the first suitable applicant being offered employment. The use of this method reduces the cost of employment but is not likely to produce the most suitable candidate.

(b) After eliminating candidates who are obviously unsuitable, interview the remainder with a view to identifying the most suitable, provided the minimum acceptance standard has been attained.

Traditionalists will claim that the second method is preferable because of the comparative element which is incorporated in the procedure and is consequently not so dependent upon the subjective judgement of the interviewer. The use of the assessment process detailed in Section 7 below permits the use of either method provided the minimum acceptable standard is raised if the first method is used.

5. Selection of Staff – Interviews

A manager of a hairdressing salon is required to select:

(a) Apprentices, who will be employed and trained under a written contract of not less than three years.

(b) Operative hairdressers, who will be mainly engaged in hairdressing.

(c) Supervisors (chargehands) and junior managers, responsible to the management for control and supervision of staff.

(d) Ancillary staff, e.g. receptionists, store-keepers, book-keepers.

In each case there is a requirement to assess the degree of professional competence or, in the case of an apprentice or junior hairdresser, professional potential. Additionally, in each case it will be necessary to assess whether the applicant's personal attributes are complementary to the current staff and will be acceptable to the clientele. It is generally found that the recruitment of apprentices and junior hairdressers forms the major proportion of all interviews and, therefore, this section is based on the interview for this type of vacancy. Interviews for more senior positions follow the same general pattern, but evidence of a more highly developed professional ability, personality and social awareness in the applicant is required. Likewise, the candidate will be more aware of the need to determine the true conditions, scope and opportunities offered by the employer.

The interview itself is an important meeting in which both interviewer and applicant need to ask questions in an endeavour to explore. The first thing looked for by the interviewer is essentially general appearance. Impressions gained from the initial meeting are very important. There may be many applicants, and the stronger impressions gained help to keep an applicant in mind when arriving at a choice of the most suitable. Next, how is the applicant dressed? Is he or she clean, fashionable, suitably dressed, overdressed, unkempt, untidy or carelessly dressed? If the applicant is neat and tidily dressed, showing care and some overall balance between choice of style, colour and make-up, then good impressions may be created which may be to the advantage of the aspiring young applicant. At this stage the young, inexperienced entrant is just that – inexperienced. All that can be looked for, with reason, is the indication that there is potential and that the young person is likely to succeed.

The next factor looked for by the interviewer is the way applicants express themselves. The way they speak, the emphasis given to why they wish to make a career in hairdressing, their reasons and aspirations etc., are all important in creating the impressions which might make them the 'right' candidate. Appearance, speech, forthrightness, individual personality, degree of enthusiasm, ability to listen, contributions to the conversation, are some of the criteria and subjective aspects by which judgements are made.

It is not easy for those interviewing to be able to 'see inside' those being interviewed. The interviewer is trying to find the person who will be most suitable and successful in the job in question. The candidate will need to be able to cope generally, help to create and enjoy the environment of the salon and be able to give something of themselves in creating the personal relation-ships so vital to the many situations that arise in the salon. They will need to learn practical skills to progress, be able to grasp opportunities in an effort to fulfil themselves, and derive a measure of satisfaction from social attainment. Appearance, good health, patience, understanding, pleasant and cheerful personality – these are just some of the attributes involved. It is necessary for these to be apparent at the interview, or for the candidate to show the potential to develop them.

The interview format varies from place to place and from one occasion to another. Different positions and jobs require different individual personalities. Too often, young beginners have little idea of what is required of them. Fortunately, more emphasis is now given in schools to careers, but still, too often, available sources of information regarding career structures are disregarded. Those who take the trouble to look at the variety of courses and training prospects, who make inquiries into different salons and who generally try to find out what is involved in a career in hairdressing, are likely to be amongst those that interview well. At least they will be better informed and able to respond to the interviewer's questions.

6. Selection of Staff – Personality

It is considered important that staff in the service industries dealing with other people have the right personality. A great deal is said and written about personality. By 'personality' is meant the total attributes of an individual, as seen by others. It includes both the physical and mental attributes with which one is born, and the effects of socialisation, i.e. the educational and environmental influences of upbringing.

The question as to what is the right personality for a career in hairdressing is not an easy one to answer. Different hairdressing environments need different personality types. Generally, a person who is able to give of themselves, recognise the needs of others, be sympathetic and prepared to help people and cultivate balanced and harmonious relationships, is more likely to be right for a career in a personal service industry.

For young entrants, learning how to behave, to listen or to express themselves without offending, does not come automatically. It has to be learned, just as much as the practical skills of cutting and styling, and requires as much effort, if not more. Social skills generally involve being able to conduct oneself in a manner which is not objectionable. Being polite, helpful and courteous, without being self-demeaning, is an indication that a person wishes to be accepted by the social group. Often a young person is in too much of a hurry to become accepted. To be too gushing, to undertake too much work so that quality declines, to talk too much, particularly at the least convenient of times, or to make oneself noticed at the expense of others, often results in rejection rather than acceptance.

A short trial period is sometimes necessary during which time the opportunity is afforded to the employer to decide whether the applicant is suitable, or the applicant to decide whether the employer and position are acceptable. This period may last from a few hours to a whole day. Occasionally it may be necessary to extend this to a couple of days. It is rarely necessary, or practical, to extend trial periods over a longer period of time.

There are adequate periods of trial employment included in most contracts of employment during which a final decision on suitability can be made.

During these periods of trial employment other members of staff can have the opportunity of assessing the new entrant. Often, their comments are very helpful, and since they are involved, it may be good policy to invite their co-operation.

7. Selection of Staff – Interview Assessment

As a result of conducting an interview it rests on the interviewer to assess whether or not the candidate is suitable. When a series of interviews for the same vacancy have been conducted it is necessary to arrive at a decision as to which candidate is most suitable. The traditional use of the interviewer's subjective judgement is sufficient to identify the unsuitable candidates, but the choice between a number of suitable candidates is frequently reduced almost to a lottery. It is rare to find a candidate who is superior in all aspects with which the interviewer is concerned and, therefore, the final selection depends on the following:

(a) The interviewer's assessment, mainly from memory, of the comparative strengths and weaknesses of each candidate.

(b) Adequate coverage of each required quality.

(c) 'Convenience factors' not being given undue weighting in the assessment, e.g. the immediate availability of one candidate as compared with a four-week delay for another more suitable one.

(d) The opinion of a third party, e.g. a senior employee, being obtained on some of the candidates and not others.

(e) The assessment and its recall in the mind of the interviewer, must have remained constant throughout the entire interview period – which may have been a matter of weeks.

To overcome these difficulties it is suggested that a formal assessment process should be used. The method detailed below is easily compiled during the course of the interview and equally easily allows an *assessment rating* to be calculated for each candidate.

A certain amount of planning is involved in preparing a listing of the qualities required in candidates. In practice, a listing of all the qualities required in all personnel employed in the salon, whether as managers or cleaners, would be prepared, and the irrelevant qualities for a particular vacancy given a zero *assessment factor*. An assessment factor is determined for each quality according to the requirement of the vacancy. Oral communication, for example, may be graded as shown below.

Type of Vacancy	Assessment Factor
Apprentice	2
Hairdressing Operator	3
Supervisor	5
Receptionist	4
Book-keeper	1
Cleaner	0

During the interview, individual ratings are awarded by the interviewer in respect of each quality for each candidate, normally on a scale from 1 to 10. On completion of the interview the individual ratings given are multiplied by the respective assessment factors which, when totalled, give a final assessment rating for that particular candidate. The format of the required document for an experienced hairdresser is shown in Fig. 4.1.

FIG. 4.1   Interview Assessment Rating

Job: Hairdresser	Date of Interview:		Candidate's Name:
A *Quality* *Required*	B *Interview* *Rating 1–10*	C *Assessment* *Factor*	D *Assessment* $B \times C$
Hairdressing Ability		10	
Personality		5	
Appearance		2	
Dress		2	
Oral Communication		3	
Enthusiasm		2	
Supervisory Experience		2	
Salon Administration		2	
TOTALS:		28	

In this case, the 'perfect' candidate could achieve a rating of 280. It would be reasonable to set a minimum acceptance level of 100 if a selection of candidates were interviewed but if the interview process was to be concluded once a satisfactory candidate was identified it would be prudent to require a rating of 120 to be achieved.

8.   Management and Staff Relationships

Too often, the managers of salons adopt a dictatorial stance which is reflected in their attitude to employees, who are considered inferior and there only to be taken advantage of. This is not conducive to the retention of good loyal workers or the building of a lucrative and successful business. The manager's role is to recognise available talent in the staff, utilise this and try to involve each of them in a capacity that is going to fulfil them individually. This may satisfactorily allow expansion of the clientele at the same time. The manager must ensure that latent potential is realised by each individual employee. This may involve further training, practice or assistance with personal problems. The better the work that each of the staff is capable of achieving, the better the prospects of the business are likely to be.

Additionally, staff are individually responsible for creating the desired atmosphere of efficient competence within the salon which is readily detected by the discerning client. Although the staff are carrying out the employer's policies it is the interpretation of these policies that is important. It falls to the professional, caring hairdresser or beauty therapist to ensure that the client is safely and competently attended to, and that, at all times, the general and personal hygiene is of a sufficient standard to prevent the spread of bacteria etc. It is also the staff who ensure that the service to the client is carried out in an agreeable social environment.

Staff vary in age and range of experience. Some may have recently completed their apprenticeship. Some may be in their first years as operatives. Others may have had many years of varied experience in hairdressing. They all have their own special individual contributions to make to the success of the salon. There is, however, another aspect of the staff that affects the running of the business. For each individual member of staff there will be a number of external, private factors which will influence the dispositions they display in the salon. Younger operators may be at the stage of making friends, which often takes a great deal of emotional effort. Mature staff may be involved with marriages, families etc. The general worries of living – renting flats, or buying houses and running them, together with a myriad of other social and living factors, all take their toll of the concentration and energy of the staff.

It is not always possible for these worries to be 'turned off' when the staff enter the salon. It would be most unreasonable to expect this. At best, the private and social life of the staff should complement life at work. Hopefully this will reflect in the way the work is carried out and the benefits obtained. Where the lives of the staff are conducted in such a way that personal problems affect work in the salon adversely, then a great deal of damage can be done. This affects both the individual's career and the prospects of the business. It is essential that the effects of staff problems and social lifestyle on the conducting of the business are minimised.

The longer staff are employed in a business, the more they expect to derive for their long and loyal service. It is true that constant and dedicated service should be well regarded. It is good management to reward good work and efforts for proven abilities and attainment. This also encourages members of staff to remain in the business. Mobility of staff between salons is often due to this not being fairly done. Although it may be good policy to encourage and pay for effort made, to overpay staff without the desired results being attained can be an unnecessary drag on the business. This could adversely affect the earning capacities of other staff. Overpaying, and overstaffing, must be avoided since it tends to reduce staff advancement and stifles incentive generally. The manager often acts as an interpreter, buffer and co-ordinator between the staff and the employers. The managing directors make known their aims and objectives to the manager. It is then his job to explain these general policies and gain the willing acceptance of the staff. If the aims of the management can also be those of the staff there is much to be gained for all concerned.

The staff should be able to approach the manager with their problems and difficulties encountered in carrying out agreed policies. The relationship between manager and staff should be one where there is reciprocal support. For this to be achieved at all times is perhaps a little too much to expect but generally it is an ideal to aim at. The manager must recognise that the apprentices will require help, training and education. Junior assistants will need to gain further experience. The stylists will require recognition of their positions and abilities. The cleaning and support staff will need to see that the manager is looking after their interests. At the same time the clients, too, must feel that there is someone overall looking after their interests and needs.

The main issues which can influence management/staff relationships are considered in greater detail in Sections 9–14 of this chapter.

9. Staff Remuneration

How staff are rewarded for the work performed in the salon is arguably the most important factor in the relationship between management and staff. In general terms, payment schemes have evolved from one of two principles:

(a) Time payment. Employees are paid a set amount per hour for their attendance at the salon. It is the responsibility of management to ensure that work is available to the employee and that it is performed in an adequate manner.

(b) Work payment. Often called 'piece work', this is a scheme which involves payment being made to the employee in respect of the performance of each and every clearly defined and recorded task or operation. A regular basic wage is not assured to the employee but the advantage from management's point of view is that in times of poor trading the wages are proportionately low.

The latter system, in a pure format, has been eliminated by statutory regulations (see Hairdressing Undertakings Wages Council) which guarantee employees a minimum wage, paid holidays, overtime payments and compensation for termination of employment for commercial reasons. Unfortunately, this standardisation of conditions of employment has reduced the opportunities of management to offer financial incentives to encourage more efficient working on an individual basis. Some managements have introduced bonus or commission schemes which award a percentage of the takings above a minimum level to individual hairdressers. Such schemes are effective where all employees are hairdressers of equal status, and overtime is not worked, but difficulties are encountered where ancillary workers, apprentices and trainees support the operative hairdressers.

The problem of lack of incentive to employed personnel is to be found in all sections of industry and commerce but within the salon, with its limited number of employees performing one general function, a service to clients, an opportunity exists for enterprising managements to implement a group productivity scheme.

The principle of such schemes is that as a result of diligent work by the staff and good management, the profit made by the salon is greater than that which would normally be expected. A portion of this increased profit is returned to the employees as a bonus or additional payment. Such a scheme involves the need for management to consult with the staff in producing a clearly defined scheme and to keep employees informed on such matters as turnover and profit margins. The establishment of such a scheme is dependent upon having readily available management data to determine:

(a) The normal anticipated profit.

(b) The basis of division of the increase in profit between owners, management and employees.

(c) The frequency of payment to employees and the basis of its allocation.

It should be noted that a group productivity scheme only provides a means of rewarding the employees as a group for above-normal co-operation with a competent management over a period of time. The increment in total remuneration received by each employee is not apportioned on a personal basis and cannot be regarded as a personal salary rise. For both contributions and benefits associated with State and private insurance schemes, earnings which arise from participation in a group productivity scheme are ignored. Additionally, managements have to avoid the possibility of a group incentive scheme superseding any personal salary review schemes which are intended to reflect the worth of individual contributions to the working of the salon.

10. Staff Advancement and Promotion

One of the features of modern society is that all its members expect to receive a continual increase in relative earnings throughout their working lives. This need is not satisfied by a general increase to all workers employed within an industry since such rises are correctly regarded as 'cost of living' increments by all but the most naive. The increments resulting from a group productivity scheme, outlined in Section 9 above, only satisfy one group of employees as compared with other groups within the industry. There is still a desire for individual advancement within the group; i.e. the employees within a particular salon wish to be rewarded individually for good work and ability by either upgrading or promotion to a higher status than their less conscientious and gifted colleagues.

In the case of new entrants to hairdressing the Hairdressing Undertakings Wages Council stipulates a minimum wage for apprentices and for the first three years as a hairdresser. The increments are, however, dependent upon time served in the industry and not upon individual performance and consequently do not completely solve the problem even if the increments given are greater than the statutory minimum.

Increments for hairdressers of over five years' standing are entirely at the discretion of managements and the awarding of such increments is worthy of greater management attention than it is often given. The award of an increment is motivating to the recipient but frequently produces resentment and discontent amongst those employees who have either not received an increment or have been given a smaller one. It is, therefore, incumbent upon management to justify the award of increments and subsequently to be able to generally discuss the rationale with the staff.

To achieve this objective a system of ongoing staff assessment has to be undertaken, the principal features of which are:

(a) The preparation by management of an assessment rating for each member of staff at regular intervals – at least one per year.

(b) The qualities assessed are identical to those looked for in the interview assessment (see Section 7 above). Indeed, the same format can be used.

(c) The assessment has to be discussed with each employee with particular reference to areas of improvement or deterioration since the previous review.

(d) Increments should be in proportion to the improved assessment ratings.

(e) The results of the assessments are to be used in determining suitability of staff for promotion when vacancies occur.

11. Relationships Between the Staff

Relationships created by the staff are in part a reflection of management. There are, however, many factors which occur that cannot be placed at the feet of management. Likes, dislikes, professional jealousies, sometimes downright envy, must be contained. From time to time these may be the root cause of salon work disruption. It must be recognised that these may exist and that efforts must be quickly made to deal with them. Other members of staff, perhaps not directly involved, can be most helpful in these matters and often the means by which the problems can be resolved. It can be to no one's benefit if these problems are not contained, as they are often one of the main causes of client loss and eventual curtailment of business. It is essential that staff disagreements are kept out of the salon and never allowed to affect the clients.

12. Relationships Between Staff and Clients

These could and should be enjoyed. The manner in which the staff conducts itself can be the means of attracting the clients back to the salon regularly. Good manners, efficient and competent working and a sincere wish to achieve good results for all are ideals to aim for. Often, even though the standard of work is not of a high level, the manner in which it is carried out is sufficient for the client to return regularly. It can never replace, or be used to excuse bad work, but manner of working does go a long way. The extremely clever and expert worker has still to present what they are able to do and unless it is done in an acceptable manner they may never get a second chance to do so. It is important to display the right attitude – which will involve a careful choice of words. There are times and places to give full vent to what one feels and would like to say. These rarely occur in the process of tending a client. So often it is better to avoid discussing politics, religion or other people. These subjects may involve personal prejudices and dislikes, possibly affecting the client's ability to relax and enjoy the service being provided. Clients should always be treated respectfully and professionally. Whether the client is a relative, personal friend, a close neighbour, or complete stranger, there should be no difference to the manner or approach in which the service is carried out. Some clients are easy to befriend but this should not alter the manner of working in the salon. It is usually better to keep personal friendships outside business so that others may not be antagonised by them. Spending an unnecessary amount of time on a friend at the expense of another client can only result in loss of clientele or recommendation. Likewise, to gossip to those who can be 'trusted' often results in upsetting other clients. Respecting the confidences of others without repeating them is the least that can be expected. Readily repeating what one has been told often 'bounces' back hurtfully at some future time. To be professional in approach to clients is to respect them. Mutual respect is then soon earned. This often results in an increased clientele as well as an enhanced reputation. There is no doubt that hairdressers with both the ability and correct manner are always the most successful and popular with the clientele.

13.   Relationships Outside the Salon

These should be conducted in a way that does not affect the salon. When meeting a friend, arrange for this to take place somewhere other than the salon, so avoiding the unnecessary clutter and inevitable interruptions that this causes. Professionalism extends outside the salon. Meeting people at various social functions is often a means of attracting clients. But it is easy for one's conduct to discourage people seeking the services of the salon. If the personal lives of staff can be conducted in a pleasant, considerate and thoughtful way, then the means of success may be more assured. Where boyfriends and girlfriends are allowed to impinge on working time continually then problems are created rather than resolved. Contacts with all outside the salon should be kept to a minimum when working and only be permissible in emergencies.

14.   Relationships Generally

The creating of amicable relationships requires a degree of maturity and understanding. It is important to try to look at situations as seen by others. As a person enters a room, the way they walk, the manner of dress worn, the fashion of hair, the demeanour or disposition displayed and facial expression worn will produce all kinds of responses from others. If a person walks in an affected way then it is likely to be noticed and to be distracting. The clothes worn may be extremely fashionable, causing others to feel underdressed or insignificantly attired in comparison. Reactions may vary from admiration to envy. If condescending looks or facial expressions are used then negative responses are likely to be evoked which are not conducive to the creating of good relationships. Each individual contribution to a relationship is essential. The look, proximity, smell and sound of an individual will all contribute to the relationship for good or otherwise. When the factor of speech is added to the interaction then a multitude of other responses are evoked. The question of communication is a very important one. What is intended to be said is not always interpreted as such. Not only is what is said vital to understanding; but the way it is said, combined with other mannerisms and gestures verbally or non-verbally communicated is also involved. It is important that as many as possible of the sort of things that antagonise or create adverse reactions are recognised and avoided if good relationships are to be established. The interaction and interchange between two persons becomes even more complicated when three or more individuals are involved.

The working of staff in the modern salon, particularly one of the open type, is clearly seen by all. Exclamations or comments made and unknowingly heard can produce all kinds of surprising reactions from clients. Consideration must be given to the possible reactions of other people in the salon. Although it is not possible or desirable to analyse each of the relationships entered into, it can be fruitful to think about them from time to time.

In a business which consists of the interactions and reactions of so many people it is most important that some time be given to the effects of the variety of relationships that the salon or business environment produces. These are often the root cause of problems. Nurturing care and understanding between oneself and others is an important aspect of salon management. It is invariably appreciated by clients and can only be conducive to achieving success in business.

15. Staff Training and Education

Many formal training schemes, given in a variety of establishments are available to new entrants into the hairdressing profession and are suitable for entrants of all ages. The majority of these schemes are designed to teach the technical aspects of performing the hairdressing services but, increasingly, courses are being made available for experienced hairdressers to improve their expertise and also to acquire scientific and managerial skills. The generally accepted forms of training are:

(a) **Apprenticeship** in a salon which involves a period of learning the practical skills and techniques, as well as the business of hairdressing. It deals with the handling of a variety of people and principles of administration. (A copy of an indenture for a hairdressing apprentice is to be seen in the Appendix, which details some of the duties of an apprentice.) For many years now, a three-year basic apprenticeship has been the norm. During this time the apprentice agrees to learn and the employer agrees to teach, or have taught. What has never been universally accepted is just what the apprentice should learn as basic skills. Some consider that fashion is the main concern. Others require the learning of a narrow set of skills which will allow more money to be taken in the salon, more quickly. Still others like to see a variety of basic skills taught which allows the greatest adaptability at a later stage of apprenticeship. From the apprentice's point of view the ability to progress throughout a career in a variety of salons is necessary. From the point of view of some employers, only those skills that enhance their prospects and their businesses should be considered. The enlightened employer will ensure that the interests of both the apprentice and the business are balanced and will encourage all that is necessary to equip the young apprentice for a successful career in an industry of which their business is a part.

In addition to being trained in the salon the apprentice can attend the local technical college, where there should be courses to augment the practical skills. Generally, these courses ensure practice of basic skills and learning of related subjects which help the student to understand more fully what they are doing. It is also frequently necessary to broaden the basic educational standard of the apprentice so that more advanced subjects may be assimilated in the later stages of hairdressing training. The right balance between practical work, theory and educational subjects has been a constant source of discussion, argument and downright disruption since hairdressing training in colleges began. Repeatedly, syllabuses laid down by such bodies as the City and Guilds of London Institute, devised and contributed to by the representatives of the various craft organisations, have, almost as soon as they are printed, become subject to criticism, often from those very organisations whose contributions helped to determine them. Despite this, the combination of both salon and college training and education of young apprentices has produced a more professional approach which has begun to permeate the various levels of the industry. It has contributed to a greater value being placed on the skills and abilities in the industry. It has been the pattern of success on which other industries have been founded – the future of its young entrants.

(b)   Full-time college training is an alternative to a salon apprenticeship. For a period of two years the practical and theoretical skills of hairdressing are studied. Included in this period of learning is the development of basic education and the acquisition of professionalism. The first stage introduces the student to the principles of analytical study and the careful planning of the application of the variety of techniques that can be involved. This allows for speedier working in simulated salon conditions. The aim is to achieve all that an apprentice would achieve at the end of their training, namely, a good grounding in basic hairdressing, the ability to adapt to the requirements of a variety of salons and types of styling, and generally to begin to apply that basic knowledge required of a professional hairdresser in the world of commercial hairdressing.

(c)   Private school training is another alternative to the three-year training as an apprentice. In the private schools a variety of condensed courses are available which may involve attendance for a period of a day to several months. Generally, the private schools offer the best means of adult training and often this is the only means of entry to hairdressing for the mature student. Generally, it might be considered that the apprenticeship and full-time college training schemes fit the young school leaver's requirements better than private school training. For the specialised, more advanced styling courses, the private school is generally unequalled. As with the salons and colleges, there are a variety of schools available, each with their own standards of excellence and repute. Good training in the best of any of them will assure the required results.

(d) Differences between the training schemes. To serve an apprenticeship in a good professional salon which provides practical hairdressing experience, together with the necessary ongoing instructions which may be augmented by day-release to the local technical college, is a sound way to become a competent hairdresser. Throughout the training period, wages are paid, as laid down by the Hairdressing Undertakings Wages Council.

Provided at least half of the timetable is devoted to practical periods of hairdressing, full-time attendance at a college is an equally good way to become a hairdresser. A student does not, however, receive wages during the period of training, but some grants may be available from certain local education authorities.

For the young person entering hairdressing and attending a private school of hairdressing there is a variety of courses available. Mistakes are often made when young people attempt to become qualified and expert stylists in two or three months. The younger student requires a period of practice and learning, generally spread out over a period of time. Some people, however, are stimulated to quicker learning when they are involved with paying the total costs. No wages, or grants are made in private school training. Fees are payable which vary between the different schools.

There are two important factors which contribute to the effectiveness of training, whether apprenticeship, full-time college training, or private school training. One is in the manner in which the entrants to hairdressing conduct themselves throughout the course. If the time is devoted to practice and learning there is every chance of achieving good standards. Although the facilities may vary with the variety of environments, the successful students of hairdressing often make their own opportunities. It is easy to waste time and be diverted by a myriad of other interests only to realise too late that time has passed and the anticipated results have not been achieved. Unfortunately, many students do this and then resort to blaming others for their own inadequacies and lack of ability.

The second factor involves those responsible for the training. In many salons there is neither planning nor purpose in what is taught or the way in which it is taught. The apprentice too often has to 'pick up' what should be formally taught. In other salons there is neither the time nor the opportunity to acquire the basic skills required. The professionally run salons, however, make every endeavour to ensure that good practical training is carried out, and where these salons do not send their apprentices to college for day-release they themselves impart the theoretical instruction required. Generally, however, the training is integrated with college-based schemes.

Similarly, there are colleges that do not have the balance of staff or the time to produce the co-ordinated level of training required to fit the full-time student for a successful entry into the commercial hairdressing salon. However, in those establishments where staff are professionally trained by good, experienced, qualified teachers, there is a good, balanced and generally acceptable training schedule. Whether in the salon or the college or school it is the integrity of the personnel responsible for the training which is often at the root of the issue. There are those who, because of the poor standards of some salons, colleges or schools, consider that all these forms of training are a waste of time. These criticisms usually come from those who have neither the knowledge of alternative schemes nor the ability or understanding to effect improvements in the 'training packages' available.

In most cases, however, it is not what is taught but the way in which it is taught that matters. In the days of the private, voluntary academy, where the skills of masters were freely given to young, aspiring hairdressing students, there was a degree of enthusiasm which could not fail to motivate even the weakest. Fortunately, much of this attitude survives today in salons, colleges and schools throughout the country and this has probably bound the industry of hairdressing together throughout its most traumatic periods. The education and training of students is an investment in the future of the hairdressing industry as well as affording stable career prospects for the successful student.

(e)   General staff training.   Having attained a basic training in hairdressing, it is necessary to maintain and improve the standards achieved. Many consider upon completion of the basic training that they are complete hairdressers and there is no need for further practice or training. To others who take a keener interest in the developments and innovations of the fashion world there is no end to learning. To them there is always something more to practise, to enthuse over and take pride in achieving. For those who are this interested in their work – usually the most successful – new ideas are readily assimilated and carried out in practice sessions or in application on clients. For them there is much interchange and discussion with colleagues about the work of the moment and ways to achieve it. Those that apply their basic training and knowledge, coupled with a thoughtful approach to their work, generally soon become the sought-after stylists of their salons and areas.

Managements who wish to achieve successful operations will encourage and nurture in the staff a desire to continue to develop their professional expertise. This may take the form of sending staff at management's expense to courses held at local technical colleges, private academies and manufacturers' technical tuition centres. Generally, short updating courses of one to three days are the most popular, both with the staff, whose personal routines are not too disturbed, and with management, who avoid the effects of understaffing. These courses cater for those wishing to acquire the most recent innovations and techniques, particularly in cutting and styling. Further training is achieved for other members of the staff when these new skills are demonstrated to the staff who did not attend the course.

The commonest type of training is that done in salon training sessions after business hours. During these sessions the various members of staff work on different techniques and generally analyse and experiment. The younger members of staff are guided and encouraged too. In many instances special tutors are invited into the salon for these sessions. This has the appeal of new ideas being introduced from outside the salon. In most cases this proves to be most stimulating and rewarding. It can be done by the individual, or a group of salons. An exchange of a member of staff with another salon can be arranged, which may be on a reciprocal basis, to encourage enthusiasm and help develop good practical skills and attitudes. This, and other training schemes and ideas, may be attempted, but whatever scheme is used it is most important that some training provision is made for all the staff.

(f) Other training. Apart from stylists and other specialist operators the training of others needs to be undertaken. The manager must keep abreast of developments in the law, costing, insurance and the variety of changes of tax systems. Periodic reviewing of general management techniques is probably a good investment. The ability to deal with staff and their problems requires periods of thought and consideration which some management seminars can provide.

As new staff are acquired so the principles and policies of the business need to be imparted. This can be achieved in the form of special induction sessions during which it can be assured that all those starting have received similar instructions and the latest information. So often this is neglected, with the result that misunderstandings arise between old and new staff.

General administration of the salon is the responsibility of management and staff. Systems of storing, stock-taking, dispensing, dealing with special equipment, maintaining cleanliness and hygiene, and general reception need periodic overviewing. Regular sessions should be set aside for this to be done. It might prove invaluable to include in these sessions the recent work of the craft organisations and the role they play in the industry. How they directly affect the salon running can be of general interest, and how the staff may be encouraged to support, or make their contribution, might be usefully discussed. So often it is left to a few volunteers to get things done, with the result that too much is done by too few. This often results in other opinions and viewpoints not being generally reflected. If members of an organisation have any criticisms to make then they should be adequately represented. This usually means participating in some way in the organisation.

Training for juniors, seniors, managers, receptionists and cleaners requires thought and planning. It is in the interests of all concerned to ensure that this is carried out. Clients usually appreciate, and look forward to trying out the innovations that training sessions produce. Training helps to develop the employees as people and this is often reflected in their loyalty to the salon and their colleagues and clients. Reputations and standards generally may be determined by the amount, type and quality of the training. Although often dismissed because of costs, much business is lost if it is not undertaken.

The fifteen matters outlined above all need careful consideration to help establish the correct relationships between management, staff and clients. It shows that the management of a salon is not wholly concerned with the practical and artistic carrying out of a hairdressing service. Neither is it entirely dependent upon the application of formal business and commercial practices such as stock-keeping, accountancy etc. Important though both these aspects are, the success of a modern hairdressing salon relies heavily on the staff employed. Like the hotel and catering industry, hairdressing is a 'people' industry. It involves the interaction of people; it is a service to people. For success, people have to be tended and satisfied. Without this essential ingredient of the satisfied client returning for further service, the hairdressing business could not survive. To ensure a satisfactory outcome of service the technical staff should have the necessary practical skill and ability, and the means of presentation, which will meet the requirements of clients. Additionally, the staff should have the type of personality that allows them to be readily acceptable, to maintain their enthusiasm and to update their expertise. Further to this is the ability to ensure the clients' comfort, recognise their needs and be able to interpret their requests when dealing with them in practical situations. Such an environment can only be obtained by team work involving all employees, whether deemed management or staff. Mutual trust should exist between everyone associated with the salon. Management is responsible for originating, developing and maintaining policies and social practices which will create an environment in which the individual's personal requirements are satisfied and in which the salon as a business can prosper.

CHAPTER V

Work Study in the Salon

The objective of *Work Study* is to ensure the best possible utilisation of both human and material resources in carrying out the specified activities. Work study may be regarded as a combination of two things: *Method Study* which is the recording and critical examination of existing and proposed methods of doing work, together with the development and application of improved methods; and *Work Measurement* which establishes the work content of a specified job by finding the time required to undertake it to a defined standard by a suitably qualified worker.

Work study techniques have been widely applied to industrial processes during the twentieth century and by the 1950s similar techniques were being applied to commercial and administrative functions, under the title of 'Organisation and Method Studies'.

Unfortunately, the introduction of Work and/or *Organisation and Method Studies* has often not occurred until the business was well established and working methods and practices had been accepted by the employees, whether management or staff. The introduction of work study to replace familiar practices with more efficient methods is often only introduced when the trading results are showing an adverse trend. In such circumstances it is natural for staff to view the introduction of work study as a threat to their earnings and possibly to their future employment prospects with the enterprise.

In the hairdressing industry very little use has been made of formal work study and organisation and method techniques although, undoubtedly, the professional hairdressing operations taught in formal training establishments have in recent years been developed as a result of method study rather than the practical skills of individual instructors. Many college-trained students find it difficult to apply effectively the techniques they had been taught in training within the environment of the commercial salon. One of the prime causes for the newcomer's difficulties is often the layout of the working area which has generally been arrived at as a result of evolution rather than as a result of a systematic plan developed from method studies.

The problems of the newcomer in adapting to the salon working methods may often be an indication of the inefficiency of the methods which have developed within the salon, rather than the more commonly assumed inability or inexperience of the newcomer. Newcomers are accordingly advised to follow blindly the example of their longer-serving colleagues and adapt to the prevailing working methods. Neither the management nor the newcomer has the evidence with which to prove or disprove the validity of the process used.

53

Such evidence would be available to management if a method study had been used to develop the working systems employed.

The scope of work study and 'organisation and method' is not, however, confined to the performance of hairdressing operations, where the introduction of method study alone may be directly conducive to the development of an efficient salon. The introduction of work measurement will produce a time for each hairdressing operation and also the time spent on associated tasks, e.g. reception duties, stock-keeping etc. In addition, work measurement provides a management tool for the setting of standards and for the making of costing and pricing decisions. It also provides a basis for awarding merit increases in remuneration. In addition, any need for more staff will be discovered; the tasks to be performed by the newcomers may also be identified.

In the larger salons the division of administrative work between the hairdressing operatives and the administrative employees may need clarification and standardisation to enable the hairdressers' time to be concentrated on their professional duties and, at the same time, to preserve the personal hairdresser/client relationship.

The introduction of work study provides management with:

1. The means of producing a realistic plan of future activities.
2. A means of measuring actual performance against the plan.
3. The means with which to develop an economically efficient enterprise.

It has already been stated that the introduction of work study can cause resentment amongst the staff and the introduction of a dedicated work study practitioner will usually be uneconomical as well as unwise. If a work study analysis is carried out by the manager or supervisor a feeling of being 'spied on' can prevail amongst the staff; this may be transmitted to the clients.

The willing co-operation of all members of staff is a prerequisite for the successful introduction of the work study techniques. To achieve this co-operation management have to:

1. Select the right time to initiate works study. Ideally this time would be when trade was buoyant but not overwhelming.
2. Provide a measure of security to the staff: this may be in the form of increased remuneration, preferably in the form of a profit-sharing scheme or a lengthy contract.
3. Fully explain to the staff the objectives of the 'study' and the techniques to be employed and invite their suggestions in their application within the salon.
4. Introduce the various aspects of work study on a gradual basis.

METHOD STUDY

In general the introduction of *Method Study* is recommended as the first stage because method study is directly associated with the performance of the day-to-day hairdressing operations. The hairdressing operatives will, therefore, be familiar and practised in the detailed operations or elements which comprise a particular hairdressing service or treatment. If staff training sessions for juniors are part of the normal salon activities it is recommended that method study should be introduced at these sessions, with senior operators being trained in the relevant techniques. To achieve this aim it is necessary for the training supervisor to break down the hairdressing service being taught into elements (see Fig. 5.1).

The senior operators should be given an opportunity to discuss and, if necessary, amend the listing of elements which comprise the complete service. During the training session the trainee method study practitioners should observe the activities being performed and:

1. Identify the individual elements.
2. Observe the performance of the elements by both the instructor and the student.
3. Note any variation between the listed elements and activities performed.
4. Identify any differences between the training activities and the actual salon conditions, e.g. all preparations used set out in a segregated area.
5. Note any difficulties or delays experienced by either the instructor or the student in performing a particular element.

At the conclusion of the hairdressing operation or service, the findings of all participants should be freely discussed; recommendations for overcoming the general difficulties and sources of delay identified should be prepared and submitted to the management. If practical within a short time-scale, all services provided by the salon should be subjected to a similar examination. It is then for management to consolidate the recommendations and, where they are not contradictory, to implement the changes as soon as is practically possible, whether these changes are to methods of working, work area layout, salon layout, salon equipment or administrative procedures. In instances where the recommendations are contradictory, further discussion with the staff and possibly further exercises may be necessary.

It can, therefore, be said that method study is an organised and systematic review of practical methods of working by reducing each job, task, operation or service to easily identifiable segments or elements. An individual can, therefore, apply the principles of method study to their own routine tasks, provided they are of a repetitive and defined nature. In small salons where formal in-house training sessions are not the norm, self-applied method study should be the first stage in the introduction of work study.

The division of the hairdressing services into elements may be made by management or by individual hairdressers. Ideally, it should be made by individual hairdressers and consolidated and agreed by management. This should ensure that a mutual and common agreement on the basis of the study is established between all participants and personal anomalies are identified and corrected or adjusted before the study commences.

Ideally, the next and final stage of method study should be the review of one particular hairdresser performing a hairdressing service within the practical salon environment by a colleague. The roles in this process can be reversed

FIG. 5.1

Definition of the Method Study Element

For the purposes of method study an element is considered to be a part of the service which will be provided by one member of the salon staff. The method study element, therefore, equates to the normal teaching term of 'parts' and for a Cut and Set the elements or parts would be:

1. Preparation of the client
2. Preparation of the client's hair
3. Discussion with client
4. Interpretation and consideration of style
5. Shampooing
6. The cut
7. The set
8. Drying and processing
9. The dressing

Each of the above divisions may be sub-divided into smaller parts or elements, for instance:

Number 6 – The cut

(a) examination of natural hair-growth, fall and direction
(b) discussion with client
(c) selection of tools
(d) selection of techniques
(e) sectioning of hair
(f) determination of first cut and length required
(g) determining guideline or guidelines
(h) cutting the guideline
(i) completing the first section
(j) cutting subsequent sections
(k) completing the back
(l) completing the sides
(m) completing the front
(n) completing the top front
(o) completing the top crown
(p) checking the complete cut
(q) client care and hygiene

when an opportunity presents itself. The work-load within the salon will frequently preclude such reviews, but a study by an independent person should be arranged when the individual hairdresser's study produces results that are at variance to those found by the other operators. These differences will be confined to certain elements of the service; the check study should be confined to these elements unless its findings affect other associated elements.

As a result of method study a salon will achieve:

1. An update on working methods.
2. The establishment of a shared working method.
3. An indication of the defects in salon equipment and layout.

WORK MEASUREMENT

At this stage the 'scientific' approach to management through the use of work study has only been applied to the direct hairdressing operations, although it is possible that routine and repetitive aspects of administrative or 'overhead' activities may have been partially encompassed within the method studies. It is through the introduction of *Work Measurement* that the significance and extent of overhead or indirect supplementary activities are identified.

The introduction of theoretical work measurement would necessitate obtaining an exact timing for each element of a service. The accumulation of these elements would give a total time for that particular hairdressing service. Such an operation is likely to produce considerable friction between the staff and management and, undoubtedly, the service to the clients would deteriorate because the outstanding feature which will produce a variance to any standard time for a service is the individuality of the client. Additionally, a broad idea of the time spent on hairdressing operations can be obtained from a study of the appointments book and receipt slips. Work measurement in the widest sense can and should be used to establish:

1. The amount of time spent on the direct hairdressing service.
2. The amount of time spent on indirect hairdressing operations, e.g. cleaning working areas, laundry operations etc.
3. The time spent on administrative activities, e.g. stock issuing and receiving, appointments and reception duties etc.
4. Idle time awaiting clients, i.e. absence of business
5. Idle time awaiting completion of an automatic process, e.g. with a client under the dryer.
6. Lost time due to sickness, holidays etc.
7. Lost time due to personal reasons, tea-breaks etc.

As in the case of method studies, success in obtaining meaningful work measurement times depends upon the full co-operation of the staff. Management has to give careful thought to the work measurement data recording process which has to be conducted simultaneously and concurrent with the provision of the normal salon services to clients. The methodology to be employed in obtaining the required data is dependent upon the individual salon's environment and organisation structure. However, the objective is always the same, i.e. to record the activities and the time spent on their performance during a given operating period, whether a day, week, month or year.

The first requirement in establishing the method to be employed in the data collection process is to determine the total activity of each employee. An employee designated as a hairdresser has as a principal activity the task of providing a hairdressing service; but this person may also be required to perform duties such as training of apprentices, reception of clients and control of stock issues.

Within another salon environment a person may be employed as a receptionist; but this position may include: control of the cash register and the associated banking and book-keeping duties; stock ordering and the maintenance of stock records; and responsibility for the maintenance of general salon services, e.g. laundering of protective clothing and provision of refreshments.

The activities required of each employee can be listed by the manager either from personal knowledge or, if job descriptions have been prepared (see Chapter IV), directly from these records. Each employee should be given the opportunity to review and, if necessary, discuss amendments to their individual task listings. In practice, it will often be found that the significance of such a clinically analytical approach to routine activities will not be appreciated by many of the employees and, therefore, their participation in the definition of tasks will be limited. To overcome this difficulty the listings prepared by management should be distributed to the employees well in advance (at least a month) of the finalisation date. During this time the employees should be asked to delete any tasks not performed and add those tasks performed but not identified on the listings.

The finalisation of the task listings which should be done in conjunction with the employees, both individually and, finally, collectively will highlight many anomolies. These can be classified as follows:

1.   Definition and Consolidation

Tasks may be described under a common heading but may relate to different facets of the salon's activities, e.g. cleaning:

(a) A hairdresser will identify as a cleaning task the tidying of the working surface between the departure of one client and the arrival of another.

(b) An apprentice will identify as a cleaning task the wiping down of dryers and tidying of the drying area.

(c) A receptionist will list as cleaning, the task of collecting magazines and periodicals which have become dispersed within the reception/waiting area, together with tidying tasks such as emptying ashtrays etc.

(d) A large amount of cleaning time will be identified outside of salon opening hours in respect of general salon cleaning. This task may be performed by a dedicated cleaner or by other employees as a secondary task.

Management has to decide whether these cleaning duties should be reported as individual items, e.g. working-area cleaning, grouped under only one heading (Cleaning) or divided up into two expenditure categories, i.e. Indirect Labour Cleaning (items (a) and (b) above) or Overhead Cleaning (items (c) and (d) above). In general for work measurement purposes the one heading would be used and subsequent financial apportionments and allocations would be made as part of the costing and control systems (see Chapters IX and X).

2. Primary and Secondary Tasks

The division between *primary* and *secondary* tasks is on a functional basis and not on a personal one. Most hairdressing salons have one prime function, i.e. the provision of a hairdressing service to clients. The retailing of associated products and preparations is a secondary function except where these activities require the dedicated attention of one or more persons. The prime tasks are, therefore, those directly associated with the provision of the hairdressing service. These have already been identified and broken down into elements using method study. The provision of these elements is a prime task whether provided by a person designated as a hairdresser, manager, apprentice or any other functionary. For costing purposes these prime tasks represent the total *Direct Labour Time.* All other tasks are secondary whether they are directly associated with the provision of the service, e.g. cleaning the working area after the service or indirectly, e.g. management's preparation of employees' pay-packets.

3. Normal and Abnormal Tasks

A person's job description, if accurately compiled, will detail the tasks normally to be performed by that person. However, during periods of staff absence or extreme activity an individual may be required to perform additional tasks. The time recorded by the irregular operators is an integral part of the total work-loading and consequently should not be excluded from the total time records.

4. Specialised Functions

There are certain tasks normally associated with the administrative function of the salon which can only be performed by one individual member of staff in addition to the manager; e.g. the receptionist may also be responsible for preparing the routine financial records and would consequently include as tasks the following:

(a) Daily update of Cash Book and Ledger Accounts

(b) Preparation of Wages

(c) Trial Balances

(d) Bank Reconciliations

Initially, due to their specialised nature, it is usual to classify these tasks under one heading for work measurement purposes, i.e. 'Finance General'.

Even after the grouping of administrative tasks as indicated in Section 4 above, the list of tasks will be long and as such will represent a requirement for the expenditure of considerable personnel resources in obtaining the required work measurement data. Managements should, therefore, identify what information is already available from the salon records and, if possible, extend current records to satisfy the work measurement requirements. In this category are records of:

Paid Hours

Statutory laws relating to employment, Trade Council regulations and accepted business customs have resulted in the specified paid hours for:

(a) Full-time employees   (Employees working in excess of 20 hours per week): to consist of:

(i) Guaranteed pay for attendance during normal working or contractual time whether work is available or not.

(ii) Payment for attendance hours beyond the extent of the contractual time, i.e. for overtime.

(iii) Normal pay per day for statutory holidays and personal holiday entitlements.

(iv) Normal pay per day when absence is due to sickness. (Optional.)

(b) Part-time employees.   (Those employed for less than 20 hours per week): payment to be in respect of hours worked only.

Holidays

These are of two types:

(a) Statutory holidays, e.g. Christmas Day, are days upon which the salon is normally closed and for which full-time staff are paid at their hourly rate. However, if the salon is open on such days it is statutory law that the hours worked by staff are paid at overtime rates (normally double time) and in addition such staff are entitled to a paid day-off in lieu of the statutory holiday worked.

(b) Annual holidays are a personal entitlement, being paid absence for full-time employees, additional to statutory holidays. In general, such holidays are arranged in advance and are mutually agreed by the employee and management. Records are normally retained of both intended holidays and actual holidays taken, but there may be a requirement to amend the holiday records to include half-day or part-day holidays often taken at short notice.

Absence due to Sickness

Unless the absence is due to some prearranged medical treatment, management is normally unaware of the absence until it occurs. If the illness is not of a serious nature the likely period of future absence will be known or predictable. Such data should already be recorded in the general salon records and therefore any further recording would be unnecessary.

Out of Salon Training and Meetings

The general salon records should already include details of agreed employee absence to attend events for which the salon receives no tangible benefits. It may, however, be necessary to consolidate such records in the case of part-day absence in respect of actual time absent when this differs from the previously agreed period of time.

REST ALLOWANCE

The recording of abnormal hours of attendance is frequently not included in the salon control systems, the regulation of actual time-keeping, both in respect of lateness at the commencement of the working day and strict adherence to the time-span of unpaid midday break, is left to the integrity of the employees and their immediate supervision. Additionally, it is often common practice for employees to leave the salon for short periods of time when there are no client requirements. Other employees remain within the salon but perform no salon tasks both during slack periods and in their personal midday breaks.

In a salon with a good rapport between management and staff, in times of great client demand, staff may take few or no breaks from salon-related tasks during the complete time-span of the normal working day. Overtime payments are not claimed by the staff for lunch-time working, it generally being accepted that such time will be offset by any temporary absence which occurs.

To formalise the 'give and take' informal arrangements that exist as regards actual hours worked during the course of a working day and to avoid management/staff conflict which might arise from the introduction of work measurement it is prudent for a daily *rest allowance* to be established for each employee. Such an allowance has to represent the minimum unpaid break in continuous working stipulated by law but enlightened managements should encompass within the allowance paid time in which employees would normally take refreshments etc. For example, if the working day extends over a nine-hour time-span (8.45 a.m. to 5.45 p.m.) a rest allowance of 1½ hours may be established, i.e. 10 minutes of each hour of normal attendance time. Such an allowance is applicable to both full-time and part-time staff. Work measurement should include a measurement of the actual time taken by staff against this allowance. For practical purposes the measurements should be recorded by individual members of a staff under the following headings:

1. Temporary Absence from Salon

This includes time lost due to lateness and time spent outside the salon during working hours for personal reasons.

2.   In-House Rest

This comprises time spent within the salon during the working day when, for personal reasons, the employee was not available to perform salon duties.

SECONDARY TASKS

Measurement of time spent on salon tasks other than the direct hairdressing operations (primary functions) can most expediently be performed by grouping the tasks identified in the job descriptions under one of the following general headings:

1.   Indirect Hairdressing Tasks

These are tasks which arise within the salon as a result of providing the service of hairdressing but exclude the commercial aspects which are dealt with in Sections 3–5, below. They include such tasks as: cleaning the working area, cleaning the salon generally, cleaning fixtures and fittings, equipment maintenance, laundry and preparation of clients' refreshments etc.

2.   Training

The in-salon training may take many forms and encompass training in secondary functions in addition to the direct hairdressing operations. All training involves at least two members of the staff – an 'instructor' and a 'trainee' each of whom should record the time spent as either 'training given' or 'training received' as appropriate. If, however, a 'productive task' is performed in the course of the training session, the normal or estimated normal time for the performance of the task should be recorded against the appropriate category by the 'trainee' with the balance of the actual time spent being recorded against training received.

3.   Reception of Clients

The tasks performed by the receptionist are both numerous and variable but for the purpose of work measurement should be regarded as the tasks which involve direct communication with people other than salon employees. Such tasks include: reception of all visitors; making of appointments both as a result of personal visits and telephone calls; answering all telephone calls and enquiries; maintenance of any clients' records; responsibility for cash register etc. Many of the tasks performed are of a repetitive nature and in such instances it may be appropriate to establish a set time for each task; e.g. the making of an appointment may be given a set time of 3 minutes thus if 31 appointments are made in a day, a total time of 93 minutes is recorded as part of the 'Reception of Clients' time.

4.   Stock Tasks

The control of stock whether for retail or for use during the hairdressing service is one of the most important secondary functions within the salon and one that usually involves the participation of all the staff. The tasks involved are: establishment of stock requirements, placing of orders, collection and receipt of goods, storage of goods, issuing of materials to work or sales areas, arranging or preparing materials for use etc. Most of the tasks relating to stock control are easily identifiable and generally occupy a significant period of time, i.e. in excess of 15 minutes.

5. Management Control Data

It is normally anticipated that time booked in this category will have been expended by managerial or supervisory staff who maintain financial records, prepare wages, interview staff and prospective staff, investigate complaints, prepare business plans etc. Bookings against this category by other employees are usually made on the specific direction of management and may arise as a result of: attendance at interviews; performing special tasks, e.g. vouching cash received against sale receipt slips; completing work measurement records etc. To avoid recording discrepancies, it is important that each employee is instructed as to which work measurement classification of secondary functions each of their identified tasks have been assigned.

DIRECT HAIRDRESSING OPERATIONS

The measurement of the hours devoted to the direct hairdressing operations which will comprise the major portion of all time spent on salon work may be ascertained by:

1. Deducting from total actual attendance time the sum of all other times recorded.

2. Recording the time spent performing direct hairdressing in the same manner as recording time for any of the secondary functions. This will necessitate an individual booking for each series of operations except if the performance of direct hairdressing is a continuous process.

3. In addition to recording the time spent on direct hairdressing operations, details of the elements of the service performed for each and every client should be recorded.

The complete records obtained as a result of instituting No. 3 above enables the actual time for each complete service to be calculated. From a series of times for a particular service, preferably containing times recorded by all qualified hairdressers employed, an average time for the performance of the service can be obtained, i.e. a *Standard Time* is established. Standard times can be a valuable aid to business planning both in the long term (see Chapter X) and for short-term planning, e.g. the frequency of appointments and general salon workloading. Standard times also provide a means of measuring performance of an individual hairdresser and if recordings as described in paragraphs 1 and 2 above are made, an indication of the overall performance of the salon staff may be obtained.

The completing of records as described in paragraphs 2 and 3 above is very time-consuming and in the case of 2 only confirms that all time has been accounted for by the individual employee. It is considered that method 3 should only be used until sufficient times have been obtained to calculate a realistic standard time for each service and then method 1 should be adopted. It should be noted that actual service times may vary with the level of activity within the salon; managements should ensure that times taken should not be taken in isolation for one particular service by one or more hairdresser over a particular period unless detailed timings of all other services provided over the same time scale are incorporated into the standard time calculation.

IDLE TIME

Many managements are reluctant to recognise that employee *Idle Time* is partly attributable to factors other than personal idleness or inefficiency in the staff. These factors may be summarised as:

1.   Uneven Flow of Business

Idle time is incurred when staff are available to perform the hairdressing service but there is no demand for these services. Often such slack periods are dispersed between periods when the resources of the salon are unable to meet the client demand; this will result in a loss of part of the potential share of the available trade.

2.   Uneven Throughput of Work

This can result in idle time being incurred by staff and clients who are awaiting the availability of specialised equipment or facilities which are already being utilised by other members of staff and their clients.

3.   Unco-ordinated Support Services

This may result in loss of productive time, e.g. a failure of the water-heater system would cause a delay to almost all direct hairdressing operations.

The accurate recording of idle time is an important aspect of work measurement and should not be amalgamated with the time lost due to the personal requirements of employees; that comprises the rest allowance. It is necessary for management to ensure that this distinction is clearly understood by all employees and this may best be obtained by applying the rule that if an employee is available for work and no work is done, the time should be recorded as idle time. Idle time generally may be divided into two categories: time spent waiting for clients; and time spent waiting to use facilities.

DATA RECORDING

To facilitate the recording of the data not contained in the normal salon records it is recommended that a special form should be designed for use by the recording staff. The typical layout of such a form is shown in Fig. 5.2, and this

layout contains provision for collection of data for the calculation of standard
times. As previously stated, this detailed information is not required for the
computation of routine control data, and in practice the 'Direct Hairdressing'

FIG. 5.2   Work Measurement – Daily Time Sheet

Employee's Name:			Date:			
Category of Activity:			**Notes:**			
(a) *Ineffective Time* (i) Authorised Absence .... (ii) Temporary Absence .... (iii) In-Salon Rest						Hours
				Total Ineffective Time		
(b) *Idle Time* (i) Absence of Clients .... (ii) Awaiting Facilities						
				Total Idle Time		
(c) *Secondary Tasks* (i) Indirect Hairdressing .... (ii) Training (Given) .... (iii) Training (Received) .... (iv) Reception .... (v) Stock Control .... (vi) Management						
				Total Secondary Tasks		
(d) *Direct Hairdressing*						
Client Ref.	Service Provided (No.)	Elements Performed (Nos.)	Time Started	Time Finished	Time Taken	
			Total Direct Hairdressing			
			Total Daily Attendance Time			

section may be contained on a separate form which will be utilised only when a standard time review is required. The results of any check measurements conducted by management or an independent member of the staff may also be reported on this document.

ANALYSIS AND INTERPRETATION OF WORK MEASUREMENT DATA

The data contained in the Daily Time Sheet is a report of the activities performed by an individual employee and, therefore, by consolidating the reports of all employees for each day, a daily report on the complete salon activities can be determined. Further consolidation of each daily report can determine the activities of the salon per week, per month, per year or over any other time scale. Frequently, the data is only used to evaluate an individual's performance as compared to other employees or against an expected performance level. The principle use of such information is, however, to provide management with immediate data on adverse business trends so that prompt corrective action may be taken.

Since hairdressing is a labour-intensive industry an ongoing analysis of the activities of employees will not only indicate at an early date the existence of an adverse trend, but also the reasons for such a trend. A trend is indicated by comparison with the results of other, similar periods. The longer the time-scale of each period, the greater the effect of levelling out of individual facts. For example, a month's analysis will show an increase or decrease in direct hairdressing hours compared with previous months. But it will not show that these were incurred during a particular week or on certain days of the week.

The basic analysis should be performed over a weekly time-span and the results compared to the average result of previous weeks or a targeted result set by management. Such targets are normally expressed as percentages, e.g. the *Efficiency Rate* should be 85 per cent. If adverse results are obtained, more detailed analysis may be required. At the end of this chapter is a worked example which shows a routine weekly analysis and specifies some control percentages.

As a result of the work measurement analysis, management decisions can be based on known facts, not 'hunches', and consequently are more realistic and acceptable to the affected personnel. Analysed Work Measurement results can be utilised for the determination of:

Number of employees to be engaged.
Tasks to be performed by employees, i.e. extent of specialisation.
Salon business hours.
Holiday arrangements.
Training time-table.
Personal performance.
Indication of the adequacy or otherwise of salon facilities.
Indication of the adequacy of salon methods and procedures.
Development of realistic business plans, financial programmes and personnel policies.

Further reference is made to the use of work measurement data in Chapters IX and X of this Book.

WORKED EXAMPLE OF WORK MEASUREMENT ANALYSIS

Narrative

Histyles Hairdressing Salon is jointly owned and managed by H. and I. Styles, who each draw a salary as working managers and, with the exception that this salary is based on a 48-hour, 6-day week, their conditions of employment are identical to the rest of the staff. The salon is open to the public between 9.30 a.m. and 5.30 p.m. on the six weekdays. The permanent staff, here referred to as A, B, C, D, E, F, M and N, are contracted to work a 5-day week, between 9.00 a.m. and 5.45 p.m., i.e. a 40-hour week. This figure excludes an unpaid lunch-break. The precise timing of this break is flexible, but it averages 45 minutes. In addition, two part-time staff, X and Y, are employed on a regular basis on Wednesdays, Thursdays, Fridays and Saturdays, X between the hours of 10.0 a.m. and 1.0 p.m., and Y between 1.0 p.m. and 5.0 p.m.. A third part-timer, Z, may be employed by arrangement. If part-time employees are required to attend for a continuous period of time exceeding 5 hours they are entitled to a 45 minute unpaid 'lunch-break'. The normal 'days off' for the permanent staff are:-

Mondays	—	A and B
Tuesdays	—	C and D
Wednesdays	—	E and N
Thursdays	—	F and M

It has been agreed that, partly in lieu of a formal lunch-break, a rest allowance of 12 minutes in each hour of attendance time should be regarded as normal. During week 14 of Year 19–, which contained Good Friday, the following deviations from normal attendance were recorded as part of the established salon reporting system:

1. On Monday, H and I were absent, attending a Trade Council Meeting, between 1.0 p.m. and 4.0 p.m.

2. On Monday, M (an apprentice) was on day-release to the local technical college.

3. On Tuesday, N (a senior apprentice) attended a hair nutritional lecture between 1.45 p.m. and 5.45 p.m.

4. C was injured in a road accident on Tuesday and was 'absent sick' for the rest of the week.

5. Z works between 10.0 a.m. and 5.45 p.m., Thursday to Saturday.

6. The overtime worked was:
   Wednesday – A and D, 30 minutes each
   H and I, 1 hour 15 minutes each
   Thursday – A, B, D, E and N, 1 hour each
   H and I, 1 hour 15 minutes each

7.   A was absent – agreed part of annual holiday entitlement.

A consolidation of the individual work measurement returns for each employee for each day worked showed the following:

Work Measurement Returns

Category of Activity	Hours
Authorised Absence	18.75
Temporary Absence	36.50
In-Salon Rest	17.50
Absence of Clients	4.00
Awaiting Facilities	11.00
Indirect Hairdressing	53.00
Training Given	2.00
Training Received	1.00
Reception	27.50
Stock Control	19.00
Management	8.00
Direct Hairdressing	170.75

From this information the following analysis to arrive at the complete performance data for Histyles operations in Week 14 can be made:

1.   Paid Hours

(a) Managerial Basic: 2 at 48 hours 96
     Overtime: 2 at 2.5 hours 5
(b) Full-time staff: Basic – 8 at 40 hours 320
                       Overtime 6
(c) Part-time staff: 1×3 days at 3 hours 9
                       1×3 days at 4 hours 12
                       1×2 days at 7 hours 14

                                        Total Paid Hours: 462

2.   Gross Contracted Attendance Hours

(a) Managerial Staff: 2×6 days
     at 8.75 hours 105.0
(b) Full-time Staff: 8×5 days
     at 8.75 hours 350.0
(c) Part-time Staff: 1×3 days at 3 hours 9.0
                       1×3 days at 4 hours 12.0
                       1×2 days at 7.75 hours 15.5

                                        Total Contracted
                                        Hours: 491.5

3. Approved Absence Hours

(a) Statutory Holidays: 9 at 8.75 hours 78.75
(b) Annual Holidays: 1 at 8.75 hours 8.75
(c) Staff Training: 1 at 8.75 hours .... 8.75 ⎫
                 1 at 4.00 hours .... 4.00 ⎬ Agree with total of 18.75 hours authorised absence on staff work measurements returns.
(d) Meetings: 2 at 3.00 hours .... 6.00 ⎭
(e) Sickness: 1×4 days at 8.75 hours 35.00

               Total Approved
               Absence: 141.25

4. Effective Hours Available

i.e. Gross Contracted Attendance Hours, minus Approved Absence, plus Temporary Absence, plus In-Salon Rest:

$$491.5 - (141.25 + 36.50 + 17.50) = \underline{296.25}$$

5. Effective Labour Rate

This is given by the formula

$$\frac{\text{Effective Hours}}{\text{Paid Hours}} \times 100 = \frac{296.25}{462} \times 100 = \underline{64.12\%} \text{ for } Wk.\ 14$$

Further analysis will show that the 35.88% ineffectiveness is attributable to the following:

(a) Statutory Holidays $\dfrac{78.75 \times 100}{462} =$ 17.05

(b) Annual Holidays $\dfrac{8.75 \times 100}{462} =$ 1.89

(c) Authorised Absence $\dfrac{18.75 \times 100}{462} =$ 4.06

(d) Sickness $\dfrac{35.00 \times 100}{462} =$ 7.58

(e) Paid Rest $\dfrac{(36.50 + 17.50) - (491.5 - 462)}{462} \times 100 =$ 5.30

                                               35.88

6. Efficiency Rate

The percentage of Effective Hours in which salon work was performed is given by the following formula:

$$\frac{(\text{Effective Hours} - \text{Idle Hours}) \times 100}{\text{Effective Hours}}$$

In Wk.14 when Idle Hours = 4 (Absence of Clients) + 11 (Awaiting Facilities)

Efficiency Rate $= \dfrac{(296.25 - 15.00) \times 100}{296.25}$ = Efficiency Rate = 94.94%

7. Percentage by Activity

Is given by the following formula:

$$\frac{\text{Hours devoted to activity} \times 100}{(\text{Effective Hours} - \text{Idle Time})}$$

In the case of *Direct Hairdressing* the *Activity Percentage* is:

$$\frac{170.75 \times 100}{(296.25 - 15.00)} = \underline{60.71\%}$$

A similar series of calculations will establish the following:

Activity	Percentage
Indirect Hairdressing	18.86
In-Salon Training	1.06
Stock Control	6.75
Reception	9.78
Management	2.84
Total Indirect Activity	39.29%

CHAPTER VI

Procurement and Control of Salon Materials and Equipment

Considerable reference has been made in previous chapters of this book to the management of personnel and to personnel-related activities, i.e. the dynamic factor associated with the operation of a salon or any other enterprise. There is, in addition, a static or inanimate factor which requires careful management attention and this is the control over the procurement, receipt, storage, utilisation, maintenance and eventual disposal of, materials and equipment. The nature and extent of management involvement can vary with each individual item of material or equipment used by the salon, but in general terms all items can be categorised under one of the following headings:

1. Capital Equipment

This may also be referred to, particularly in financial terms, as 'fixed assets', under individual headings such as Fixtures and Fittings, Salon Furniture, Salon Equipment, Office Equipment and, if appropriate, Motor Vehicles. The items in this category are an aid to the hairdresser in providing a hairdressing service and the associated retail operations. They are not expended during the performance of any one business transaction, but with the passage of time, they will deteriorate and require maintenance and eventual replacement. In addition, before they become unserviceable due to 'fair wear and tear' they may have become inefficient as compared with alternative equipment which utilises a more advanced technology. Equipment may also become redundant due to a change in working methods, often made necessary by a change in clients' demands upon the salon.

Management of capital equipment requires particular attention to:

(i) A realistic assessment of the requirement and use to which the item of equipment will be put.

(ii) A professional approach to the placement of the order, i.e. the obtaining of quotations from alternative sources of supply.

(iii) Safeguarding and maintaining the equipment after acquisition.

2. Expense Items

These are items that are not directly connected with the provision of the hairdressing service but are used frequently on a repetitive basis to maintain the general salon facilities and its associated commercial and administrative operations. Where the requirements are of a repetitive nature, for example, appointment cards, staff wage-packets etc., they may for control purposes be treated as stock items (see Section 3 below). The majority of items in this category are either required for a special purpose, e.g. electric light bulbs or are consumable, e.g. tea, coffee, milk etc., and are of little value individually. They are also of a proprietary nature, i.e. obtainable from many retail or wholesale outlets on an 'as required basis'. Consequently, the salon management is concerned with the extent of usage and amount of expenditure incurred, rather than the establishment of stocking levels and procurement policies.

3.   Stock Items

These are by far the most numerous items of material held within the salon and consist of:

(a)   Salon stock, which may be further divided into:

(i)   Consumable items, which are those materials that are used by the hairdresser during the provision of the hairdressing service, e.g. shampoos, setting lotions, tints, dyes, lacquers, creams, neutralisers etc. Such items are usually purchased in large 'trade' packs or quantities either in a usable form or in a form which may require a preparation mix prior to application during the hairdressing service.

(ii)   Semi-consumables are items that can be used by the hairdresser more than once but over a fairly short time-span will get lost, be broken or deteriorate into an unusable condition, e.g. hairpins, rollers, clips and hairnets.

(iii) Protective clothing and service equipment can be used by the hairdresser for more than one service but, in addition to being semi-consumable, will require regular servicing (normally laundering), e.g. towels, gowns and overalls.

(iv)   Tools may be supplied free of charge by the salon to the individual hairdressers or, alternatively, each hairdresser may be expected to purchase, either from the salon or elsewhere, items such as scissors, brushes and combs.

(b)   Resale stock consists of items which are intended for direct sale to clients. They are usually far more expensive, both in type and range than the items in the category of salon stock, and are normally in retail packs and quantities.

The control of the stock items represents the main challenge to the materials management expertise of the salon management, and requires the employment, to a greater or lesser extent, of all the techniques developed in other commercial undertakings, whether retail, service or manufacturing, to effect the required level of control.

In the small salon the complete process of material control will be undertaken by one individual, normally the owner/manager. In such instances much of the documentation necessary to the control system described below may be either dispensed with or consolidated into one or two control documents, namely, a stock record card to control physical stock movements, and an accounts record, which shows committed expenditure, as well as a record of payments, and bills outstanding. In the salon which is a department within a store or hotel, it is probable that a number of people will be involved in material control. The salon storekeeper will be responsible for determining the requirement (the requisitioner); the salon manager will be responsible for authorising the demand (the authoriser); the buyer may be part of the centralised purchasing staff; the goods may initially be received by a centralised goods receiving section prior to delivery to the salon; suppliers' invoices are paid by a centralised accounts department; finally, the salon stores issues stock to each individual hairdresser. It will be a prerequisite of any control system that each individual employee involved in the control of material is advised of the actions taken by the other participants which will, in due course, affect the activities of that individual.

In the pages that follow, an attempt is made to detail the factors which have to be addressed in the control of materials, whether the salon is large or small. The references to systems and documentation are of a general nature and will require modification to suit the individual requirements of each salon.

THE REQUISITIONING OF MATERIAL

1. Capital Equipment

The procurement of capital equipment is normally only commenced after a careful study of the requirement has been made. The purchase of capital equipment usually involves the expenditure of a comparatively large amount of money and in most salons the authorisation of such amounts is restricted to the highest level of the executive structure. Consequently, the main task of the 'requisitioner' is to prepare an economically viable proposal which will justify the expenditure involved. This activity may involve prior consultation with the 'buyer' in addition to the obtaining of the concurrence of the authoriser. The requisition, therefore, becomes a pure formality but is a necessary document to initiate the official purchase order and subsequent receipt documentation.

2. Stock Materials

These include both salon and retail stock, and may also include goods which are termed expense items if they are repeatedly in use and a supply of these items is normally retained in the salon. The fact that a stock is held within a salon should indicate that there is a regular demand for that item and the salon has obtained the stock items in anticipation of future sale or use in the hairdressing service. To this end, an investment of working capital has been made. It is, therefore, important that this investment should be recovered, together with a return on the investment in the form of a profit mark-up. Under ideal circumstances, stock would be obtained at the commencement of the trading day and sold at a profit during that day, and replacement stock sufficient for the following day ordered for immediate delivery. In practice, it is impossible to forecast the actual demands for material that will be made during the course of the working day. In addition, the cost of ordering, even if the material was obtainable from a 'Cash and Carry' warehouse located nearby, would be prohibitive in terms of employees' time, if not in price of material.

It is common practice for all vendors of materials to retail outlets (hairdressing salons) to reduce the price charged to the retailer in proportion to the value of the order placed with them, if above a minimum order value. This decrease in price is referred to as a *Quantity Discount*. The receipt of such a discount for large purchases has to be balanced by each individual retailer against the available storage space, the cost of storage, the profitability of utilising the storage space for other products or activities, and the length of time that the material may be in storage. The latter factor in addition to adversely affecting the cash turnover also presents a risk of loss by deterioration or obsolescence.

For routine requisitioning of the large numbers of stock items held in the salon, it is necessary to establish a methodical system which will enable the employee responsible for provisioning to initiate the procurement procedure at the appropriate time. This time is best indicated by establishing a holding quantity for each item of stock. When the stock holding drops to this level, a further requisition should be raised which will result in the placing of a purchase order upon the material supplier. This stock level is known as the *Reorder Level,* the establishment of which requires the determination of:

(a) The number of items which comprise a normal order quantity, often referred to as the *Reorder Quantity.*

(b) The length of time between the raising of the requisition to the receipt of the goods. This is normally called the *Reorder Period* and is often ranged, e.g. 3–5 weeks.

(c) The rate of usage of the item over a predetermined time-span, normally a week or a month. The average rate of usage is known as the *Normal Consumption* but if the periodic consumption shows great variances, *Maximum Consumption* and *Minimum Consumption* rates are also established.

With the exception of the reorder quantity, all the data referred to in (a), (b) and (c) above is variable; but the current performance levels can be determined from the data recorded on the Stock Record Card (see Fig. 6.2). This information can be recorded on the card, but it is more common to omit it and only record the derived data which is essential to the initiation of the requisitioning process. This derived data is:

1. *The Reorder Level* which is calculated using the formula:
   Maximum Consumption × Max Reorder Period

2. *The Minimum Stock Level* is calculated by the formula:
   Reorder Level minus (Normal Consumption × Normal Reorder Period)

3. *The Maximum Stock Level* is obtained from the formula:
   Reorder Level plus Reorder Quantity minus (Minimum Consumption
   $\times$ Minimum Reorder Period)

The inclusion of both minimum and maximum stock levels on the stock card provides management with the means of identifying items which require remedial action. If a stock holding reaches minimum level, either an order is overdue or the consumption rate has dramatically increased. In either case, action is needed to avoid a shortage of material. If the maximum stock holding is reached, demand has declined. Management then has to decide whether to revise the reorder level, reorder period or consumption levels. Often, such action has to be concurrent with a disposal programme, possibly in the form of a reduction in the price charged to customers (i.e. a 'sale price'). In cases where storage space is critical, a maximum stock level may be mandatory, in which case the same formula may be used to determine the reorder quantity which is the determining factor. For illustration purposes there follow two worked examples of the calculations required to determine reorder levels and maximum and minimum stock holdings.

1. Product X has a Reorder Quantity of 180 units
        Reorder Period of 3–5 weeks
        Maximum Consumption is 45 units per week
        Normal Consumption is 30 units per week
        Minimum Consumption is 15 units per week
   Reorder Level is 45 units $\times$ 5 weeks = *225 Units*
   Minimum Stock Level is 225 units minus (30 units $\times$ 4 weeks) = *105 Units*
   Maximum Stock Level is 225 Units plus 180 Units minus (15 Units $\times$ 3 weeks) = *360 Units*

2. Product Z has a Reorder Quantity of 250 Units
        Reorder Period of 1–2 days
        Maximum Consumption is 40 Units per day
        Normal Consumption is 30 Units per day
        Minimum Consumption is 20 Units per day
   Reorder Level is 40 Units $\times$ 2 Days = *80 Units*
   Minimum Stock Level is 80 Units minus (30 Units $\times$ 1.5 Days) = *35 Units*
   Maximum Stock Level is 80 Units plus 250 Units minus (20 Units $\times$ 1 day) = *310 Units*
   If management restricts the maximum stock level to 200, the reorder quantity can be determined from the maximum level formula, i.e.
   200 Units Maximum Stock Level = 80 Units, plus Reorder Quantity minus (20 Units $\times$ 1 day)
   Therefore, Reorder Quantity = 200 − 80 + 20 = *140 Units*

Having established the requirement to place an order for additional stock, the storekeeper, if a different individual from the person responsible for authorising salon expenditure, has to obtain the agreement of the authorising manager. When a further staff member performs the duty of buyer it is necessary to inform them of the goods to be purchased and that management concurrence has been given to the proposed purchase. The document used is a Purchase Requisition (P.R.) which is passed by the storekeeper (the requisitioner) via the authorising manager to the buyer as authority to enter into a purchase agreement with a material supplier. Upon completion of the procurement process the P.R., annotated with the Purchase Order Number is either retained by the buyer or is passed to the Accounts Department as 'payment authorisation'.

The purchase requisition, which should be identifiable by a unique serial number, should contain three sections:

(a) *To be completed by the Requisitioner*
   (i) The date of origination.
   (ii) The quantity of goods required.
   (iii) The description and/or reference number of the goods requested.
   (iv) The date delivery is required.
   (v) The signature of the requisitioner.

(b) *To be completed by the Authoriser*
   (i) Approved or Reject should be clearly marked.
   (ii) In the case of the former the signature of the authoriser.

(c) *To be completed by the Buyer*
   (i) Purchase order number and date of order origination.
   (ii) Signature of the buyer.

THE PURCHASE OF MATERIAL

Within any commercial organisation, the negotiations with outside suppliers and contractors are performed and co-ordinated by an employee who is termed the 'buyer'. The function of the buyer will vary, according to the nature of the enterprise, the size of the enterprise and its own particular organisation and distribution of responsibilities. In the case of the buyer who is responsible for the purchase of materials required by a small hairdressing salon, the 'buying function' will be very much part-time and of a repetitive, order-placing nature. In other salons, it is possible that the buyer will also be responsible for the assessment of the potential market for retail sales, as well as the strict buying of stock. In general terms, however, the buyer's function is to obtain, through the placement of orders in the most expedient manner, the materials required by the salon, to the required quality, at the correct time and at the lowest cost to the salon.

In theory, the buyer should, before placing an order have established, possibly by seeking quotations, that the price is the cheapest obtainable and that the delivery will be in accordance with the salon's requirements. In addition, it is necessary for the buyer to be satisfied that the goods will be to an acceptable quality. Such a detailed procedure would, however, be both time-consuming and expensive for each and every transaction involving the regular procurement of stock items which are of comparatively little monetary value individually. In the case of such items, it is often expedient to group them into one purchase commodity category, e.g.

hairdressing preparations, shampoos, rinses etc., and to agree a 'block' contract with the supplier who offers the best overall terms with regard to price, including discounts, delivery etc. In such cases the buyer's regular task is reduced to a clerical order-placement process, but it is important that the buyer should periodically (at least once a year) investigate the alternative suppliers available with a view to maintaining an economical procurement contract.

From time to time the salon will require the purchase of an item of material or equipment of individual high value, e.g. a new bank of dryers or a new cash register. In such cases, the range of alternative designs and types of goods may be extensive and obtainable from a large number of sources whose prices and delivery show large variations. In such instances, the traditional methods of buying become an economical proposition. The buyer must:

1. Establish a firm and definite specification of the goods required.

2. From catalogues and other forms of suppliers' advertising literature, identify the possible source of materials or equipment that will conform to the requirement.

3. Obtain quotations from a selection of the suppliers – these should contain:
   (a) Price to be charged.
   (b) Terms of payment, including cash discounts allowed, e.g. a percentage reduction for prompt payment.
   (c) Delivery time from the date of placement of an order
   (d) Service or maintenance conditions which may include guarantees in respect of the quality of the goods supplied.

4. Evaluate the financial viability of the alternative forms of procurement available, i.e. purchase of the goods as compared with leasing or renting.

5. Raise a purchase order on the selected supplier or enter into a rental agreement as appropriate.

In instances where a rental or lease contract is entered into, the buyer should advise the requisitioner of the expected arrival of the goods and also the fact that they are rented and as such will be maintained by the vendor, either by means of regular service visits or upon request. It is normal practice for the hire agreement to be passed to the accountant for retention and reference for the duration of the contract, since subsequent transactions between the vendor and purchaser will be principally of a financial nature.

When it has been decided to purchase the material or equipment, the buyer is responsible for raising a document which is theoretically a *Contract of Purchase* but is generally known as a *Purchase Order*. The document raised should show:

1. The nature of the document, i.e. be headed Purchase Order.

2. The name and address of the enterprise placing the order.

3. The order number taken from a unique series of numbers.

4. The date of the order.

5. The name and address of the supplier upon whom the order is placed.

6. Particulars of goods to be supplied, i.e. quantity, description and supplier's reference number.

7. The agreed price, including any quantity or trade discounts but excluding cash discounts.

8. Date on which delivery is to be made.

9. Conditions and instructions, i.e. place of delivery, conditions of delivery, submission of advice notes and invoices and payment conditions.

10. An internal reference, i.e. stock code number, internal expense code and requisition number.

11. The signature of the buyer or responsible manager.

The purchase order copies sent to the supplier may contain a tear-off acknowledgment slip which is to be completed by the supplier and returned to the purchaser to confirm agreement to the contract.

In addition it may be necessary for the buyer to forward copies of the order to:

1. The Receiving Department

2. The Accounts Department

3. The Requisitioner

In the larger salons, or when the buyer is acting for a chain of salons, the individual order may be used regularly for the purchase of stock items. In such cases it will not be uncommon for the order to specify that deliveries should be made at various dates and in various quantities over a time-span which may cover the next twelve months. Such an order enables the supplier to plan his production and, in theory, reduces the purchaser's administration costs as well as offering the possibility of obtaining a greater quantity discount on the total order value. In practice, however, fluctuating demand can result in frequent delivery schedule adjustments, and whilst most suppliers are content if the adjustments are forward, if they produce an extension of the delivery period beyond the original completion date, in times of inflation an increase in contracted price is sought. To overcome this feature, and to encourage the ordering of a greater range of goods, many suppliers offer an *Annual Turnover Discount* which takes the form of a cash rebate to customers the size of which is proportional to the volume of business actually transacted between the two concerns in the previous twelve months.

The smaller independent salon's turnover will be generally far below the value at which such discounts are offered and, in addition, these salons are unlikely to have available the financial resources to fund the large stock-holding which is associated with such contracts. In addition, the buying function may only occupy a small proportion of the responsible person's total time. The result is that the majority of stock requisitions are satisfied by:

1.   Purchases from Local Wholesalers

In the majority of cases the business is conducted on a 'Cash and Carry' basis where approved retailers, i.e. the salons, receive a *Trade Discount* on the recommended retail price of the goods. Trade discounts, in contrast to the other discounts mentioned previously, are of significant proportions (between 20 and 50 per cent). The size of the discount obtainable from a wholesaler may be increased in respect of cash transactions (cash discount), goods collected upon order and payment (delivery charge avoidance) and for individual purchases of large value (quantity discount). In addition, an annual turnover discount on the annual sum of purchases may be made to encourage regular patronage. In the case of Cash and Carry transactions, part of the accumulated discounts received will be absorbed by the cost to the salon of an employee travelling to the wholesale outlet, collecting the goods and returning to the salon. The salon's buyer has the task of continually reviewing the terms offered by the various wholesale outlets. Such an evaluation is affected by the volume of material requirements of the salon, the value of discounts offered, the base price of the proprietary items offered by the wholesalers, the range of goods offered and their availability, and the 'cost of purchase' incurred by the salon.

One of the major difficulties which such purchases present is often a loss of some of the documentary controls necessary to maintain full control over the stock materials. It will be normal for one visit to the wholesaler to involve the purchase of many individual items for which it would be inappropriate to raise individual orders. If 'omnibus' orders are raised, difficulties can occur if one or more individual items are not available. The employee collecting the goods will require a 'shopping list', the storeman will require a listing of goods received and the accountant will need to know the price paid for each individual item, as well as the total expenditure which is sometimes all that is shown on the receipt of payment obtained by the collector of the goods. For such purchases it is recommended that a special purchase order format should be designed as shown in Fig. 6.1.

In such cases the buyer originates the order by entering:

(a) the name of the wholesaler, the date of the order and an order number which is allocated from a series. (This order number is entered on any relevant purchase requisitions.)

(b) The description of the goods required (if this is not preprinted), together with the size of containers required and the quantity of containers to be obtained.

In addition, the buyer will authorise or obtain the signature of the authorising executive. The collector will, during the course of obtaining the goods, enter the following:

(a) The quantity purchased.

(b) Either or both of the price columns for each item purchased.

(c) The net receipted payment which will agree with the cash paid and the amount entered on the wholesaler's receipt.

(d) Their signature, in the space provided for the expeditor.

The cashier will allocate a payment voucher number to the wholesaler's receipt and cross-reference the payment voucher with the purchase order number.

FIG. 6.1

Histyles Hairdressing Salon Wholesale Purchase Order Form						
Date:	*Wholesaler:*			*Order No.:*		
Description of Goods	Size	Qnty Reqd	Qnty Prchsd	Qnty Entrd on Stock Card	Unit Price	**Total Price**
Total Value of Goods Purchased:						
Less: Special Discounts Received:						
Plus VAT:						
Cash Receipt Number			Net Receipted Payment			
Expenditure authorised by:			Date:			
Expended by:			Date:			
Goods received by:			Date:			

Upon receipt of the goods and the purchase order, the storeman will check the quantities received against the quantities shown as purchased, entering the quantity received onto both the order form and the stock record card. After signing the copy order he will return it to the accountant for completion of the financial records.

2. Purchases Using Suppliers' Documentation

Included in this category of purchase are mail-order transactions and the placing of orders for goods with suppliers' representatives during their visits to the salon. Whether such purchases are on a credit or 'cash with order' basis, the details of the goods being purchased are recorded on the suppliers' order form, which is frequently of a similar format to the 'Wholesale Purchase Order

Form' shown in Section 1 above. This form will require signing by a responsible executive of the salon but will frequently not provide a space for the salon's reference (purchase order) number, and it will very rarely have the facility to record actual receipts. In the case of such transactions it is important for the buyer to ensure that the purchase is commercially viable and that the originating documentation provides adequate information for the performance of the control operations arising from the receipt of the goods in the salon. It may be necessary to increase normal salon purchase documentation to complement the supplier's order form. This action should not be avoided in an attempt to save time, since in all but the smallest salons the initial increase in administrative work will be more than compensated for by time saved in the future.

3. Direct Orders

When a direct order for stock is placed on a supplier for delivery at a future date, such an order may be for many items with varying delivery dates. In such cases it is often appropriate to provide a separate listing of the individual itemised requirements, the normal purchase order being annotated in the appropriate columns with a reference to the listing for all except the total agreed price, which should be clearly shown on the formal purchase order.

THE RECEIPT OF MATERIAL

Because receipt of material is closely related to purchasing, it may be considered as a separate function of material control rather than as an aspect of stock-keeping. In practice, the responsibility for the receipt of material rests with the storekeeper who has to validate that all items received have been correctly entered onto the stock records, and that these records accurately reflect the stock available in the stores. We have already shown that the storeman is also responsible for originating the purchase requisitions for additional stock requirements and to perform this task it is necessary to be able to confirm that all the goods requisitioned and subsequently ordered have been delivered. The performance of this task involves the maintenance of a record of receipts against each order and for the appropriate purchase requisition to ensure that suppliers effect a timely delivery of the ordered goods. Non-delivery of goods at the anticipated time should be referred to the buyer so that the reason for the delay may be established and/or remedial action can be taken. Alternatively, early delivery and the subsequent payment may produce storage or cash flow problems which may be avoided, upon management instructions, by the return of the goods.

It is also necessary for all materials received to be checked to ensure that:

1. Goods advised have been received.
2. Quantity advised has been received.
3. Goods are in accordance with the ordered description or specification.
4. Items are received in an undamaged condition.

The corrective action in respect of any of these deficiencies should be initiated by the buyer, who, after liaison with the supplier, will advise the storeman of any action to be taken, e.g. the return of defective goods. It is important that only satisfactory and correct materials are taken into stock and entered in the stock records.

In the large salon the above may be the extent of the storeman's responsibility as regards the receipt of goods, but in the smaller salon, where the duties of buyer, storeman and accountant are combined, the resolution of anomalies associated with the receipt of goods will involve the following actions:

1. Non-receipt of a Consignment

Salon management may become aware of a missing delivery:

(a) As a result of querying with the supplier the reason for not meeting an agreed delivery date.

(b) The receipt of an advice note or invoice for which no goods have been received.

In the latter case, it is necessary for the matching of invoices to receipt documentation to be an ongoing process within the salon's administrative procedures so that suppliers may be immediately advised of non-receipt of goods. Most suppliers will accept no responsibility for financial loss if such notification is not made within 14 days of the dispatch date. If correctly notified, the suppliers and/or their agents must 'prove delivery' or withdraw the invoice, which is usually done by raising a credit note for the invoiced amount.

2. Quantity Discrepancy

When a discrepancy is found between the quantity received in stores and the quantity in respect of a 'cash and carry' purchase no recourse can be made to the wholesaler, except possibly in the case of manufacturer's prepacked goods. In such cases, care should be taken not to destroy all evidence of the deficiency and a claim should be made as for delivered items.

When deliveries are made directly to the salon and a signature is required by the carrier as proof of delivery, it is important that unless the goods are unpacked and counted in the presence of the carrier, the receipt given is clearly marked 'Received Unchecked'. If discrepancies are found upon checking the contents of such a delivery, notification is usually required by the supplier on the same day as delivery is made before any liability is accepted. The adjustment, if agreed, is made by means of a credit note in the case of shortages, and an additional invoice in the case of over-deliveries.

3. Defective Goods

If the goods are found to be at variance with the description or specification ordered, or to be damaged, notification has to be made to the supplier within 3 to 7 days from the date of dispatch. Normally the goods will be returned under cover of a dispatch note which is clearly marked with the reason for the return.

If the rejection is accepted, the supplier should forward a credit note to cancel the original invoice in total or in part for the returned items.

In the larger organisations where the responsibility for the receipt of goods rests with a person other than the individual who is responsible for making payment to suppliers, it is necessary to advise the accountant of all goods received. This is normally done by the origination of a Goods Received note which will show:

(a) Supplier's name and purchase order number.

(b) Supplier's advice note or consignment note number.

(c) Description of goods received.

(d) Quantity of goods received and quantity on advice note if different.

(e) Quantity returned to supplier and return note reference number.

In addition to the accountant, copies of the Goods Received note may be sent if appropriate to the organisation to:

(a) The buyer to confirm the status of the order.

(b) The storeman or requisitioner to whom the goods are passed.

A copy is retained which has been signed by the storeman or requisitioner as proof of receipt of the goods.

PHYSICAL STOCK-KEEPING

Many salon managers have in the past paid scant attention to the physical maintenance of the stock held within the salon. It is often not appreciated that at any one time the value of the stock in the salon is greater than the contents of the cash register and safe, and that it therefore requires an equal amount of safeguarding. In general, the stock is of use to almost everyone and, in addition to the possibility of excess usage, damage or deterioration if exposed to the elements, salon stock may be misappropriated or pilfered by both staff and clients.

To reduce the possibility of excessive stock losses it should be a general salon practice to have the minimum amount of stock within the salon working areas or the retail sales area. Retail stock, if displayed, should be in glass cases so that it can be easily seen by clients but not touched. An employee should be responsible for each and every item of stock outside the stores, and control can be maintained by the stores issuing, and possibly receiving back, excess stock on a daily basis. Access to the stores area should be limited to the storekeeper and the responsible manager.

Within the stores the most difficult problem is to be able to readily identify the location of any particular item of stock. Adequate storage space has to be provided, whether this is in the form of shelved cupboards or open racking. The storage space provided should be divided up into appropriately sized locations and each location given a reference number which should be clearly marked on the fitting in an easily visible and sequential manner. The size of locations should be appropriate to the size and quantities of the items to be stored. There are two systems of locating stock:

1. Random Locations

Each quantity received is located in the first available empty location. To effect access for issues, a *Location Ticket* is raised which shows the stock number and/or description and the location number employed. The tickets are filed in part-number or description sequence and if issues are required to be on a 'first in, first out' basis the tickets should be in date order.

2. Fixed Locations

Locations are designated for each individual item held in the stores and, upon receipt, the storeman consults the stock card for the item to establish the location in which the goods are to be placed.

In general, the use of fixed locations is the most appropriate method to be employed in the salon stores but care has to be taken that items which are likely to deteriorate with long storage are used first, i.e. when new stock is received it is placed at the rear of the storage area. Care should also be taken that locations are not occupied by small quantities of slow-moving or redundant stock which may result in an excess of storage space. The advantages of fixed storage locations are:

(a) The location can be suitable to the storage of a particular stock item.

(b) It is not necessary to maintain separate location tickets for each receipt.

(c) By packing the items in a pre-arranged order into the location, it is possible to show the area to be occupied by stock which has attained reorder level, using coloured adhesive tape.

It is important that all receipts and issues to and from the stores should be counted and recorded on the stock card. The entries on the stock card should be supported by the relevant documents, whether these are Goods Received notes or stores issue requisitions.

STOCK RECORD CARDS

For control purposes it is necessary to retain an ongoing record of the stock held in the salon, its location and information regarding the past demand and future availability of stock to meet anticipated demands. To meet this requirement, a stock card is maintained. As a minimum, this shows for each item of stock the date and quantities of each receipt and issue made, and the resultant quantity of stock held in the stores. It is also normal to record on the stock card the reference number of the document which authorised the movement of stock, together with the location(s) where the stock is stored if a fixed location system is employed within the stores.

When the storeman is responsible for requisitioning and/or ordering of stock items, the stock card may be extended to include details of the reorder level, reorder quantity, maximum stock level and minimum stock level, together with the details of orders raised, whether completed or not. It is also possible to extend the stock record card to include the price paid for the stock and to complete, after each movement, an entry which shows the value of the

FIG. 6.2 Stock Record Card

DATE	ORDERED			STOCK			AUTHORITY
	Quantity	Order No.	Qty. Outstanding	Qty. Received	Qty. in Stock	Qty. Issued	
25 Jan.					116		Balance Forward
25 Jan.					89	27	Stock Issue Request 477
26 Jan.					68	21	Stock Issue Request 495
26 Jan.	140	H.8274	140				
27 Jan.					43	25	Stock Issue Request 536
27 Jan.				140	183		Goods Received Note 11399
27 Jan.			40		143	40	Reject Note 48-wrong contents
28 Jan.					126	17	Stock Issue Note 571
29 Jan.					94	32	Stock Issue Note 614
29 Jan.			NIL	40	134		Goods Received Note 11463
30 Jan.					99	35	Stock Issue Request 55

Reorder Level 80	Max Stock	200	Location(s)	PART NUMBER
Reorder Quantity 140	Min. Stock	35		SO14

PART Description

200 ml bottles Allsoaps Medicated Shampoo

stock in the stores. Unless there is a reason to regularly evaluate the stock holding on an individual item basis, sufficient valuation information should be available from the normal financial records for normal control information to avoid the need to maintain such costed stock record cards.

To illustrate the use of the stock record card, Fig. 6.2 shows the stock record card for Histyles Salon for item reference SO14 which is 200 ml bottles of Allsoaps Medicated Shampoo and during the week 25–30 January the following movements occurred:

25 Jan.: 27 of the outstanding balance of 116 bottles were issued.
26 Jan.: 21 bottles were issued and an order for 140 was raised.
27 Jan.: 25 bottles were issued and 140 were received, but 40 of these were found to contain Beer Shampoo and were returned for replacement.
28 Jan.: 17 bottles were issued.
29 Jan.: 32 bottles were issued and 40 replacement bottles received.
30 Jan.: 35 bottles were issued.

STOCK-TAKING AND PERPETUAL INVENTORY CHECKING

It has been a traditional practice to conduct, at the completion of the financial year, a one hundred per cent physical count of all the stock held within the salon and salon stores. This activity normally entails overtime working by the entire salon staff, and whilst the size of a stock discrepancy may be established, no indication is obtained as to the reason for the shortage and nor is the time-span over which it occurred identified.

To overcome these disadvantages it is becoming increasingly common for managements to institute a system of ongoing checks of a randomly selected proportion of the items held in controlled stores. These checks are carried out by an employee other than the storeman. If a large discrepancy is identified a check of the arithmetical accuracy of the stock record card against the original authorising documents is made. In practice it will be found that many of the discrepancies result from clerical errors which can be corrected immediately.

If, over the course of the year, all items have been checked at least once and the average discrepancy rate is very low (below 1 per cent) the need to conduct a physical count of the stores stock can be eliminated. It will, however, be necessary to evaluate and sum the outstanding balances shown on each stock record card, together with a physical count and evaluation of the stock held outside the stores to validate the balance on the stock account which is maintained as part of the financial records of the salon.

CHAPTER VII

General Salon Administration

Certain important facets of salon administration have to be performed on a regular basis to support the main tasks of the salon. These are discussed in separate sections below:

VALUE ADDED TAX

In April 1973 Value Added Tax (VAT) was introduced in Great Britain in place of Purchase Tax, the intention being to tax all goods and services deemed by the Government to be non-essential rather than a selected number of 'luxury' items. The business impact was that all concerns other than the extremely small became 'tax collectors' whereas previously, only manufacturers were required to perform this task. Indirectly, the introduction of VAT compelled small traders to keep records so that they could compute the payments due to H.M. Customs and Excise, the collecting authority, to effect the statutory quarterly payments and also retain supporting documentation for audit by H.M. Customs and Excise.

The following paragraphs contain a broad outline of the impact of the VAT regulations upon hairdressing salons and the resulting administrative work required, reference is only made to general principles since the details are subject to change in each annual Finance Act. It is, therefore, of great importance for new proprietors to obtain copies of the General Guide (VAT Notice 700) and other relevant Notices from the local Customs and Excise VAT Office before commencing business, and for current proprietors and/or managers to ensure that their copies of the regulations are up to date.

1. Principles of VAT

VAT is a tax upon the consumer expressed as a percentage increment to the supplier's charge for the goods or services supplied. For example:

If Hairdresser A purchases a container of hair conditioner from Wholesaler B at 40p plus VAT and subsequently sells the conditioner to Client C for 60p plus VAT then:

(a) C is the ultimate consumer and if VAT is set at 10 per cent of sales price then the VAT due to H.M. Customs and Excise is 6p.

(b) The price paid to A by C is, therefore, 66p, of which 6p is due to H.M. Customs and Excise.

(c) A, when making the purchase from B, paid 44p, which included 4p VAT. Since A is not the ultimate consumer, the 4p VAT is claimable from H.M. Customs and Excise, thus making A's net payment 2p (6p minus 4p).

(d) In the same manner, B is allowed to offset the 4p payable as the VAT component of any purchase.

From the above example it can be seen that whilst the tax is ultimately paid by the consumer, the tax due is collected in part by each supplier involved in the manufacturing distribution chain. Each of these suppliers has to maintain a record of tax paid on resaleable items and tax charged on sales.

2. VAT Rates

When VAT was introduced, certain items were termed 'Exempt' from VAT; certain others were allocated a zero rate; and the remainder were charged at a standard rate. Since that time, subsequent Finance Acts have established different rates of VAT for different goods and services. It is, therefore, appropriate to consider VAT as being applicable to all items being either at a *zero* or *positive* rate and, therefore, the amount rather than the rate is the significant factor.

3. VAT Registration

The VAT regulations stipulate a turnover value above which an enterprise must be registered for VAT purposes. This value limit, in general, is such that other than the small one-man business, all hairdressing salons will require registration. Unregistered concerns are not allowed to charge VAT and, therefore, become for tax purposes the ultimate consumer. They are, therefore, not allowed to reclaim VAT charged to them. If the turnover is below the stipulated value, the proprietors may if they wish be registered, in which case they can charge and claim tax in the normal manner. But they also have to maintain auditable records, thus losing a degree of privacy in their affairs.

4. Tax Invoice

A registered taxable person must normally issue a tax invoice for each taxable supply and must keep a copy of the invoice. In practice, a non-registered customer will not require an invoice, which in the case of the hairdressing salon is often in the form of a cash receipt. Provision should, however, be made for the client who requires tax invoices: this may be achieved by always providing an invoice or receipt for the client, in addition to the salon's copy of the 'output document'. Similarly, it is important that the salon obtains acceptable tax invoices for all 'inputs'.

A taxable invoice, whether input or output, should show:

(a) The supplier's unique invoice number.

(b) Date of supply (i.e. the tax point).

(c) The supplier's name, address and, most importantly, its VAT registration number.

(d) Quantity and amount payable (excluding VAT) for each item.

(e) Rate and amount of any VAT charged.

It should be noted that special dispensations are granted by H.M. Customs and Excise within these broad criteria, and the practising manager should constantly update himself on these dispensations, either from published documentation (VAT Guides etc.) or by personal reference to the local Customs and Excise VAT office. Some of the more important dispensations which affect the hairdressing salon are:

(a) The issue of tax invoices which show a total charge which is inclusive of VAT, provided a statement is made on the invoice, saying that 'All charges include VAT at X per cent.'

(b) Cash and Carry wholesalers may adopt the till rolls produced by their cash registers to serve as tax invoices, provided all the required details are shown.

(c) For certain kinds of taxable supply, input tax may be claimed without a tax invoice, provided that the cost, including VAT, does not exceed £10, and that there is no doubt that the supply was made by a registered taxable person.

5. Tax Returns

In order to spread the flow of Tax Returns evenly over the year the three-month tax periods covered by each return are staggered, and upon registration every taxable person is allocated to a particular stagger group. The finishing date of the first tax period and the dates of subsequent tax periods are notified on the certificate of registration. The opportunity exists for these dates to be realigned to coincide with the end of the registered trader's financial year.

Prior to the end of the tax period a 'Return of Value Added Tax' is sent from the VAT Control Unit for completion and return, together with the remittance for the Net Tax Payable. The information to be entered on the Return of VAT Form is:

(a) Accounts of tax payable or repayable which consist of:
  (i)   Tax due in the period on outputs (sales etc.).
Plus (ii)   Underdeclarations or underpayments from previous periods.
Minus (iii) Tax deductable – being the credit claimed for input tax allowable (on purchases etc.).

(b) A Statement as to:
  (i) Value of outputs excluding VAT for the period (3 months).
  (ii) Value of inputs excluding VAT for the period (3 months).

The accounting entries required in the salon records are shown in Chapter VIII 'Financial Accounting', but where such detailed records are not retained by a particular salon, the minimum requirements should be established after consultation with the local Customs and Excise VAT Office.

MAINTENANCE OF THE CASH REGISTER

It is beyond the scope of this book to describe the many types of cash registers or 'tills' that are available to the modern retail enterprise. In its simplest form the cash register may be a drawer in a table or desk, or even – in the case of the 'sole barber' – his back pocket; in its most sophisticated form it may be a mini-computer capable of printing receipts and performing much of the subsequent financial analysis required by salon management.

The cash register is only a 'tool' used for the control of cash and cash transactions within the salon, and the form that it takes is dependent upon the size of the salon and the management control procedures and methods employed. There are, however, fundamental features which must exist in any cash control system and these are:

1.   Security of Cash

Where possible, all salon cash should be kept in one place which is not easily accessible to the general public and can be kept under constant scrutiny by responsible members of the staff. Large amounts of cash should not be retained in the cash register. It is a sound precaution to bank all cash, with the exception of a small cash float, at the close of each day's business. If it is not possible to bank the cash it should be removed from the till and kept in a safe or other secure container, preferably away from the business premises.

Where possible, it is also desirable that only one person should be responsible for effecting cash register transactions. For example, a dedicated receptionist is situated by the cash register and receives all clients' remittances and makes restitution to members of staff for all minor expenditure. In addition, another person, normally the Manager or senior supervisor should be responsible for reconciling the cash contained in the register to the transaction records at the end of each day.

2.   Cash Records

In general, all cash register transactions are receipts from clients and it is important that a record is maintained of the value charged and the service provided, not only to complete the salon financial and control records, but also to provide evidence of VAT charged to the appropriate authorities when required. Although management should avoid making cash payments from the register, from time to time it may be expedient to make minor payments in cash. In such instances a payment slip should be inserted in the register which can be used as part of the salon's financial records.

3.   Cash Register Reconciliation

At least daily at the close of business a 'cash reconciliation' should be conducted. This activity should involve:

(a) Calculating the amount of cash, i.e. receipt slips, minus payment slips, plus opening float.

(b) Physically counting cash, which should agree with (a) above.

(c) Counting back into the till the agreed float and making out a 'Bank Paying-in Slip' for the balance.

(d) Banking net receipts.

4. Entry to Financial Records

Although each payment into the bank should be recorded in the cash book individually, it is often found expedient to make detailed accounting entries, for the sales receipts and cash payments, both financial and cost, on a weekly rather than daily basis. Whatever method is adopted, it is important to be able to refer to the individual transaction document. To facilitate this a separate sequential series of numbers should be allocated to each and every transaction document.

PAYROLL PREPARATION AND PAYE DEDUCTIONS

The various Employment Acts require employers to pay their employees on a regular basis, normally either weekly or monthly, and to supply the employee with a statement as to:

1. The composition of gross pay, i.e. basic hourly rate for standard contracted hours worked, overtime payments, bonuses, commissions etc.

2. The deductions, both statutory (Income Tax and National Insurance contributions) and voluntary (union subscriptions etc.), which when deducted from the above give the net amount paid to the employee.

The volume of detail to be compiled by employers was greatly increased by the introduction in Britain in 1944 of the Pay As You Earn (PAYE) system whereby a proportionate amount of Income Tax is deducted by the employer and handed over to the Inland Revenue before wages are paid. Tax reliefs due to individual employees are notified to the employer by the tax office in the form of code numbers. As a result of the establishment of the state welfare schemes in the period 1946 to 1949, employers were also required to deduct and contribute to the financing of these schemes through the payroll systems in respect of all employees.

Payroll systems and related activities have, due to the intervention of statutory regulations, been standardised. But the methods employed are still in detail very numerous. The extremes are: the manual system, where the Manager or responsible person completes all the documentation and physical funding of pay packets; and the computerised package system which completes the documentation for each employee and raises credit transfers for payment direct to the recipient's bank account.

The range of systems and their advantages and disadvantages are beyond the scope of a book of this size and general content, but it is important to understand the general operation functions. Even the brief résumé of the features of a payment system, outlined below, shows the large amount of non-standard and variable data which has to be input for each payroll calculation, and which in turn makes a large degree of manual operations mandatory.

1. Gross Payments

The amount of gross pay has to be in agreement with the employee's contract of employment and each addition or deduction has to be authorised by responsible management and notified to the employee (particularly if it is a deduction).

2. Statutory Deductions

The extent of such deductions is determined largely by the amount of gross salary or payment received by the individual employee in the statutory financial year in relation to his/her personal circumstances, as shown by the Inland Revenue records. Detailed instructions are contained in the Employer's Guide to PAYE and National Insurance, which can be obtained from the local Inland Revenue Office. These include:

(a) Amount of National Insurance deduction shown by a table listing per category of employee the gross pay per payment period in units of £1, and the related deduction to be made, together with the employer's contribution. These make up the National Insurance element of the subsequent remittance to the Inland Revenue.

(b) Tables to facilitate the calculation of Income Tax to be deducted in accordance with the code number allocated to each employee, i.e.:

    (i) Table A shows, with relation to the code number, the amount of pay which for the taxation year to date is free of tax. (A table is given for each of the tax weeks contained in the tax year.)

    (ii) Table B shows the amount of tax due on the total taxable pay to date (total gross pay to date minus (i) above).

By deducting the amount of tax deducted previously in the tax year, as shown in (ii) above, the amount of tax to be deducted from this payment is determined.

(c) A Deduction Card (Form P.11) has to be maintained for each employee, which ultimately is forwarded and retained by the Inland Revenue at the end of the year. This card shows:

    (i) National Insurance contributions.

    (ii) Total pay for pay period.

    (iii) Total pay to date in tax year.

    (iv) Total tax-free pay to date.

    (v) Taxable pay, i.e. (iii) minus (iv).

    (vi) Amount of tax applicable to (v) above.

    (vii) Amount of tax deducted, i.e. the amount entered in the previous period's value of (vi), deducted from the current period's value of (vi).

3. Voluntary Deductions

All voluntary deductions should be authorised by the employee.

4. Pay Advice

Each employee should be supplied with a statement which shows the amounts by category which result in the net amount being paid to them.

5. Payment

If cash payments are made it is necessary to:

(a) Draw from the bank a cheque equivalent in value to the sum of the payroll and in such monetary denominations as to facilitate payment of each individual amount.

(b) Make up individual pay packets and distribute to employees.

(c) Maintain adequate security over the cash at all times.

As an alternative, many employers make payments to employees by means of Credit Transfers directly to the employees' personal bank accounts.

6. Payment to Inland Revenue

Monthly, a payment of all deductions from employees plus employer's contributions is made to the Inland Revenue and supported by the Deduction Cards which are sent with the remittance. The cards are initialled and returned in time for the next payment.

7. Wages Book

This is a record of all payments and deductions made to employees and is usually a duplication of the Deduction Card (2.(c)). Such information is required by law to be retained for seven years independently of the Inland Revenue who retain the Deduction Card at the completion of the tax year.

The related accounting entries in the books of account of the salon are outlined in Chapter VIII, 'Financial Accounting'.

RECEPTION AND CLIENTS' RECORDS

Even in the smallest salon, i.e. the one-person 'barber's shop', there is a requirement for a separate area in which the related commercial transactions may be conducted: e.g. settlement of clients' accounts for services received. Traditionally, the first extension to the barber's trading is the introduction of retail sales as part of the salon's activities, and this generally results in the cash desk becoming part of a display area. In modern times the small one-man barber's shop, except in small communities, is becoming increasingly rare, and where it does exist the clientele are no longer prepared to spend time waiting for service. In such circumstances and with the increase in the range of hairdressing services being offered, much of the hairdresser's time is reserved for clients who have arranged an appointment in advance of the time of the service.

The introduction of an appointments system adds a further administrative function to the hairdressing salon activities. A record has to be maintained of the appointments made, and a time has to be allocated for the provision of the service by the hairdresser. In the case of the one-person business the making of future appointments, whether as a result of a telephone call or a personal visit by the future client, is often a distraction from the service being performed at the time of the call. Consequently, in the larger salon employing more than one hairdresser the making of appointments is the responsibility of either a dedicated member of the staff or a hairdresser who at the particular time is free of clients. In the larger salons, whether Men's, Ladies' or Unisex, it is usual to employ a dedicated person, usually termed a receptionist, who is responsible for all client-related administrative and commercial activities. Reference has already been made previously in this book to the display and cash register maintenance duties normally allocated to the receptionist, so this section is confined to the client-related activities listed below.

1. Making Appointments

The receptionist has to maintain an appointments register, usually in the form of a book in which one double-sided page has been designated to each of the salon's future working days. The extreme left-hand column is annotated (often preprinted) with the periods of the working day, each period being 15 minutes, e.g. 9.00 – 9.15 – 9.30 – 9.45 – 10.0 etc. A column is ruled against these times for each hairdresser who is employed within the salon, and the name of the client and service required is entered in the column appertaining to the particular hairdresser, as and when the appointment is made. For the appointment system to be effective it is necessary for:

(a) The appointment book to be 'marked up' as soon as possible with the times of absence of each member of the hairdressing staff, whether this is for complete days or parts of days, including holidays, sickness, training time, lunch-breaks etc. It should be noted that it is management's responsibility to ensure that this information is made available promptly, since failure to do so can be detrimental to client relationships.

(b) A system of taking appointments needs to be determined so that each hairdresser's designated or appointed time can be shown in the appointments book. More importantly, the times available for assignment to further clients can then be seen. The system will be dependent upon the working arrangement within the salon, the abilities of the individual hairdressers, the facilities available in the salon and the type of service which the class of clientele requires. In its simplest form bookings may be taken after a predetermined time for the previous appointment, the length of time being dependent upon the nature of the previous service. Alternatively, appointments may be taken to suit the work flow arrangement within the salon, although this will sometimes involve bookings for more than one hairdresser and for more than one client at a particular time.

(c) All members of the staff are familiar with the booking system employed. It should be noted that the work measurement techniques described in Chapter V are an important aid in determining the booking system to be employed in a particular salon.

2. Clients' Record Cards

To ensure a continuity of service to regular clients, particularly to those who make their appointments with one individual hairdresser, it is important that a record is kept of the services given to the client for the information of the replacement hairdresser in the event of the regular hairdresser being absent. For this purpose, a record card should be made out for each regular client which will include details of any allergies and known likes and dislikes, as well as personal information such as address and telephone number. The record cards should normally be in alphabetical order. They should be maintained and held by the receptionist so that a degree of privacy is assured between clients but the information is available when required to any member of the staff who is called upon to attend the client. It should be noted that the information contained on the cards will also be useful when any sales promotion events occur, e.g. special offers, displays and exhibitions.

3. Maintaining Communications

The reception area is the communications centre of the salon. It should be so situated that everyone entering the salon is immediately aware of the existence of a reception area and a receptionist who is employed to help them. All visitors should be discreetly monitored by the receptionist. In the case of clients who have called to avail themselves of the salon services, it is the receptionist's task to pass them onto the hairdresser or to keep them within the reception area until the salon staff are available to serve them. Visitors such as trade representatives etc., should not be allowed to freely enter the main salon in search of the responsible member of staff. It is the receptionist's task to arrange for such visitors to meet the person they need to see in the reception area. It is also the receptionist's task to prevent personal callers entering the salon and interrupting the hairdressers while they work.

The reception area is also the telephone exchange for the salon, although most of the incoming calls will usually be in connection with appointments. Telephone calls will also be received for individual members of staff and for clients. Unless it is known that the member of staff is available to accept the call, e.g. the Manager is alone in the office or a hairdresser is not attending to a client and is in the rest-room, a message should be taken and the member of staff informed at the earliest possible moment. The same general approach should be taken in respect of calls for clients. The general rule is that only in cases of emergencies should the client be disturbed whilst receiving the service.

It is also the receptionist's task to control the outgoing calls, which should be limited to business calls only. It should be impressed by management on all staff that the use of the telephone lines for personal calls can prevent or delay the receipt of incoming calls. Enlightened managements often provide a separate pay-phone for the personal use of staff.

The reception area is also a convenient place to retain information regarding other business addresses, telephone directories and trade publications of general interest to clients.

Although the span of reception activities is wide, care should be taken that business and salon personnel records or documents are not maintained in this 'public' area where they are freely available to all members of the staff and also to visitors to the salon. These records should be retained in the office (see below).

OFFICE RECORDS

The modern hairdressing salon, in common with all other business concerns, enjoys the benefits of improved communications and control techniques but also experiences the difficulties in storing data in such a manner that easy reference may be made to it when required. In addition, to avoid excess storage space or the use of expensive processes such as microfilming or computer data storage, it is necessary to be able to identify and dispose of old or unimportant records.

Due to the individual nature of each concern it is not possible to define in detail the records required to be retained, the means and method of retention or the location where they should be retained. The following are however general points which require attention.

1. Accessibility

Access to documentation and information should be restricted to those personnel who require the data to perform their designated tasks. Not only is this factor important in maintaining confidentiality in delicate matters – e.g. the personal circumstances of one member of staff should not be available to other staff members apart from the Manager – but also to safeguard the documents from loss, damage or misplacement. In a large salon, access to the stores and stock records should be restricted to one or two members of the staff who are familiar with all aspects of stores routines.

2. Storage

Large quantities of loose papers stacked on table tops, chairs or window ledges are not only untidy and unsightly but are likely to lead to loss, damage and misplacement of important documents. The requirement is therefore twofold: firstly a means to collect and retain documents of a like nature, i.e. to file; and secondly a means of retaining the files in such a manner that reference can easily be made to the contents.

The most common form of file storage is in filing cabinets in which the files are suspended in wallets which are annotated with the title of the file. If the drawers or layers of files are numerous, an index can be maintained which shows the exact location. In practice, this form of filing is expensive due to the cost of the cabinets, but they have the advantage that they can be locked and are thus useful for storing confidential files, e.g. the personal file on each member of staff. The cost of file storage can be greatly reduced by the use of box files which can be stored on open shelves. For economy of space it is necessary to have omnibus files since an almost empty box file occupies as much space as an almost full file. For ease of usage it is often expedient to retain record cards, e.g. stock record cards, in open-topped boxes. In such cases it is appropriate to include index cards, so that the required card may be easily identified.

3. Files and Records

Careful consideration has to be given to the items to be contained and the order in which they are arranged within the file. In general, this will be determined by the frequency of reference to the data and the information to the user in the form of reference criteria. Some examples of data which may be filed within a salon and the method and order of retention within the files are given below:

(a) Personal files on members of the staff. The reference point is the name of the employee. Therefore, a file is raised for each individual, with the files being retained in alphabetical order. The contents could include: initial job application, initial and subsequent staff assessments, changes in rates of pay, training courses attended etc. Within the file it may be expedient to group the documentation into categories, e.g. training; but the general order would be the date of the document or letter.

(b) There are many documents which may be appropriately described as business forms, which should be filed together and in a strict sequential order. Reference will be made to these documents for several purposes, and in a large salon it is likely that more than one member of staff will require access to perform the particular function for which they are responsible. Some examples are:

(i) *Purchase orders.*   These will normally bear a serial number which has been allocated by the buyer in strict numerical sequence. It is logical to retain copies of the orders in a numerical sequence so that the storeman can check receipts and the accountant can check the agreed price and, if necessary, the outstanding committed expenditure (orders which are yet to be fulfilled).

(ii) *Sales receipts.*   These should also be sequentially numbered and filed in this order. It is perhaps particularly pertinent to mention the big advantage of numerical filing when considering sales receipts: that is the ability to quickly identify when a document is missing. For example, when the cash register is reconciled daily it is necessary to check that all documents are present and they equal the cash addition. These documents have to be retained for possible VAT audit as well as internal control reference.

(iii) *Invoices payable and cash receipts.*   Although these documents will bear a supplier's reference number, such a number is of little use for reference purposes; within the salon. It is suggested that a number is allocated to these documents upon receipt in the salon, with reference being made to this number in the accounting and stock records. The documents themselves should be filed in the allocated number sequence, although initially, two files will have to be retained: one for paid invoices and the other for unpaid invoices.

(iv) *Stock cards.*   At first sight it is likely that alphabetical order would be considered most effective, i.e. Shampoo followed by Tints. However, since there are likely to be large numbers of each of these items stored, and since they may vary in type, size or manufacturer, a logical sequence of retention will soon be lost. In such cases it is suggested that a 'salon material number' should be allocated to each stock item and a separate index kept to indicate the description. Often the number can be used to signify the type of item. For example, in a six-digit number the first two digits could signify the type of product, the second two digits the size, and the third two digits the supplier.

(c) Documents of a like nature will require filing, e.g. staff time-sheets as outlined in Chapter V, 'Work Study in the Salon'. These will be received weekly from each member of staff and consolidated into one complete summary for the salon as a whole. It is therefore appropriate to file all returns together in week order and possibly alphabetical order of employees' names, after each summary sheet.

(d) Much of the correspondence will be subject-related, e.g. complaints. In these cases it is suggested that items should be filed, together with the response and the related correspondence, in date order per complaint within the alphabetical complainant order.

(e) It is likely that much documentation may be in the form of circulars, e.g. from trade organisations. In such cases it is likely that a file should be retained for each correspondent and the documents filed in date order.

CHAPTER VIII

Financial Accounting

The requirement to maintain financial records that will provide the basis for the completion of the Statutory VAT Returns which are auditable by VAT officials has already been identified in an earlier chapter. The introduction of this legislation effectively eliminated the use of 'single-entry' or 'incomplete' accounting systems which were frequently found in operation in very small businesses. The proprietors of any business consequently have to be familiar with the principles of *Double-Entry Book-Keeping* and the completion of final accounts i.e. *Profit and Loss Account* and *Balance Sheet.* Alternatively, they may employ, at least on a part-time basis, a suitably qualified person.

There have been numerous books published which adequately detail the principles and practice of book-keeping and accounts using the double-entry system, so it is inappropriate for this book to duplicate their contents in detail. This chapter is, accordingly, a guide to the application of a financial accounting system, based on records, which conforms to the double-entry principle which may be applied to the practical situation encountered in a hairdressing salon. It should be clearly understood that the details of any one system employed should be suitable for the particular circumstances of the business. The business should not be run to suit the requirements of an accounts system, no matter how sound that system may be.

Theoretical book-keeping requires that in addition to the ledger accounts, a journal should be maintained that gives, in chronological order, a record of each transaction, and lists the ledger accounts which have been debited and credited. In practice, the journal takes many forms e.g. the Wages Book referred to in Chapter VII is a 'journal' as also are the Sales Receipt Notes after they have been annotated and tabulated as described in the Sales Receipts Section of this chapter.

The main transactions which require book-keeping and accounting actions are shown below, and for illustration purposes we shall again attribute them to our hypothetical salon 'Histyles – Ladies' and Men's Hairdressing'.

1. Wages and Associated Employment Costs

In Chapter VII it was established that a wages book has to be maintained which shows not only the calculation of the gross wages due to each employee but also the subsequent distribution of this sum to:

(a) The Inland Revenue in the form of PAYE and Employees' National Insurance deductions.

(b) Net wages paid to the employees.

In addition, the wages book also shows the value of the employer's contribution to be paid to the Inland Revenue in respect of each employee on the payroll. Thus, for Week 36, Histyles' wages book shows:

		£
(a)	Gross wages	420
(b)	PAYE Deductions	77
(c)	Employees' N.I. Contributions	25
(d)	Net Wages	318
(e)	Employer's N.I. Contribution	42

The following entries are required to be made in the ledger accounts in respect of these journal entries:

(a) On 1 December, 19–8 after completion of the payroll calculations:

	£	
Debit – Employment Cost Account	462	(See Fig. 8.12)
Credit – Wages Account	318	(See Fig. 8.11)
Inland Revenue Account	144	(See Fig. 8.31)

(b) On 2 December, 19–8 after paying the employees with cash withdrawn from the bank:

	£	
Debit – Wages Account	318	
Credit – Cash Book	318	(See Fig. 8.10)

(c) On 3 December, 19–8 payment is made to the Inland Revenue for the deductions/contributions in respect of Weeks 33–6, i.e.:

	£
Debit – Inland Revenue	535
Credit – Cash Book	535

2. Cash Sales and Cash Purchases

In general, the hairdressing salon can be described as a 'retail outlet' and consequently the majority of sales receipts are in the form of cash reimbursements made at the time of the sale or upon completion of the service. Likewise, many of the payments are in the form of cash, whether they are in respect of purchases, e.g. stock items obtained from the local Cash and Carry or expenses, e.g. expenditure on coffee, tea, milk etc., for both staff and clients. In Chapter VII we established that each individual transaction which passed through the till should be supported by either a till tabulation if such a feature was incorporated within the till, or a till voucher detailing each receipt and payment. Arising from cash transactions it is necessary to develop the financial records of the salon to show:

(a) The cash held in the till.

(b) The cash held in the bank (being reconcilable to the bank records).

(c) The value of sales by category.

(d) The value of purchases and expenses by category.

(e) Value Added Tax (VAT) records in accordance with the requirements of H.M. Customs and Excise.

These requirements may be achieved with the minimum of book-keeping entries by the adoption of the following procedures:

(a) Maintain a *Cash Register Journal* which records and analyses on a daily basis the transactions entered into.

(b) Update the cash book and relevant ledger accounts with the totals of the cash register journal analysis columns on a periodic (recommended weekly) basis.

To illustrate the above procedures in the week commencing 28 November 'Histyles' had the following transactions:

(a) Sales receipts

Date	Salon Service (£)	Retail Sales (£)
28 Nov.	100.00	20.00
29 Nov.	70.00	30.00
30 Nov.	140.00	10.00
1 Dec.	130.00	40.00
2 Dec.	160.00	—
3 Dec.	185.00	15.00

(b) Payments

Date	Stock Purchased (Salon)	Stock Purchased (Retail)	Meals and Refresh-ments	Salon (Equip-ment)	Period-icals	Laundry
28 Nov.	4.00	—	—	—	0.50	—
29 Nov.	—	11.00	3.00	—	—	—
30 Nov.	—	—	—	20.00	—	10.00
1 Dec.	13.00	—	2.00	—	—	—
2 Dec.	—	18.00	—	—	—	—
3 Dec.	—	—	—	—	—	—

(c) Cash. A cash float of £5 is maintained and all cash in the till in excess of this amount is banked at the end of each day.

(d) Value Added Tax. All payments were either exempt from VAT or bore VAT at a rate of 8 per cent. All receipts included an 8 per cent VAT increment.

The resultant daily bookings made in the cash register journal are shown in Fig. 8.37. It should be noted that this journal's layout is only suitable for the transactions that were actually experienced. In practice, provision would be made for a greater number of analysis columns, the headings of which would only be entered if a transaction occurred in that particular week.

Further study of the sample journal will show:

(a) It is effectively divided into five segments excluding the Cash Float column (13) which is recorded for reference purposes only.

    (i) Narrative Sections (Cols. 11 and 12) which show the date and the relevant Sales and Purchase (Receipt and Payment Voucher) reference numbers. All vouchers of each type for a particular day are allocated the same reference number.

    (ii) Receipts/Sales Analysis (Cols. 14 and 15).

    (iii) Payments/Disbursements Analysis (Cols. 4–10). Col. 10 shows the daily takings net of daily payments and should reconcile with the cash in the till minus the £5.00 float.

    (iv) VAT Output (Cols. 16 and 17). Separates the VAT charges (Col. 17) from the remaining charges (Col. 16). The sum of these columns should agree with the sum of the columns in paragraph (ii) above.

    (v) VAT Input (Cols. 1–3). Separates the reclaimable VAT (Col. 3) from the VAT to be absorbed (Col. 2) and the value of inputs excluding VAT (Col. 1). The sum of these columns should agree with the sum of the columns in paragraph (iii) above excluding the 'cash banked' (Col. 10).

(b) The bookings to the ledger accounts for the week can be summarised:

Action	Account Title	Journal Col. No.	Value £	Fig. No.
Debit	Purchase Stock (Salon)	4	17.00	8.14
	Purchase Stock (Retail)	5	29.00	8.13
	Meals and Refreshments	6	5.00	8.26
	Salon Equipment	7	20.00	8.5
	Laundry	8	10.00	8.27
	Stationery	9	0.50	8.28
	Cash Book	10	818.50	8.10
	Customs and Excise	3	4.58	8.32
	VAT Output	17	66.65	8.18
			971.23	
Credit	Salon Sales	14	785.00	8.16
	Retail Sales	15	115.00	8.15
	VAT Input	3	4.58	8.17
	Customs and Excise	17	66.65	8.32
			971.23	

(c) No immediate action is taken in respect of Cols. 1, 2 and 16, but this information will in due course be required for the completion of the quarterly 'Return of VAT' to H.M. Customs and Excise which requires:
 (i) Total value of outputs (Sales) excluding VAT.
 (ii) Total value of inputs (Purchase plus expenses) excluding VAT.

3. Credit Sales

It will generally be found that credit sales only comprise a small proportion of the total sales; thus each transaction may be treated on an individual basis throughout the financial records as is shown in the example below:

Histyles provided a hairdressing service for the models taking part in a Fashion Show at Newday Department Store the cost being borne by Newday. On 29 November the service was performed and Histyles forwarded their invoice for £27 including VAT to Newday. Subsequent payment was received on 2 December.

The sequence of administrative events associated with this transaction is:

(a) Since no cash payment is made at the time of the service, the sales vouchers cannot be passed through the cash register.

(b) An invoice, sequentially numbered, in this instance No. 643, is raised on Newday, and a copy of the invoice, together with the relevant sales vouchers are filed as a journal record. From the financial accounting viewpoint a debtor has been created in respect of services provided. Thus, the action in the ledger is:

Debit	Outstanding Debtors A/c.	£27.00	(Fig. 8.33)
Credit	Salon Sales A/c.	£27.00	(Fig. 8.16)

(c) Since invoice No. 643 charges VAT, and the tax point is the date of the invoice, Histyles is liable to Customs and Excise for the £2 VAT from the date of the invoice, irrespective of whether payment has been made. Customs and Excise, therefore, become a creditor and the following ledger bookings are required:

Debit	VAT Output A/c.	£2.00	(Fig. 8.18)
Credit	Customs and Excise A/c.	£2.00	(Fig. 8.32)

(d) When payment is received on 2 December the ledger bookings are:

Debit	Cash	£27.00	(Fig. 8.10)
Credit	Outstanding Debtors	£27.00	(Fig. 8.33)

In addition to the prime actions shown above, the following supplementary activities are recommended:

(a) On the 'Debit' side of the Outstanding Debtors Account an analysis of Output VAT similar to Columns 16 and 17 of the Cash Register should be maintained.

(b) When payment is received, the 'Credit' entry in the Outstanding Debtors Account is made alongside the relevant 'Debit' entry, thus providing a means to identify easily any 'Outstanding Creditors'.

(c) When, for security reasons, the payment is lodged in the till prior to banking, an easily identifiable voucher should also be placed in the till to prevent confusion when the daily cash transaction reconciliation is performed.

(d) To facilitate the Bank Statement to Cash Account reconciliation, payments in respect of credit sales should be made under cover of a separate Bank Paying-in Slip to those in respect of normal cash sales.

4. Credit Purchases

In addition to the payment for goods after they have been received, from the book-keeping point of view, credit payments also include the payment for rent, rates and utilities which may involve an element of prepayment. The accountancy principles involved are identical to those in respect of credit sales and are illustrated by the following transaction entered into by Histyles:

(a) On 24 November, received shampoos to the value of £43.20 including VAT, for salon stock. The invoice was received from Hairdressing Supplies Ltd, on 25 November and was given the Histyle purchase invoice number 13425.

(b) On 22 November new reception chairs to the total value of £64.80 including VAT were received, together with the invoice which was given the number 13424.

(c) The electricity bill for £140, dated 16 November, was received on 22 November and was given the invoice number 13423.

(d) All three of these invoices were paid by cheque on 1 December.

The ledger bookings required are:

22 Nov.	Debit	Electricity A/c.	£140.00	(Fig. 8.19)
	Debit	Furniture A/c.	64.80	(Fig. 8.6)
	Credit	Outstanding Creditors A/c.	204.80	(Fig. 8.34)
25 Nov.	Debit	Purchase Stock (Salon) A/c.	43.20	(Fig. 8.14)
	Debit	Customs and Excise A/c.	3.20	(Fig. 8.32)
	Credit	Outstanding Creditors A/c.	43.20	(Fig. 8.34)
	Credit	VAT input A/c.	3.20	(Fig. 8.17)
1 Dec.	Debit	Outstanding Creditors A/c.	248.00	(Fig. 8.34)
	Credit	Cash A/c.	248.00	(Fig. 8.10)

5. Return of Value Added Tax (VAT)

It was identified in Chapter VII that when the quarterly return of VAT is made to Customs and Excise, in addition to the payment of the difference between 'tax charged on Output' and 'tax charged on Input', the following information is required:

(a) Total Output tax in the quarter.

(b) Total Input tax deductible in the quarter.

(c) Value of Outputs net of tax.

(d) Value of Inputs net of tax.

Consideration of the accounts developed above in respect of Histyles shows that if the quarter ended on 3 December, a sum of £793.63 would be due to Customs and Excise, i.e. the debit balance on Customs and Excise A/c. (Fig. 8.32). When payment is made in this instance on 3 December, the accounting entries are:

Debit	Customs and Excise A/c.	£793.63	(Fig. 8.32)
Credit	Cash A/c.	793.63	(Fig. 8.10)

The additional information required is readily obtainable as follows:

(a) Total Output tax — The total of the credit entries on the Customs and Excise A/c., i.e. £961.25 (Fig. 8.32).

(b) Total Input tax — The total debit entries on the Customs and Excise A/c. prior to the payment of the net tax, i.e. £167.62 (Fig. 8.32).

(c) Value of Outputs — The cumulative value shown in Col. 16 of the Cash Register (Fig. 8.37) plus the value accumulated in the analysis Col. 1 of the Outstanding Debtors A/c. (Fig. 8.33), i.e. £12 015.74.

(d) Value of Inputs — The cumulative value shown in Col. 1 of the Cash Register plus the value accumulated in the analysis Col. 1 of the Outstanding Creditors A/c. (Fig. 8.34), i.e. £1770.44.

6. Capital and Associated Accounts

Capital can be regarded as the value of the investment made in the business which, while expressed in terms of cash value, may actually take the form of tangible items, e.g. land, buildings, salon equipment etc. The capital structure of the various types of business unit has already been described in Chapter II, and the accounting entries required are shown below in respect of our hypothetical salon.

Histyles was founded on 3 December 19–6 by the amalgamation of H. Styles – Men's Hairdressers with I. Styles – Ladies' Hairdressers, each of the partners initially providing £2000 capital. The detailed composition of this capital was:

(a) H. Styles – cash £1400, salon equipment £400, furniture £150, fixtures and fittings £50.

(b) I. Styles – cash £800, salon equipment £900, furniture £200, fixtures and fittings £100.

To effect these transactions the following book-keeping entries were made:

Debit	Salon Equipment A/c.	£1300	(Fig. 8.5)
	Furniture A/c.	350	(Fig. 8.6)
	Fixtures and Fittings A/c.	150	(Fig. 8.7)
	Cash A/c.	2200	(Fig. 8.10)
Credit	H. Styles Capital A/c.	2000	(Fig. 8.1)
	I. Styles Capital A/c.	2000	(Fig. 8.2)

Subsequent additions to fixed assets, i.e. salon equipment, furniture, fittings and fixtures are normally paid for from the cash resources of the business, e.g. the purchase of additional furniture to the value of £64.80 on 22 November 19–8 by Histyles (see Section 4 above). However, on the occasion of major additions to fixed assets it may be necessary for further capital to be injected into the business, which will necessitate similar book-keeping entries to those shown above.

In theory, the profits of a business, i.e. the excess of income over expenditure, will be allocated to the owners of the business on a periodic basis, normally either annually or biannually. In the case of Limited Companies this allocation would be in the form of dividends on shares and can be regarded as a return upon capital invested. The remuneration for the executive services of any shareholder can be included as part of the employment costs of the business. In other business units the legal identity of the proprietor(s) and the business is one and the same. Consequently, the profit from the business is regarded as the proprietor's income and any definition between salary and return on capital investment is purely arbitrary.

The proprietor will, in practice, require funds for personal use more frequently than his profit may be accurately calculated and, therefore, the following book-keeping procedure is recommended:

(a) A 'Current Account' for the proprietor, or in the case of a partnership a series of current accounts for each partner, should be opened.

(b) The current accounts should be debited with all drawings, including the personal National Insurance contributions of the proprietor(s).

(c) The current accounts should be credited with the profit or the agreed share of the profits when these are determined.

(d) Finalisation of the accounts at the financial year-end should include the posting of the balance on the current accounts to the appropriate capital accounts. Thus, if drawings exceeded the share of profits the capital investment would be reduced and, alternatively, if the share of profits exceeded drawings and it was agreed to retain the funds in the business, the capital invested would be increased. It should be noted that the retention of excess funds within an enterprise is uneconomic since these funds are not 'working' and consequently provide no returns to the proprietor(s). It is, therefore, advisable to withdraw such funds from the business, i.e. increase drawings and invest outside the business on a personal basis.

For the purposes of illustration, current accounts for both H. Styles and I. Styles are included in Figs. 8.3 and 8.4 respectively.

7. Adjustments

(a) **Real accounts and depreciation.**   The accounts which contain a record of the assets owned by a business are frequently termed 'Real Accounts' and are debited with the original cost price of the asset. Depreciation may be defined as the decrease in the value of the asset through wear and tear in use, or the passage of time. Depreciation can, therefore, be regarded as an expense of carrying on the business, and requires recording in the books of accounts to:

(i) Facilitate the calculation of true profit or loss of the business during the accounting period.

(ii) Provide a realistic valuation of the fixed assets for inclusion in the balance sheet.

There are several methods of apportioning the total depreciation between the accounting periods which will occur during the 'life' of an asset. It is considered that the most practical method is the *Reducing Balance Method of Depreciation* under which the total depreciation is spread over the anticipated useful life of the asset by taking a fixed percentage of the book value of the assets at a particular date, normally the business year-end. The accounting action is:

> Debit Profit and Loss A/c. for year
> Credit Fixed Asset A/c.

If a particular item becomes unrepairable or is sold during the depreciation period, a special depreciation allowance equal to the outstanding book value should be raised and actioned as above. If the asset is sold, an 'Asset Sales A/c.' should be raised which is credited with the proceeds of the sale. To facilitate these transactions it will be necessary to maintain, in the form of loose-leaf cards, an asset register which shows for each item:

(i) Purchase price and the date of purchase.

(ii) Value of depreciation provisions and the adjusted 'book value', i.e. purchase price minus depreciation provisions.

(iii) Date of sale and value obtained.

The cumulative value of the loose-leaf cards is reconciled with the balances brought forward annually on the fixed asset accounts in the financial records.

(b) Nominal accounts. Nominal accounts are those which record the expenses, losses, incomes and gains of a business. At the end of each trading period, normally yearly or half-yearly, the debit and credit balances on these accounts are transferred to the Profit and Loss Account.

To obtain the true trading result it is essential that the whole of the expenditure or losses and all income and gains whether actually paid or not during the period should be reflected in the Profit and Loss Account. It is invariably found that at the closing date of the trading period:

(i) Expenses have been incurred but not yet charged in the accounts.

(ii) Expenses recorded in the accounts cover a period beyond the end of the trading period concerned.

(iii) Income applicable to the period has not been received.

(iv) Income received during the period relates wholly or partly to the succeeding period.

Accordingly, adjustment of entries is required to ascertain the true total of income and expenditure applicable to the period to which the accounts relate. Detailed examples of such adjustments are shown in the Profit and Loss Account section of this chapter.

8. Trial Balance

One of the advantages of double-entry book-keeping is that the arithmetical accuracy of the accounting records can be checked by the preparation of a statement of the outstanding balances on the accounts which shows both the value of the balance and whether it is a debit or credit balance. Such a statement is called a *Trial Balance* and since every individual transaction requires both a debit and a credit entry in the financial records the sum of the debit balances should equal the sum of the credit balances.

The first step in the preparation of period-end accounts, i.e. Profit and Loss

Histyles — Trial Balance As at 3 December 19–8		
Account Name	*Debit £*	*Credit £*
H. Styles – Capital Account		2250.00
I. Styles – Capital Account		2250.00
H. Styles – Current Account	3566.13	
I. Styles – Current Account	3422.45	
Salon Equipment (Depreciated Value to 4.12.19–8)	1326.09	
Furniture (Depreciated Value to 4.12.19–8)	446.71	
Fixtures and (Depreciated Value to 4.12.19–8) Fittings	243.00	
Salon Stock (as at 4.12.19–8)	315.54	
Retail Stock (as at 4.12.19–8)	1118.90	
Cash at Bank	1887.36	
Cash in Hand	5.00	
Employment Costs	24 032.00	
Purchases – Retail Stock	7221.90	
Purchases – Salon Stock	1795.66	
Retail Sales		11 843.94
Salon Sales		45 816.80
VAT Input		880.08
VAT Output	4611.25	
Electricity	563.24	
Rent	6000.00	
Rates	482.00	
Gas	361.83	
Telephone	217.33	
Insurance	1159.33	
Agency Labour	1312.86	
Meals and Refreshments	288.00	
Laundry	583.96	
Stationery	189.80	
General Maintenance	314.28	
Salon Cleaning	1576.20	
TOTALS:	63 040.82	63 040.82

Account and balance sheet is to extract from the ledger accounts a trial balance. In practice, it is prudent to prepare a trial balance at frequent (monthly) intervals so that errors may be detected at an early date and also to reduce the clerical work at the time of preparing the final accounts. For illustration purposes the above is a trial balance in respect of Histyles as at the close of business on 3 December 19–8 which was Histyles' financial year-end.

9. Profit and Loss Account

The main function of the Profit and Loss Account (P. and L. A/c.) is to ascertain the net profit resulting from the trading operations in a given period. The required result is obtained by debiting the Profit and Loss Account with purchases and expenses and crediting that account with sales and other income. Since the double-entry book-keeping system requires an 'equal and opposite' entry to be made, the effect is to reduce to a zero balance the nominal account concerned, i.e. in the case of Histyles the following accounts are thus reduced:

Employment Cost .... Fig. 8.12

Retail Sales .... Fig. 8.15

Salon Sales .... Fig. 8.16

VAT Input .... Fig. 8.17

VAT Output .... Fig. 8.18

Rent .... Fig. 8.20

Agency Labour .... Fig. 8.25

Meals and Refreshments .... Fig. 8.26

Laundry .... Fig. 8.27

General Maintenance .... Fig. 8.29

Salon Cleaning .... Fig. 8.30

Whilst the major portion of the information needed for the completion of the Profit and Loss Account is contained within the books of account there are instances where additional information is required. In the case of Histyles it is necessary to establish:

(a) The value of both retail and salon stock in hand at the close of business on the 3 December 19–8 (subsequently found to be £1064.10 and £347.68 respectively).

(b) The value of stationery held on 3 December 19–8 (estimated to be £19).

(c) The rates of depreciation to be applied to the fixed assets. (The partners agreed that the depreciation on salon equipment should be 20 per cent of the outstanding book value and 10 per cent in the case of fixtures, fittings and furniture.)

The subsequent entries are shown in the following accounts:

Profit and Loss for the year ending 3 Dec. 19–8 . . . . Shown Below
Salon Equipment . . . . Fig. 8.5
Furniture . . . . Fig. 8.6
Fixtures and Fittings . . . . Fig. 8.7
Salon Stock . . . . Fig. 8.8
Retail Stock . . . . Fig. 8.9
Purchases — Retail Stock . . . . Fig. 8.13
Purchases — Salon Stock . . . . Fig. 8.14
Stationery . . . . Fig. 8.28

Histyles – Profit and Loss Account
(for the year ending 3 December 19–8)

	£	£		£
Salon Stock at 4 Dec. 19–7	315.54		Salon Sales	45 816.80
Plus Purchases	1795.66		Retail Sales	11 843.94
Less Stock at 3 Dec. 19–8	347.68	1763.52	VAT Input	880.08
Retail Stock at 4 Dec. 19–7	1118.90			
Plus Purchases	7221.90			
Less Stock at 3 Dec. 19–8	1064.10	7276.70		
Employment Cost – Permanent Staff		24 032.00		
Employment Cost – Temporary Staff		1312.86		
Gas		401.83		
Electricity		613.24		
Laundry		583.96		
Telephone		254.52		
Rent		6000.00		
Rates		584.00		
Insurance		991.33		
Stationery Purchase	189.80			
Less Stock 3 Dec. 19–8	19.00	170.80		
General Maintenance		314.28		
Salon Cleaning		1576.20		
Meals and Refreshments		288.00		
Depreciation – Salon Equipment		265.22		
Depreciation – Fixtures and Fittings		24.30		
Depreciation – Furniture		44.67		
VAT Output		4611.25		
Balance being Net Profit		7432.14		
		58 540.82		58 540.82

Additionally, it will always be found that at the end of a financial period there are:

(a) Expenses accrued but not yet charged to the business.

(b) Expenses paid in advance, a proportion of which are in respect of, and are chargeable to, the next succeeding trading period.

In these instances, to obtain the expenses relating to the financial period concerned, it is necessary to proportion the charges either incurred or prepaid to the appropriate Nominal Account prior to clearing the outstanding balance to the Profit and Loss Account. It is suggested that the most expedient method is to establish 'Suspense' or temporary accounts to record these adjustments.

Fig. 8.35 shows the Accrued Expense Account of Histyles and the entries required during the preparation of the Profit and Loss Account for the year ending 3 December 19–8, together with the subsequent clearance entries on the 4 December 19–8, the start of the new financial year. Similarly, Fig. 8.36 shows the Accrued Prepayments Account.

10. Profit and Loss Appropriation Account

In the case of a sole trader's accounts the net profit as shown by the Profit and Loss Account may be transferred directly to the trader's Capital Account as a 'Credit', it being normal practice to debit any drawings throughout the period directly to the Capital Account. In the case of both Partnerships and Limited Companies the division of profits is subject to an executive decision by the appropriate partners or directors. The accounting action is to transfer the net profit to a Profit and Loss Appropriation Account, which in reality is an extension of the Profit and Loss Account, as a 'Credit' entry and to debit the account with any distribution which may be agreed, whether subsequent or retrospective.

For purposes of illustration, H. and I. Styles agreed that their drawings, as represented in the books of account by their current accounts, should be equal, and that any residual profit should be divided equally to their Capital Accounts. The resultant entries in the Profit and Loss Appropriation Account are shown below:

Histyles – Profit and Loss Appropriation Account (for the year ending 3 December 19–8)			
	£		£
H. Styles – Current Account	3566.13	Net Profit from P and L A/c.	7432.14
I. Styles – Current Account	3422.45		
I. Styles – Accrued Drawings	143.68		
H. Styles – Capital	149.94		
I. Styles – Capital	149.94		
	7432.14		7432.14

11. Balance Sheet

The main objective of the *Balance Sheet* is the presentation of a concise summary of the liabilities and assets of a business, as at the date of the statement, so that the financial position may be clearly ascertained.

The liabilities which are shown on the 'Debit' side of the balance sheet may be regarded as the value of the investment in the business and include:

(a) Invested capital which in the case of a company is share capital.

(b) Retained profits.

(c) Loans.

(d) Liabilities which may be Creditors or Accrued Expenses.

The assets which are shown on the 'Credit' side of the balance sheet may be regarded as a listing in order of permanence of the use to which the investments (liabilities) had been put. The listing is normally classified into the following:

(a) Fixed Assets, e.g. Salon Equipment

(b) Current Assets, e.g. Stock

(c) Liquid Assets, e.g. Cash

The items shown in the balance sheet are effectively those accounts upon which there is an outstanding balance after the Profit and Loss A/c. and associated adjustments have been actioned. Accordingly, Histyles' balance sheet as at 3 December 19–8, prepared from the accounts developed above is shown at Fig. 8.38.

12. Trader's Income Tax

The contents of this Section apply to the taxing of businesses which are either Sole Traders or Partnerships where income tax is charged individually on the owners. In the case of a company, profits are subject to Corporation Tax but since the majority of hairdressing salons are either sole traders or partnerships, Corporation Tax has been excluded from this book.

In view of the likelihood of change with each successive Finance Act (at least annually) it is appropriate to detail only the basic principles of the taxation of proprietors of businesses. These are:

(a) Income Tax charged on an individual business person is in respect of the profits arising in the year preceding the year of assessment, which, with the concurrence of the Inland Revenue authorities, may be set back to the business' year-end rather than the statutory authorities' year-end, i.e. 5 April. Thus, the profits of Histyles for the financial year 19–7/19–8 would be the basis for H. and I. Styles' Income Tax for the statutory year April 19–8 to April 19–9.

(b) Business profits assessable are not usually the profit shown by the accounts since certain expenses are not allowed by the Inland Revenue. Such items have to be added to profits or deducted from losses. In the case of Histyles the outstanding item is depreciation.

(c) In lieu of excepting depreciation as an allowable expenditure, the Inland Revenue gives an 'Allowance for Capital Expenditure' at the rate of 25 per cent per annum on the outstanding Capital Balance.

Accordingly, it is necessary to prepare an adjustment statement to be forwarded to the Inland Revenue, together with a copy of the Profit and Loss Account and Balance Sheet. The following statement is pertinent to Histyles and its proprietors H. Styles and I. Styles:

Histyles (H. Styles and I. Styles) – Tax Adjustment Statement Based on Profits and Loss Account (for year ending 3 Dec. 19–8)			
	Total (£)	H. Styles (£)	I. Styles (£)
Net Profit and Loss A/c.	7432.14	3716.07	3716.07
Plus Depreciation	334.19	167.10	167.09
Total Net Taxable Profit	7766.33	3883.17	3883.16
Less Capital Allowances on:			
Furniture 95.76			
Fixtures and Fittings 50.63			
Salon Equipment 311.12	457.51	228.76	228.75
Taxable Profit.	7308.82	3654.41	3654.41

FIG. 8.1

DR. _____ H. Styles - Capital _____ ACCOUNT _____ CR.

DATE	REF	AMOUNT	ANALYSIS				DATE	REF	AMOUNT	ANALYSIS			
							19-6						
							3rd Dec.	Initial Input	2000 . 00				
							19-7						
							3rd Dec.	Retained Profit	250 . 00				
							4th Dec.	Balance F/W	2250 . 00				
							19-8						
							3rd Dec.	Retained Profit	149 . 94				
							4th Dec.	Balance F/W	2399 . 94				

FIG. 8.2

DR. _____ I. Styles - Capital _____ **ACCOUNT** **CR.**

DATE	REF	AMOUNT	ANALYSIS				DATE	REF	AMOUNT	ANALYSIS			
							19 - 6						
							3rd Dec.	Initial Input	2000 . 00				
							19 - 7						
							3rd Dec.	Retained Profit	250 . 00				
							4th Dec.	Balance F/W	2250 . 00				
							19 - 8						
							3rd Dec.	Retained Profit	149 . 94				
							4th Dec.	Balance F/W	2399 . 94				

FIG. 8.3

DR. _____ H. Styles - Current _____ **ACCOUNT** **CR.**

DATE	REF	AMOUNT	ANALYSIS				DATE	REF	AMOUNT	ANALYSIS			
19 - 8							19 - 8						
22nd Nov.	Balance F/W	3534 . 63					3rd Dec.	P/L Appropriate	3566 . 13				
27th Nov.	Drawings	31 . 50											

FIG. 8.4

DR. _____ I. Styles - Current _____ **ACCOUNT** **CR.**

DATE	REF	AMOUNT	ANALYSIS				DATE	REF	AMOUNT	ANALYSIS			
19 - 8							19 - 8						
22nd Nov.	Balance F/W	3387 . 29					3rd Dec.	P/L Appropriate	3566 . 13				
25th Nov.	Drawings NI	10 . 16											
27th Nov.	Drawing	25 . 00											
3rd Dec.	Provision	143 . 68											
							4th Dec.	Write-back P.F.	143 . 68				

FIG. 8.5

DR.				Salon Equipment ACCOUNT						CR.			
DATE	REF	AMOUNT	ANALYSIS				DATE	REF	AMOUNT	ANALYSIS			
19-6													
3rd Dec.	Initial Input	1300 . 00											
11th Dec.	Inv. 10005	280 . 00											
19-7							19-7						
14th June	Inv. 10816	38 . 29					3rd Dec.	Depr. Prov.	326 . 52				
6th Oct.	Cash Pur.	14 . 32											
4th Dec.	Bal. F/W	1306 . 09					19-8						
19-8							3rd Dec.	Depr. Prov.	265 . 22				
3rd Dec.	Cash Pur.	20 . 00											
4th Dec.	Bal. F/W	1060 . 87											

FIG. 8.6

DR.				Furniture ACCOUNT						CR.			
DATE	REF	AMOUNT	ANALYSIS				DATE	REF	AMOUNT	ANALYSIS			
19-6													
3rd Dec.	Initial Input	350 . 00											
19-7							19-7						
22nd Nov.	Inv. 10478	74 . 34					3rd Dec.	Depr. Prov.	42 . 43				
4th Dec.	Bal. F/W	381 . 91					19-8						
19-8							3rd Dec.	Depr. Prov.	44 . 67				
22nd Nov.	Inv. 13424	64.80											
4th Dec.	Bal. F/W	402.04											

FIG. 8.7

DR.				Fixtures and Fittings ACCOUNT						CR.			
DATE	REF	AMOUNT	ANALYSIS				DATE	REF	AMOUNT	ANALYSIS			
19-6													
3rd Dec.	Initial Input	150 . 00											
19-7							19-7						
15th Jan.	Inv. 10082	120 . 00					3rd Dec.	Depr. Prov.	27 . 00				
4th Dec.	Bal. F/W	243 . 00					19-8						
							3rd Dec.	Depr. Prov.	24 . 30				
19-8	Bal. F/W	218. 70											

FIG. 8.8

DR.   _Salon Stock_ ACCOUNT   CR.

DATE	REF	AMOUNT	ANALYSIS			DATE	REF	AMOUNT	ANALYSIS		
19 -7						19 -8					
4th Dec.	Bal. F/W	315 . 54				3rd Dec.	Stocktake/FWD	347 . 68			
19 - 8											
3rd Dec.	Purchases	1795 . 66				3rd Dec.	Bal. Stock used	1763.52			
19 - 8											
4th Dec.	Bal. F/W	347 - 68									

FIG. 8.9

DR.   _Retail Stock_ ACCOUNT   CR.

DATE	REF	AMOUNT	ANALYSIS			DATE	REF	AMOUNT	ANALYSIS		
19 -7						19 - 8					
4th Dec.	Bal. FWD	1118 . 90				3rd Dec.	Stocktake/FWD	1064 . 10			
19 - 8						" "	Bal. Stock used	7276 . 70			
3rd Dec.	Purchases	7221 . 90									
4th Dec.	Bal. FWD	1064 . 10									

FIG. 8.10

DR.   _Cash_ ACCOUNT   CR.

DATE	REF	AMOUNT	ANALYSIS				DATE	REF	AMOUNT	ANALYSIS		
			Cash	Bank						Cash	Bank	
19 - 8							19 - 8					
28th Nov.	Bal. FWD	2941 . 49	5 . 00	2936 . 49			1st Dec.	Inv. 13423/4/5	248 . 00	-	248 . 00	
2nd Dec.	Newday	27 . 00		27 . 00			2nd Dec.	Wages	318 . 00	-	318 . 00	
3rd Dec.	Cash 29/11 + 3/12	818 . 50		818 . 50			3rd Dec.	Customs & Excise	793 . 63	-	793 . 63	
							" "	Inland Rev.	535 . 00	-	535 . 00	
							" "	Bal. B/S	1892 . 36	5 . 00	1887 . 36	
4th Dec.	Bal. FWD	1892 . 35	5 . 00	1887 . 36								

FIG. 8.11

| DR. | | | | | | | | Wages | | | ACCOUNT | | | | | CR. |

DATE	REF	AMOUNT	ANALYSIS				DATE	REF	AMOUNT	ANALYSIS			
19 - 8							19 - 8						
26th Nov.	Bal. FWD						1st Dec.	Payroll	318 . 00				
2nd Dec.	Cash	318 . 00											

FIG. 8.12

| DR. | | | | | | | Employment Cost | | | ACCOUNT | | | | | CR. |

| DATE | REF | AMOUNT | ANALYSIS | | | | DATE | REF | AMOUNT | ANALYSIS | | | |
			Wages	PAYE	N.I EES	NL ERS							
19 - 8							19 - 8						
30th Nov.	Bal. F/W	23570 . 00	16,220.00	3930 . 00	1275.00	2145.00	3rd Dec	P + L	24032 . 00				
1st Dec.	Payroll Wk.36	462 . 00	318.00	77.00	25.00	42.00							

FIG. 8.13

| DR. | | | | | | | Purchases - Retail Stock | | | ACCOUNT | | | | | CR. |

DATE	REF	AMOUNT	ANALYSIS				DATE	REF	AMOUNT	ANALYSIS			
19 - 8							19 - 8						
2nd Dec.	Bal. F/W	7192 . 90					3rd Dec.	Stock Retail	7221 . 90				
3rd Dec.	Cash for Wk.	29 . 00											

FIG. 8.14

DR.			Purchases - Salon Stock			ACCOUNT				CR.	
DATE	REF	AMOUNT	ANALYSIS			DATE	REF	AMOUNT	ANALYSIS		
19-8						19-8					
22nd Nov.	Bal. F/W	1735.46				3rd Dec.	Stock Salon	1795.66			
25th Nov.	Inv. 13425	43.20									
3rd Dec.	Cash for Wk.	17.00									

FIG. 8.15

DR.			Retail Sales			ACCOUNT				CR.	
DATE	REF	AMOUNT	ANALYSIS			DATE	REF	AMOUNT	ANALYSIS		
19-8						19-8					
3rd Dec.	P+L a/c	11,843.94				27th Nov.	Bal. F/W	11,728.94			
						3rd Dec.	Cash for Wk.	115.00			

FIG. 8.16

DR.			Salon Sales			ACCOUNT				CR.	
DATE	REF	AMOUNT	ANALYSIS			DATE	REF	AMOUNT	ANALYSIS		
19-8						19-8					
3rd Dec.	P+L a/c	45,816.80				28th Nov.	Bal. F/W	45,004.80			
						29th Nov.	Inv. 643	27.00			
						3rd Dec.	Cash for Wk.	785.00			

FIG. 8.17

DR.			VAT Input		ACCOUNT					CR.		
DATE	REF	AMOUNT	ANALYSIS			DATE	REF	AMOUNT	ANALYSIS			
19-8						19-8						
3rd Dec.	P+L	880.08				21st Nov.	Bal. F/W	869.30				
						25th Nov.	Inv. 13425	3.20				
						26th Nov.	Cash Purchase	3.00				
						3rd Dec.	" "	4.58				

FIG. 8.18

DR.			VAT Output		ACCOUNT					CR.		
DATE	REF	AMOUNT	ANALYSIS			DATE	REF	AMOUNT	ANALYSIS			
19-8						19-8						
28th Nov.	Bal. F/W	4542.60				3rd Dec.	P+L	4611.25				
29th Nov.	Inv. 643	2.00										
3rd Dec.	Cash Sales	66.65										

FIG. 8.19

DR.			Electricity		ACCOUNT					CR.		
DATE	REF	AMOUNT	ANALYSIS			DATE	REF	AMOUNT	ANALYSIS			
19-8						19-7						
2nd Feb.	Inv. 13063	164.28				4th Dec.	W/Back Prov.	43.00				
17th May	" 13151	127.64				19-8						
29th Aug.	" 13305	174.32				3rd Dec.	P+L	613.24				
22nd Nov.	" 13423	140.00										
3rd Dec.	Prov.	50.00				4th Dec.	W/Back Prov.	50.00				

FIG. 8.20

| DR. | | | | Rent | | ACCOUNT | | | | | | | CR. |

DATE	REF	AMOUNT	ANALYSIS				DATE	REF	AMOUNT	ANALYSIS			
19-7							19-8						
6th Dec.	Inv. 13014	1500.00					3rd Dec.	P+L	6000.00				
19-8													
6th Mar.	Inv. 13121	1500.00											
6th June	" 13208	1500.00											
6th Sept.	" 13336	1500.00											

FIG. 8.21

| DR. | | | | Rates | | ACCOUNT | | | | | | | CR. |

DATE	REF	AMOUNT	ANALYSIS				DATE	REF	AMOUNT	ANALYSIS			
19-8							19-7						
28th Jan.	Inv. 13054	264.00					4th Dec.	W/Back Prov.	88.00				
28th Aug.	" 13304	306.00					19-8						
3rd Dec.	Prov.	102.00					3rd Dec.	P+L	584.00				
							4th Dec.	W/Back Prov.	102.00				

FIG. 8.22

| DR. | | | | Gas | | ACCOUNT | | | | | | | CR. |

DATE	REF	AMOUNT	ANALYSIS				DATE	REF	AMOUNT	ANALYSIS			
19-8							19-7						
2nd Feb.	Inv. 13064	97.24					4th Dec.	W/Back Prov.	31.00				
17th May	" 13152	118.37					19-8						
29th Aug.	" 13306	82.64					3rd Dec.	P+L	401.83				
4th Nov.	" 13398	94.58											
3rd Dec.	Prov.	40.00					4th Dec.	W/Back Prov.	40.00				

FIG. 8.23

| DR. | | | | Telephone | ACCOUNT | | | | | | CR. |

DATE	REF	AMOUNT	ANALYSIS			DATE	REF	AMOUNT	ANALYSIS		
19-8						19-7					
16th Jan.	Inv. 13038	62.90				4th Dec.	W/Back Prov.	47.50			
18th April	" 13125	58.32				19-8					
18th July	" 13281	69.23				3rd Dec.	P+L	254.52			
17th Oct.	" 13346	74.38									
3rd Dec.	Prov.	37.19				4th Dec.	W/Back Prov.	37.19			

FIG. 8.24

| DR. | | | | Insurance | ACCOUNT | | | | | | CR. |

DATE	REF	AMOUNT	ANALYSIS			DATE	REF	AMOUNT	ANALYSIS		
19-7						19-8					
4th Dec.	W/Back Prov.	151.33				3rd Dec.	Prepayment	168.00			
19-8						" "	P+L	991.33			
4th Feb.	Inv. 13071	260.00									
" "	" 13072	158.00									
" "	" 13073	590.00									
4th Dec.	W/Back Prov.	168.00									

FIG. 8.25

| DR. | | | | Agency Labour | ACCOUNT | | | | | | CR. |

DATE	REF	AMOUNT	ANALYSIS			DATE	REF	AMOUNT	ANALYSIS		
19-8						19-8					
4th Aug.	Bal. F/W	916.86				3rd Dec.	P+L	1312.86			
4th Sept.	Inv. 13318	270.00									
4th Oct.	" 13329	126.00									

FIG. 8.26

DR.			Meals and Refreshments		ACCOUNT						CR.

DATE	REF	AMOUNT	ANALYSIS				DATE	REF	AMOUNT	ANALYSIS			
19-8							19-8						
19th Nov.	Bal. F/W	273.90					3rd Dec.	P+L	288.00				
" "	Cash Purchase	6.15											
26th Nov.	" "	2.95											
3rd Dec.	" "	5.00											

FIG. 8.27

DR.			Laundry		ACCOUNT						CR.

DATE	REF	AMOUNT	ANALYSIS				DATE	REF	AMOUNT	ANALYSIS			
19-8							19-8						
26th Nov.	Bal. F/W	561.23					3rd Dec.	P+L	583.96				
" "	Cash Purchase	12.73											
3rd Dec.	" "	10.00											

FIG. 8.28

DR.			Stationery		ACCOUNT						CR.

DATE	REF	AMOUNT	ANALYSIS				DATE	REF	AMOUNT	ANALYSIS			
19-8							19-8						
19th Nov.	Bal. F/W	158.04					3rd Dec.	Stock EST.	19.00				
25th Nov.	Inv. 13417	27.00					" "	P+L	170.00				
26th Nov.	Cash Payment	4.26											
3rd Dec.	" "	.50											
4th Dec.	Stock	19.00											

FIG. 8.29

DR.   General Maintenance   **ACCOUNT**   CR.

DATE	REF	AMOUNT	ANALYSIS				DATE	REF	AMOUNT	ANALYSIS			
19 - 8							19 - 8						
26th Nov.	Bal. F/W	314.28					3rd Dec.	P + L	314.28				

FIG. 8.30

DR.   Salon Cleaning   **ACCOUNT**   CR.

DATE	REF	AMOUNT	ANALYSIS				DATE	REF	AMOUNT	ANALYSIS			
19 - 8							19 - 8						
7th Aug.	Bal. F/W	1056.20					3rd Dec.	P + L	1576.20				
18th Aug.	Inv. 13281	130.00											
18th Sept.	" 13311	130.00											
18th Oct.	" 13356	130.00											
18th Nov.	" 13419	130.00											

FIG. 8.31

DR.   Inland Revenue   **ACCOUNT**   CR.

DATE	REF	AMOUNT	ANALYSIS				DATE	REF	AMOUNT	ANALYSIS			
19 - 8							19 - 8						
3rd Dec.	Cash	535.00					9th Nov.	Tax Week 33	125.00				
							16th Nov.	" " 34	126.00				
							23rd Nov.	" " 35	140.00				
							1st Dec.	" " 36	144.00				

FIG. 8.32

DR. ___Customs and Excise___ **ACCOUNT** **CR.**

DATE	REF	AMOUNT	ANALYSIS			DATE	REF	AMOUNT	ANALYSIS		
VAT	ACCOUNT	PERIOD -8/03 (contd.)									
19-8						19-8					
21st Nov.	Bal. F/w from 19	156.84				28th Nov.	Bal. F/W	892.60			
25th Nov.	Inv. 13425	3.20				29th Nov.	Inv. 643	2.00			
26th Nov.	Cash Purchase	3.00				3rd Dec.	Cash Sales	66.65			
3rd Dec.	" "	4.58									
" "	Payment	793.63									
VAT	ACCOUNT	PERIOD -8/04									

FIG. 8.33

DR. ___Outstanding Debtors___ **ACCOUNT** **CR.**

DATE	REF	AMOUNT	Output net of VAT	VAT Output		DATE	REF	AMOUNT	ANALYSIS		
19-8						19-8					
28th Nov.	Analysis F/w	—	329.07	25.93							
29th Nov.	Inv. 643	27.00	25.00	2.00		2nd Dec.	Newday	27.00			

FIG. 8.34

DR. ___Outstanding Creditors___ **ACCOUNT** **CR.**

DATE	REF	AMOUNT	ANALYSIS			DATE	REF	AMOUNT	Input net of VAT	VAT absorbed	VAT Input	
19-8						19-8						
1st Dec.	Inv. 13423	140.00				21st Nov.	Analysis F/w	—	1160.00	—	92.80	
1st Dec.	" 13424	64.80				22nd Nov.	Inv. 13423	140.00	140.00	—	—	
1st Dec.	" 13425	43.20				22nd Nov.	" 13424	64.80	60.00	4.80	—	
						25th Nov.	" 13425	43.20	40.00	—	3.20	

FIG. 8.35

DR.			ANALYSIS			Accrued Expense		ACCOUNT		ANALYSIS			CR.
DATE	REF	AMOUNT				DATE	REF	AMOUNT					
19-8						19-8							
						3rd Dec.	Rates Prov.	102.00					
						" "	Telephone.	37.19					
						" "	Gas "	40.00					
						" "	Electricity.	50.00					
						" "	I Styles Cur. "	143.68					
4th Dec.	Rates W/B	102.00				4th Dec.	Bal. F/W	372.87					
" "	Telephone "	37.19											
" "	Gas "	40.00											
" "	Electricity.	50.00											
" "	I Styles "	143.68											

FIG. 8.36

DR.			ANALYSIS			Accrued Prepayments		ACCOUNT		ANALYSIS			CR.
DATE	REF	AMOUNT				DATE	REF	AMOUNT					
19-8						19-8							
3rd Dec.	Insurance Pr.	168.00											
4th Dec.	Bal. F/W	168.00				4th Dec.	Insurance W/B	168.00					

FIG. 8.37

Histyles - Cash Register Journal

	VAT - Input Related			Purchase - Expenditure							Transaction Date/Documents		Sales Receipts			VAT Output Related	
	1.	2.	3.	4.	5.	6.	7.	8.	9.	10.	11.	12.	13.	14.	15.	16.	17.
	Input net of VAT (£)	VAT absorbed Input (£)	VAT Input (£)	Purchase Salon (£)	Purchase Retail (£)	Meals & Refresh. (£)	Salon Equip. (£)	Laundry (£)	Stationery (£)	Cash to Bank (£)	Date	Reference	Cash Float (£)	Service Sales Receipts (£)	Retail Sales Receipts (£)	Output net of VAT (£)	VAT Output (£)
	295.00	-										Brought Forward	5.00			10833.32	
	4.14	-	.36	4.00	-	-	-	-	.50	115.50	25th Nov.	Sales Voucher (243) / Purchase " (218) / Bal. to Bank		100.00	20.00	111.11	8.89
	12.96	-	1.04	-	11.00	3.00	-			86.00	29th Nov.	S.V. (244) / P.V. (219) / B. to B.		70.00	30.00	92.59	7.41
	27.78	1.48	.74	-	-		20.00	10.00		120.00	30th Nov.	S.V. (245) / P.V. (220) / B. to B.		140.00	10.00	138.89	11.11
	13.89	-	1.11	13.00	-	2.00				155.00	1st Dec.	S.V. (246) / P.V. (221) / B. to B.		130.00	40.00	157.41	12.59
	16.67	-	1.33	-	18.00					142.00	2nd Dec.	S.V. (247) / P.V. (222) / B. to B.		160.00	-	148.15	11.85
										200.00	3rd Dec.	S.V. (248) / B. to B.		165.00	15.00	185.20	14.80
	75.44	1.48	4.58	17.00	29.00	5.00	20.00	10.00	0.50	818.50	TOTALS FOR WEEK		5.00	785.00	115.00	833.35	66.65
	370.44											Carried Forward	5.00			11666.67	

FIG. 8.38

Histyles — Balance Sheet
As at 3 December 19–8

Capital Accounts	£	£	*Fixed Assets*	£	£
H. Styles			(a) Salon Equipment		
– Balance at 3 Dec. 19–8	2250.00		at Cost	1652.61	
Plus retained profit 19–8	149.94	2399.94	Less Accumulated Depreciation	591.74	1060.87
I. Styles			(b) Fixtures and Fittings		
– Balance at 3 Dec. 19–8	2250.00		at Cost	270.00	
Plus retained profit 19–8	149.94	2399.94	Less Accumulated Depreciation	51.30	218.70
			(c) Furniture at Cost	489.14	
			Less Accumulated Depreciation	87.10	402.04
Accrued Liabilities			*Current and Liquid Assets*		
Rates	102.00		Stock — Retail	1064.10	
Telephone	37.19		Stock — Salon	347.68	
Gas	40.00		Cash in Bank	1887.36	
Electricity	50.00		Cash Float	5.00	
I. Styles (Drawings)		143.68	*Prepayments*		
			Stationery – Stock	19.00	
			Insurance	168.00	
		5172.75			5172.75

FIG. 8.39

DR.							Stock Usage (Salon)			ACCOUNT					CR.

DATE	REF	AMOUNT	ANALYSIS				DATE	REF	AMOUNT	ANALYSIS			
3rd Dec.	Stock Salon	1763.52*											
		* Note :											
		This value is reconcilable to the value of Salon Stock issued plus Scrappage											

FIG. 8.40

DR.							Stock Usage (Retail)			ACCOUNT					CR.

DATE	REF	AMOUNT	ANALYSIS				DATE	REF	AMOUNT	ANALYSIS			
3rd Dec.	Stock Retail	7276.70*											
		* Note:											
		This value is reconcilable to the value of Salon Stock issued plus Scrappage											

Figs 8.39 and 8.40 complete the 'double-entry' for the Salon Stock and Retail Stock Accounts. In practice they would be divided into separate accounts to show wastage as opposed to 'cost of sales' for management reference when an integrated Cost Reporting System is not used.

CHAPTER IX

Cost Accounting in the Salon

The development of a greater range of hairdressing services to meet the demands of a larger, more fashion-conscious clientele, coupled with an increasing number of salons readily available to an individual client, has made the hairdressing industry very competitive in all but the most isolated communities. In addition, the hairdressing manager is subjected to a continual round of price increases for materials and equipment and, more important, since hairdressing is a labour-intensive industry, increasing wage demands from employees. All of these factors have a detrimental effect upon the profitability of the salon, which is frequently redressed by management implementing a general rise in the salon's charges. Increasingly, such a policy results in a loss of clientele to competitors who, having encountered the same inflationary factors, have identified the impact upon each of the hairdressing services being provided and adjusted the prices accordingly.

The manager who ignores the inflationary trend until such time as the loss of profitability is shown by the annual profit and loss account and balance sheet will usually find that it is too late to take effective corrective action. A large increase in prices or a deterioration in the standards of the salon as a result of rigid economy measures will be unacceptable both to clients and employees. The latter would already be discontented since one of the first economies would be, at best, a severe restraint on salary rises. At worst it would be a reduction in their numbers as a result of a redundancy policy that increases the work-load on each individual and also induces a feeling of insecurity within the mind of each remaining employee.

The use of an effective *Cost Accounting and Budgetary Control* system provides management with the means to:

1. Identify the causes of increases or decreases in the actual expenses or receipts compared to those anticipated.

2. Compile meaningful costs for each service upon which the 'selling price' may be determined and, where necessary, adjusted to meet the changing market conditions.

   In addition, the system may provide:

3. A basis for formulating operating policies, e.g. data may be available to provide economic justification for the introduction of a new working method using new equipment.

129

4. An integral part of an efficient material control system.

5. Information which may identify the profitability or non-profitability of each activity performed by the salon.

6. An indication of the sources of wastage or loss.

The system is in theory an amalgamation of two systems: *Cost Accounting,* and *Budgetary Control.* Each of these can be operated on its own within an enterprise. However, to be an effective aid to management control each system in practice needs to be complemented, at least in part, by the other. For ease of reference, the underlying principles and practical application of both constituent parts of an integrated cost accounting and budgetary control system are considered individually, cost accounting below, and budgetary control in Chapter X.

COST ACCOUNTING

By definition, cost accounting is the analysis of the total amounts shown in the financial accounts in such a way as to disclose the actual cost and/or the profit or loss on each individual service or operation which has been conducted during a given period.

When the analysis is conducted over successive periods, normally calendar months, a comparison between the data obtained in each period will identify not only the trend in terms of profitability of the activities performed, but also the reasons for any change, whether adverse or favourable. Managements can, therefore, take remedial action to correct any adverse trends before they have any significant long-term impact upon the business as a whole. Such action is retrospective and, ideally, managers need to anticipate what changes will occur in future periods and to plan the activities of the business accordingly. The analysis of actual performance is often compared to a planned performance to validate or otherwise the assumptions and estimates made by management at the time of preparing the plan. It is of course necessary to arrange the planned data in the same format as that in which the actual performance will be reported. Where precise actual costs are not identifiable to one particular service or activity, the method of apportionment of that total expense must be constant. (Detailed reference to apportionment is made under the heading of 'Overheads', later in this chapter.)

In general terms the costs of a salon can be considered to be the expenditure incurred and equate to the 'Debits' shown in the Trading and Profit and Loss accounts in the financial records. Costs can be divided into three elements:

Labour

Material

Overheads

Each element can be divided into *Direct* and *Indirect* costs, although in the case of a hairdressing salon it is likely that indirect labour and indirect material will frequently be considered as part of the overhead expenditure.

Overheads can in turn be classified as *Fixed* or *Variable*: fixed overheads are costs that will be incurred whatever the level of activity in the salon, e.g. rent and rates; variable overheads are those that fluctuate with the level of activity in the salon. For example, in times of low activity the payment for idle time will increase, and when the level of business increases, the value of idle time payments will show a proportionate decrease. Further amplification of these terms, together with a detailed description of the content and costing actions required is given below for each of the three elements of cost.

LABOUR

It is recommended that the labour element of salon costing should be confined to the direct cost of providing the hairdressing operations as identified by the works study techniques described in Chapter V of this book. For practical purposes, the total time spent by the hairdresser in performing these operations can be considered as the *Chair Hours* for the particular service, even if the client actually spends time in the salon chairs in excess to this time, e.g. under the dryers. The direct labour value of a hairdressing service is given by the following formula:

Time taken (to perform the hairdressing operations) × *Rate of Pay*

A constituent part of the work study analysis is to establish a *Standard Time* for each hairdressing operation which can be accumulated to give a standard time for each and every complete service offered by the salon. Unless there is a change in the working methods, very little variation from the standard time will be found to occur on a consistent basis. Discrepancies between actual time taken to perform the service and the standard time will occur, but these will generally be both positive and negative, and over a period of time, e.g. a week or month, will net out to practically zero. The establishment of the standard rate of pay to be used as the multiplicant to the standard time in order to give the standard labour value of each service provided by the salon, requires careful consideration by the management. It is shown later in this chapter that the direct cost of 'chair hours' is not only an important constituent part of the total cost of each service but is also the determining factor in establishing the amount of salon overhead costs to be allocated to each of the hairdressing services. Consequently, it is important that the standard rate of pay used to calculate the standard labour cost (Chair Hours × Direct Labour Cost) is as near as possible to the actual rates that will be paid during the forthcoming standard period (normally a year). The factors which enter into the management's considerations are:

1. Increased Rates of Pay

These can be:

(a) Inflation increases, which are awarded annually and are usually in line with the increased minimum rates quoted by the revised Orders made by the Hairdressing Undertakings Wages Council.

(b) Time-served increments.   It is common practice within the hairdressing industry to award pay increments to junior employees on a time-served basis. Official recognition of this custom is contained in the Hairdressing Under-takings Wages Council minimum rates which show an increased rate for hairdressers for each of the first three years of their employment within the industry. (For current figures please refer to the recent publication of the Order of the Hairdressing Undertakings Wages Council.)

(c) Merit increments, which are awarded to individual hairdressers as a recognition of the value of their contribution to the success of the salon.

2. Mix of Hairdressing Grades

In theory, the junior employees will perform the simple operations, e.g. shampoos, and the experienced hairdressers the more advanced tasks. In practice, whilst this principle may be followed to a limited extent, consid-erable deviation from this distribution of tasks will occur as personal client/hairdresser relationships develop and fluctuations in work-load are experienced by the salon. When developing the *Standard Labour Rate* it is inappropriate to assume that a particular service will be performed by the grades or category of hairdressers indicated by the work study analysis.

With regard to the above factors, it is suggested that the standard labour rate for a standard salon year should be developed using the principles shown in the following worked example, the narrative for which is:

Histyles Hairdressing Salon requires the full-time staff – A, B, C, D, E, F, M and N – to attend the salon for 5 days, each of 8.75 hours. H and I, the owners, attend for six 8.75-hour days. Part-timers X and Y attend the salon for 12 and 16 hours per week respectively. In addition, in the case of holidays and sickness, Z is employed on a casual basis. Each attendee is allowed 12 minutes in each hour of attendance time for personal needs including lunch-breaks to be taken when convenient. It is anticipated that H and I will only spend 25 per cent of their productive time on direct hair-dressing operations and A 75 per cent of the time on these operations. M and N, the apprentices, are receiving training, and perform no direct hairdressing operations on one day and one half-day respectively. F is a receptionist/storekeeper and performs no hairdressing. At the start of the standard year, 1 December 19–8 the rates of pay were:

Payee	Rate in £ per hour
H and I	2.00
A	1.75
B and C	1.50
D, E, F, X, Y and Z	1.40
M	0.75
N	1.00

It is intended to implement a 10 per cent rise for inflation from 1 January, and on 1 June to increase the rate for A, B, C, D and E by £0.05 per hour. On this date both M and N qualify for an increment of £0.10 per hour. Histyles' *Standard Year* runs from 1 December to 30 November of the following calendar year.

The *Standard Hourly Rate* =

$$\frac{\text{Planned Cost of Direct Labour Hours available in Standard Period}}{\text{Standard Hours available in Standard Period}}$$

In this example the standard hourly rate will have to be 'weighted' in proportion to the direct hours to be contributed to the annual total of direct hours by the employees in each salary scale and also to the length of periods when different rates may apply within each salary scale, i.e. one (the month of December); five (January to May inclusive); six (June to November). This may best be achieved by establishing:

1. Average direct labour hours available to each employee in a week. In the absence of any other data it is assumed that each individual employee in the course of the year will be absent for the same period of time due to holidays, sickness etc., and that this absence will be evenly spread over the complete year. The formula for the calculation in respect of each employee is:

   Percentage Activity $\times$ (Attendance Time minus Rest Allowance) as shown below:

(1)	(2)	(3)	(4)	(5)	(6)
Employee	Attendance Hours	Rest Allowance	Effective Hours (2) − (3)	Percentage Direct Hairdressing Time	Planned Hours − Per Week (4) × (5) ÷ 100
H	52.50	10.5	42	25	10.5
I	52.50	10.5	42	25	10.5
A	43.75	8.75	35	75	26.25
B	43.75	8.75	35	100	35
C	43.75	8.75	35	100	35
D	43.75	8.75	35	100	35
E	43.75	8.75	35	100	35
M	35.00	7.0	28	100	28
N	39.375	7.875	31.5	100	31.5
X	12.00	2.4	9.6	100	9.6
Y	16.00	3.2	12.8	100	12.8
TOTAL:	426.125	85.225	340.9	79	269.15

2. Hourly rate applied to direct hours worked per week by each employee in each of the periods when different rates per hour are applicable.

Employee	Direct Hours	December		Jan. – May		June – Nov.	
		Rate £	Value £	Rate £	Value £	Rate £	Value £
H	10.5	2.0	21	2.2	23.1	2.2	23.1
I	10.5	2.0	21	2.2	23.1	2.2	23.1
A	26.25	1.75	45.94	1.925	50.53	1.975	51.84
B	35	1.50	52.5	1.65	57.75	1.70	59.50
C	35	1.50	52.5	1.65	57.75	1.70	59.50
D	35	1.40	49	1.54	53.90	1.59	55.65
E	35	1.40	49	1.54	53.90	1.59	55.65
M	28	0.75	21	0.825	23.10	0.925	25.90
N	31.5	1.00	31.5	1.10	34.65	1.20	37.80
X	9.6	1.40	13.44	1.54	14.78	1.54	14.78
Y	12.8	1.40	17.92	1.54	19.71	1.54	19.71
TOTAL:	269.15		374.80		412.27		426.53

3. Final calculation of standard hourly rate:

(a) Weighted cost of direct labour hours throughout the standard year which consists of 48 weeks after allowing 4 weeks for holidays is:

Month		£
4 (Months – Dec.) × 374.80	=	1 499.20
20 (Months – Jan./May) × 412.27	=	8 245.40
24 (Months – June/Nov.) × 424.53	=	10 188.72
Total for Standard Year	=	19 933.32

(b) Standard Hours in the Standard Year = 48 × 269.15 = 12 919.20
Standard Hourly Rate = 19 933.32 ÷ 12 919.20 = £1.55 (to nearest £0.05).

The direct labour cost for each service is calculated by multiplying the standard time for the hairdressing service by the standard hourly rate; e.g. if the standard time for a shampoo and set is 0.5 hours, then the *Standard Direct Labour Cost* is 0.5 × £1.55 = £0.775.

For control purposes it is necessary to measure actual performances against the standard performance continually. In theory, each service provided by the salon will be individually analysed against the standard performance and differences identified. Where more than one hairdresser has contributed to the provision of the total service, the analysis will be by groups of elements or parts performed by each hairdresser. To provide more meaningful performance data the analysis of actual performance will have to be compared with the standard direct hairdressing hourly rate planned for that particular period of the standard year rather than the average standard direct hairdressing hourly rate used for planning purposes and the price to be charged to the clients.

This latter concept involves the establishment of *Planned Off-Standard Labour Variances* to account for the planned differences, normally of rates of pay incorporated in the standard direct hairdressing hourly rate. In the example quoted above, concerning Histyles, rate changes were identified to occur in January and June, and a weighted standard direct hairdressing hourly rate was established for the standard year, of £1.55 per hour. However, the standard rate for other periods was as follows:

1. December: £374.80 ÷ 269.15 hours   = £1.39
2. January to May: £412.27 ÷ 269.15 hours   = £1.53
3. June to November: £426.53 ÷ 269.15 hours = £1.58

The planned off-standard labour rate variances were:

1. December: £1.55 – £1.39   = £0.16 Minus
2. January to May: £1.55 – £1.53   = £0.02 Minus
3. June to November: £1.55 – £1.58 = £0.03 Plus

We will look at another example. In December 19–8 Mrs W. attended Histyles and received a shampoo and set, a service which had the following Standard:

Element	Time in Minutes
Preparation and Shampoo	12
Set	13
Dressing	10
TOTAL:	35

The Preparation and Shampoo was performed by M (rate of pay £0.75 per hr) in 18 minutes. The other two elements were performed by A (rate £1.75 per hr) in 20 minutes.

In this case, the variance analysis would be as follows:

Standard Cost – 35 minutes at £1.55 per hour	=	£0.904
Less: Off-Standard Variance 35 minutes at £0.16 per hour	=	0.093
Adjusted Standard Cost		0.811
Actual Cost – 18 minutes at £0.75 per hour	=	£0.225
Plus: 20 minutes at £1.75 per hour	=	0.583
Total Actual Cost		0.808

In this instance, only a slight favourable variance of £0.003 occurred over the complete service, but a more detailed analysis to identify the *Time Variance* and *Rate Variance* results in the following (A = Adverse; F = Favourable):

Time Variance given by the formula:

Time Difference (Standard to Actual) × Standard Rate ÷ 60 minutes:

$$£$$

Preparation and Shampoo $-\dfrac{6 \times 1.39}{60}$ = 0.139 A

Set and Dressing $+\dfrac{3 \times 1.39}{60}$ = 0.0695 F

Total Time Variance for Service   = 0.0695 A

Rate Variance given by the formula:

(Standard Rate minus Actual Rate) × Actual time taken (hours):

$$£$$

Preparation and Shampoo $(1.39 - 0.75) \times \dfrac{18}{60} = 0.192$ F

Set and Dressing $(1.39 - 1.75) \times \dfrac{20}{60} = 0.120$ A

Total Rate Variance for Service   = 0.072 F

From the above it can be seen that the balance between standard and actual has in this instance been achieved because the adverse time variance for the complete service has been almost equalled by a favourable rate variance, each variance being a composite of a favourable and adverse factor.

In practice, a detailed analysis of each and every service provided by the salon would be time-consuming and costly. Management should, therefore, restrict the analysis in the first instance to identifying the major variances to planned costs and then limiting further analysis to the investigation of adverse variances of significant value. The suggested method for identifying the major variances is shown with reference to Histyles, whose activities in December 19–8 were as follows:

1. Standard labour hour rate = £1.55
2. December off-standard labour hour rate = Minus £0.16
3. Actual payment rates were as envisaged when the standard labour hour rate and the December off-standard labour hour rate were calculated, i.e.:

Employee	Rate per Hour (£)
H and I	2.00
A	1.75
B and C	1.50
D, E, X and Y	1.40
N	1.00
M	0.75

4. The services provided, standard time per service, number of services provided in December and total hours standard work performed were:

Service No.	Description	Unit Std Hrs.	No. of Services	Total Std Hrs.
01	Shampoo and Set	0.583	416	242.53
02	Cutting and Restyling	0.50	220	110.00
03	Permanent Waving (Cold)	1.75	140	245.00
04	Tinting	3.00	36	108.00
05	Cut and Blow-Dry	1.25	310	387.50
06	Oil Treatment and Massage	0.75	48	36.00
07	Comb-out (Dressing) only	0.50	46	23.00
08	Bleach Streaks	2.00	64	128.00
			TOTAL:	1280.03

5. During December 19–8 N was absent, sick from the salon for a period of 12 working days. Z was employed to perform the tinting service No. 04, which was normally performed by N, and was paid the agreed rate of £1.20 per hour.

6. A summary of the actual hours booked against each service, by each employee, extended by the employee's actual hourly rate to show actual cost is as follows:

Rate per Hour £	Service 01 Hrs	Service 01 £	02 Hrs	02 £	03 Hrs	03 £	04 Hrs	04 £	05 Hrs	05 £
2.00 (H and I)	26	52.00	12	24.00	26	52.00	—	—	25	50.00
1.75 (A)	25	43.75	14	24.50	27	47.25	—	—	35	61.25
1.50 (B, C)	37	55.50	44	66.00	143	214.50	—	—	96	144.00
1.40 (D, E, X, Y)	67	93.80	50	70.00	44	61.60	—	—	154	215.60
1.20 (Z)	—	—	—	—	—	—	60	72.00	—	—
1.00 (N)	—	—	—	—	—	—	50	50.00	—	—
0.75 (M)	80	60.00	—	—	—	—	—	—	60	45.00
TOTALS:	235	305.05	120	184.50	240	375.35	110	122.00	370	515.85

(cont.)

Rate per Hour £	06 Hrs	06 £	07 Hrs	07 £	08 Hrs	08 £	All Hrs	All TOTAL
2.00 (H and I)	16	32.00	—	—	15	30.00	120	240.00
1.75 (A)	4	7.00	—	—	13	22.75	118	206.50
1.50 (B, C)	—	—	—	—	—	—	320	480.00
1.40 (D, E, X, Y)	—	—	—	—	92	128.80	407	569.80
1.20 (Z)	—	—	—	—	—	—	60	72.00
1.00 (N)	—	—	15	15.00	10	10.00	75	75.00
0.75 (M)	—	—	—	—	—	—	140	105.00
TOTALS:	20	39.00	15	15.00	130	191.55	1240	1748.30

The calculation of the direct hairdressing labour variances for the period is:

1.   Total Direct Hairdressing Labour Variance

Standard Cost of Work Performed – 1280.03 hrs. × £1.55	=	£1984.05
Less: Planned Off-Standard Labour		
Rate Variance	– 1280.03 hrs. × £0.16	=	204.80
Adjusted Standard Cost of Work Performed		=	1779.25
Actual Cost		=	1748.30
Total Direct Hairdressing Labour Variance			30.95 F

2.   Labour Time Variance (F signifies Favourable; A, Adverse)

Service No.	(Standard Time	–	Actual Time)	× Standard Rate £	=	Time Variance £	
01	242.53	–	235		=	10.47	F
02	110.00	–	120		=	13.90	A
03	245.00	–	240		=	6.95	F
04	108.00	–	110	× 1.39	=	2.78	A
05	387.50	–	370		=	24.33	F
06	36.00	–	20		=	22.24	F
07	23.00	–	15		=	11.12	F
08	128.00	–	130		=	2.78	A
TOTAL:	1280.03	–	1240.0	× 1.39	=	55.65	F

3.   Apparent Rate Variance

Service	(Standard Rate × Actual Hours) –	Actual Cost	=	Rate Variance £	
01		235 –	305.05	=	21.60	F
02		120 –	184.50	=	17.70	A
03		240 –	375.35	=	41.75	A
04	1.39 ×	110 –	122.00	=	30.90	F
05		370 –	515.85	=	1.55	A
06		20 –	39.00	=	11.20	A
07		15 –	15.00	=	5.85	F
08		130 –	191.55	=	10.85	A
TOTAL:		1240	1748.30		24.70	A

4. True Rate Variance

The only 'rate' increase occurred through the employment of Z in the absence of N, and is:

$$(1.20 - 1.00)\ £ \times 60\ \text{Hrs.} = \underline{\underline{£12.00\ \text{Adverse}}}$$

5. Utilisation Variance

Originates from a change in the actual utilisation of different grades of direct hairdressing labour to that planned. In this case the value of the variance is: £24.70 − £12.00 = £12.70 Adverse. This was largely due to the greater involvement in the performance of direct hairdressing by H and I.

The above would indicate that, overall, the actual performance was better than the planned performance and that the service charges established as a result of the planned standard would, in respect of direct hairdressing labour costs, be representative. However, the sum of the variances in Sections 2 and 3 above shows that the following variances were experienced against each service:

(1) *Service*	(2) *Total Variance £*		*Adjusted Standard Cost (Std Hrs × 1.39)*		(3)	(4) *% Variance (2)÷(3) × 100*	
01	32.07	F	242.53	× 1.39	= 337.12	9.5	F
02	31.60	A	110.00	× 1.39	= 152.90	20.7	A
03	34.80	A	245.00	× 1.39	= 340.55	10.2	A
04	28.12	F	108.00	× 1.39	= 150.12	18.7	F
05	22.78	F	387.50	× 1.39	= 538.62	4.2	F
06	11.04	F	36.00	× 1.39	= 50.04	22.1	F
07	16.97	F	23.00	× 1.39	= 31.97	53.1	F
08	13.63	A	128.00	× 1.39	= 177.92	7.7	A
TOTAL:	30.95	F	1280.03	× 1.39	= 1779.24	1.74%	F

The above data would indicate that the price for services 04, 06 and 07 may be overstated, whereas services 02 and 03 may be underpriced. Since the overall trend is 'favourable' no immediate management action is required as the variances may be attributable to the 'mix' of the labour grades in that particular month. However, if the same trend is shown in subsequent months a price adjustment may well be commercially advantageous.

MATERIAL

The *Direct Material Cost* is normally only a small part of the total cost of a particular hairdressing service, the major components of which are: the cost of direct hairdressing labour hours and general salon overheads. Consequently it is often found that in the commercially less sophisticated salons the direct material cost is included as part of the salon overheads, it being assumed that the value of materials used in the course of performing each and every hairdressing service is directly proportional to the direct hairdressing hours expended on each service. With the increase in the scope of services offered, coupled with the increase in the range of material preparations available, the validity of such an assumption is suspect.

It has also become usual for salons to diversify into retail sales. This activity normally commences on such a small scale that no additional burden is placed upon the resources of the salon, with the result that the retail 'mark-up' on the goods sold is a direct addition to the profits of the business. However, with the passage of time the range of goods offered for sale will increase, space will be used for storage and display, employment time will be spent on material sales and control tasks either additional to, or in lieu of, direct hairdressing. In such circumstances a proportion of the salon overheads becomes directly attributable to retail sales and should be treated as an adverse influence upon the profitability of retail sales, rather than being included as an overhead recoverable against the hairdressing services provided.

An effective material costing system which integrates both retail material and service material is required, to enable management to exercise the necessary controls needed to operate a profitable business. Such a system is described below:

1.   Purchased Unit

Material will be purchased in various packs or sizes of container. In general retail sales, packs or containers will be smaller in volume or quantity than the packs or containers of that material used by the hairdressing operators within the salon; e.g.: Supplier R provides Flex Balsam and Protein Hair Conditioner in 50ml, 100ml, 200ml, 1 litre and 2 litre containers, but since the cost of packaging represents a significant proportion of R's cost, the larger containers offer a lower cost per millilitre, the cost per container being:

Container Size	Cost £
50 ml	0.28
100 ml	0.34
200 ml	0.50
1 litre	1.75
2 litre	3.15

In addition, Supplier T offers a similar conditioner in 75ml containers for £0.33, 300ml containers for £0.55 and 5 litre for £7.00. If it is the salon management's intention to obtain, stock, use or sell, the eight containers listed above, then for stock and accounting purposes they should be regarded as eight separate types of material; i.e. each a separate purchased unit for which a standard cost will have to be developed.

2.   Discounts

In Chapter VI, 'Procurement and Control of Salon Materials and Equipment', it was established that a purchase may be subject to the following discounts against the supplier's recommended or listed price:

Quantity Discount
Cash Discount
Annual Turnover Discount
Trade Discount

For the purposes of establishing a standard cost for a purchased unit, these discounts, with the exception of trade discount, should be ignored since they are normally of small percentage value and are variable between each and every transaction. If savings are achieved they will be treated as favourable variances.

3. Setting of Standards

In a similar fashion to that in which *Labour Standards* are set, so *Material Standards* are set. Upon these are based the sales price for retail sales items and the material component of the 'service' prices. The need to maintain a constant sales price throughout the standard year is still of great importance, particularly in respect of retail sales, where constant price changes involve considerable administrative activity within the salon. It is, therefore, of great importance to establish a standard cost for each purchase unit which will be realistic for the complete standard year.

The traditional method of setting the standard at the level of the last purchase price can be almost immediately devalued in times of inflation, particularly if the last purchase was some time previous to the date of setting the standard. It is, therefore, prudent for management to establish an *Economic Factor* to be applied to all standards based on a historical actual purchase price. This factor will be expressed as an annual percentage increase or decrease which is equal to the anticipated rise or fall in wholesale prices. Since such forecasts vary considerably, a large element of managerial judgement is required in selecting the rate to be used as the economic factor. However, regular monitoring of actual performance will soon identify significant deviations. It should be noted that when the stock records show that a particular purchase unit is slow-moving, and that the present usage rate will not require a purchase to be made in the standard year, then the standard is not revised. If a standard has not previously been set then the actual purchase price is used to calculate the sales price and for cost analysis purposes the complete price is allocated to variance. The following example illustrates the above principles.

Histyles uses the 5 litre containers of Flex Balsam and Protein Hair Conditioner supplied by T. The salon 'consumes' approximately 1 container per month and orders in quantities of 6 when the stock-holding (reorder level) reaches 3. On 1 November 19–7 the stock in hand was 7 containers, the last purchase price being £7 per container for the consignment received that day. A stock of 1 and 2 litre containers from Supplier R existed in stores but these were only used when specified by the client. The current usage rate suggested that the stock-holding purchased at £1.75 and £3.15 per respective container is sufficient to meet the next 3 years' demand. The holding of 50ml and 75ml containers was so slow-moving that no further purchases were intended, the last prices being £0.28 and £0.33 respectively. On the remaining items a regular procurement and subsequent sales programme is anticipated, the details being:

Control Data	100 ml Containers	200 ml Containers	300 ml Containers
Last Purchase Date	30 Sept. 19–7	30 Oct. 19–7	on Order
Last Price	£0.34	£0.50	£0.55
Planned Purchase Quantities	200 Containers	300 Containers	200 Containers
Planned Purchase Dates	30 Dec. 19–7 30 Mar. 19–8 30 June 19–8 30 Sept. 19–8	30 Mar. 19–8 30 Sept. 19–8	30th of each month

Histyles' management estimate that an 18 per cent per annum inflation will apply to purchases during the course of the standard year, i.e. 1.5 per cent per month.

The standards set were as follows:

(a) Non-Repetitive Items:

Size	Price in £ per container
1 litre	1.75
2 litre	3.15
50ml	0.28
75ml	0.33

(b) Repetitive Items

			£
5 litre	6 off on 1 Mar. 19–8 at £7.00 + (1.50% × 4 months Nov. to Mar.)	=	44.52
	6 off on 1 Sept. 19–8 at £7.00 + (1.50% × 10 months Nov. to Sept.)	=	48.30
	Standard $= \dfrac{44.52 + 48.30}{12 \text{ off}}$	=	7.735
100 ml	200 on 30 Dec. at £0.34 + (1.50% × 3 months Sept. to Dec.)	=	71.06
	200 on 30 Mar. at £0.34 + (1.50% × 6 months Sept. to Mar.)	=	74.12
	200 on 30 June at £0.34 + (1.50% × 9 months Sept. to June)	=	77.18
	200 on 30 Sept. at £0.34 + (1.50% × 12 months Sept. to Sept.)	=	80.24
			302.60
	Standard $= \dfrac{302.60}{800}$	=	£0.378

200 ml	300 on 30 Mar. at £0.50 + (1.50% × 5 months Oct to Mar.)	=	161.25

300 on 30 Sept. at £0.50 + (1.50% × 11 months Oct. to Sept.) = 174.75

336.00

$$\text{Standard} = \frac{336.0}{600} \qquad = \quad £0.56$$

300 ml	*200 containers purchased on each date below*		
	30 Nov. at £0.55 (overdue)	=	110.00
	30 Dec. at £0.55 + 1.5%	=	111.65
	30 Jan. at £0.55 + 3.0%	=	113.30
	28 Feb. at £0.55 + 4.5%	=	114.95
	30 Mar. at £0.55 + 6.0%	=	116.60
	30 Apr. at £0.55 + 7.5%	=	118.25
	30 May at £0.55 + 9.0%	=	119.90
	30 June at £0.55 + 10.5%	=	121.55
	30 July at £0.55 + 12.0%	=	123.20
	30 Aug. at £0.55 + 13.5%	=	124.85
	30 Sept. at £0.55 + 15.0%	=	126.50
	30 Oct. at £0.55 + 16.5%	=	128.15
	30 Nov. at £0.55 + 18.0%	=	129.80

1558.70

$$\text{Standard} = \frac{1558.70}{2600} \qquad = \quad £0.60$$

The above process is applied to each purchase item of stock whether this stock is for in-salon use or for retail sale. The standard cost of a retail purchase item can be directly used to calculate the retail sale price, i.e. standard cost + overhead apportionment + profit. The standard cost of the in-salon purchase items is for a quantity which will be split between many individual services or treatments and it is, therefore, necessary for the average usage to be determined for each service. Records of the quantity of each item issued to the salon, and of the number of times that the purchase item was expended in the course of the various services provided, will determine the average usage; e.g. Histyles found that 25 ml of conditioner was used in the course of each conditioning operation. Therefore, the material cost to be attributed to each such operation using the 5 litre (5000 ml) purchase item whose standard cost was established as £7.735 above is:

$$\text{Number of Treatments} \frac{5000}{25} = 200$$

$$\text{Average Material Cost per Treatment} = \frac{7.735}{200} = £0.0387 \text{ or 4p to the nearest p.}$$

The sum of each such average purchased standard material used in each and every service will give the Standard Material component of the service cost to the client.

4. Purchase Variance Analysis

In a similar manner to labour expenditure, the cost of each and every purchase should be compared to the standard cost and the difference or variance, whether favourable or adverse, should be identified; e.g. the 5 litre containers of conditioner whose standard cost was set at £7.735 per container for the period December 19–7 to November 19–8, were ordered, received and paid for as follows:

(a) 4 Feb. a quantity of 6 at £7.00 ea.

(b) 15 May a quantity of 6 at £7.50 ea.

(c) 11 Sept. a quantity of 6 at £8.00 ea.

The variance analysis on an individual basis will show:

Date	Total Std Cost £	Total Actual Cost £	Price Variance £	
4 Feb.	46.41	42.00	4.41	Favourable
15 May	46.41	45.00	1.41	Favourable
11 Sept.	46.41	48.00	1.59	Adverse
	139.23	135.00	4.23	Favourable

On an individual basis this performance would indicate that from the price aspect the standard set was adequate and no management action is required. However, attention should be paid to the fact that the salon had ordered and received 50 per cent more conditioner than had been planned. In costing terms, this difference is a purchase *volume variance* and is the difference between the planned volume of purchases to the actual volume of purchases, in this case:

$$(12 \times 7.735) - (18 \times 7.735) = £46.41 \text{ Adverse}$$

Such a large adverse variance will require further management investigation and it is suggested that there are three possible causes for such an occurrence which should be addressed in the following order:

(a) *The stock holding or inventory level has increased.*   A check of the stock held by the stores will quickly identify this fact. It should be noted that this increase may be justified, e.g. an increase in supplier delivery time coupled with a fluctuating demand from the salon.

(b) *An increase in the number of services for which conditioner is required.*   The existence of such an increase and extent of the increase can be obtained from the sales records. This occurrence is advantageous to the salon but care should be taken that the increased purchases are proportional to the increased activity.

(c) *An increase in apparent usage without a corresponding increase in completed services.* This shows that either wastage is excessive, or pilfering has happened or the standard usage quantity is too low. Whichever of these reasons is responsible for the adverse variance, management action is required immediately to retain the effectiveness, efficiency and profitability of the salon.

Again, as in the case of labour, an itemised analysis is extremely time-consuming and expensive. For practical purposes it is suggested that the variances should, in the first instance, be identified on an overall basis, with detailed analysis only being conducted when large adverse variances are identified. To obtain the basis for this action a record must be made of all items received and their actual price. The quantities received should be priced at the standard cost, for comparative purposes if detailed price analysis is required, and also to obtain the total standard cost of purchases. The following example illustrates the overall variance valuations required:

In February 19–8 Histyles planned to purchase goods, the standard value of which was £320, a favourable off-standard variance of £16 being anticipated. During the month, goods charged at £440 were received, the standard cost of these goods being £460. Therefore:

Total Variance $=$ £440 $-$ £320 $=$ £120 Adverse

Purchase Volume Variance $=$ £460 $-$ £320 $=$ £140 Adverse

Price Variance $=$ £460 $-$ £440 $=$ £20 Favourable

Planned Percentage Off-Standard Variance

$$= \frac{16 \times 100}{320} = 5\% \text{ Favourable}$$

Actual Percentage Off-Standard Variance

$$= \frac{20 \times 100}{440} = 4.55\% \text{ Favourable}$$

The total adverse variance is, therefore, almost entirely due to an increase in the volume of purchases. But if subsequent investigation shows that the retail sales have increased from £364 to £506, allowing that the retail sales value is given by the formula, Cost of Sales + 35 per cent mark-up for overheads and profit, then an increase in cost of sales has occurred. The amount of increase is:

$$\frac{(506 - 364) \times 100}{135} = £105.19$$

The above can be regarded as a sales volume variance of £105.19 favourable, which, provided there has been no corresponding reduction in stock value during the period, can be offset against the adverse purchase volume variance. However, since an adverse variance of almost £35 still exists, a stock verification on the following lines should be initiated:

	Retail Stock £	Salon Stock £	Total Stock £
Opening Balance (at Standard)	740	220	960
Plus Purchases (at Standard)	340	120	460
Less Issues (at Standard)	375	125	500
Balance at 1st March	705	215	920

The above shows that a decrease in stock holding had occurred, due partly to the increase in retail sales and also to an increase in the issues to the salon. To complete the variance investigation it would be necessary to establish whether the salon services provided accounted for a material usage of £125. If a significant short-fall was identified, salon 'wastage' would require detailed management attention.

OVERHEADS

The overhead costs of a salon are all other expenses apart from direct labour and direct material, which have been discussed earlier. As opposed to direct labour and direct material, the overhead costs cannot be directly attributed to one particular service or sales transaction. It is this factor which supports the theory that 'indirect' materials, e.g. hairclips, salon cleaning materials etc., and 'indirect' labour, e.g. 'idle time', 'on-the-job' training etc., should be included as part of overheads, rather than treated as separate cost elements.

The costing of the overhead items is seldom possible on an item by item basis. Therefore, it entails examining on a regular basis the actual expenditure against the planned expenditure, and allocating the actual costs in the same manner as the planned costs. A simple example to illustrate this principle is:

The planned overhead expenditure of Salon A is £1500 and this is divided equally over the planned 1000 services each of which had a direct labour cost of £1.00 and a direct material cost of £0.05. During the actual period of operations the overhead expenditure was £1600 and 1200 services were provided. No variances were experienced in respect of direct labour and direct material and a 20 per cent uplift was applied to the total salon cost in respect of profit mark-up.

1. Planned Service Charge

	Per Service £	Total for 1000 Services
Direct Labour Cost	1.00	1000
Direct Material Cost	0.05	50
Overhead $\dfrac{£1500}{1000}$	1.50	1500

	Per Service £	Total for 1000 Services
Salon Cost	2.55	2550
Profit 20% Salon Cost	0.51	510
Service Charge	3.06	3060

2. Income Actually Received from Services Provided

1200 services at £3.06 = £3672

The recovery in respect of the individual cost elements, obtained by multiplying the Unit Service Cost by 1200 is:

Direct Labour Cost	£1200
Direct Material Cost	60
Overhead	1800
Salon Cost	3060
Profit	612
TOTAL:	3672

3. Actual Overhead Expenditure

The labour and material costs were in proportion to the plan and so was the profit element but the actual expenditure on overheads was £1600 not £1800 (£1.50 × 1200), as allowed for when the costs of services were planned. The £200 difference is referred to as an *over-recovery of overheads* and as such is additional to the planned profit in the same way as a favourable material or labour variance.

Where the actual overhead expenditure is greater than the recovered expenditure based upon a service unit planned recovery rate, an *under-recovery of overheads* has occurred which reduces the planned profit.

The above example as well as showing the principle of under- and over-recovery of overheads also shows the practical tendency of overheads to vary, both directly with the volume of activity in a similar way to total labour and material direct costs and to remain constant no matter what the activity level performed. This tendency has led purist cost accountants to refer to overhead costs as being either *fixed* (unaffected by volume of activity) or *variable* (proportional to the level of activity). In practice, however, few costs can be so easily divided, the majority of overhead items being semi-variable, and accordingly this principle is largely ignored in the following paragraphs.

Classification of Overheads

Overheads can be classified under the following headings:

1.   General Employment Costs or Labour Related Overheads

These include the following:

(a) Employer's contributions to the National Insurance Scheme, and possibly a contribution to a pension or life assurance scheme which is for the personal long-term benefit of employees.

(b) Payment of sickness benefit, additional to the statutory sickness benefits paid under the National Insurance Scheme. These usually involve a sum to make up the employee's remuneration to the normal level.

(c) Payment of holiday pay, i.e. the normal basic wage, for customary (bank) holidays and for additional days' personal holidays, a minimum entitlement being stipulated by the Hairdressing Undertakings Wages Council.

(d) Overtime premium payments, i.e. increments to the hourly rate of pay for hours worked above the standard working week.

(e) Payment for idle time, training time, i.e parts of the customary working hours when no direct hairdressing work is performed or the employee attends at the salon but no work is available.

(f) Bonuses and incentive scheme payments.

(g) The total remuneration paid to employees engaged in other than direct hairdressing operations, e.g. receptionists, storekeepers, cleaners, etc.

2.   Indirect Material Costs

These include:

(a) All materials used in the direct hairdressing operations, the value of which is too small and variable to be included as a Direct Material Cost, e.g. hair sprays.

(b) The cost of 'reusables', e.g. gowns, pins, clips, etc.

(c) Small tools, if not supplied by the individual employees, e.g. combs and scissors.

(d) The cost of expendables, e.g. tissues, etc.

(e) Wastage material whether this is due to loss, breakage, evaporation, deterioration or obsolesence.

3.   General Overheads

These are all other expenses which may be incurred by a salon. The existence of these items will vary according to the circumstances of the salon. Therefore, the following list of items should not be taken as complete; neither should it be taken as a 'minimum' or 'basic' list.

Rent
Interest or Mortgage Repayments
Rates, both General and Water
Insurances
Heating and Lighting
Telephone
Laundry

Stationery and Printed Periodicals
Advertising
Meals and Refreshments
Travelling Expenses
Repairs and Renewals
Bank Charges
Professional Charges (Accountants, Solicitors etc.)
Associated Subscriptions

Apportionment of Overheads

The total cost of all of the overhead items classified above has to be 'recovered' as part of the charges made to clients for the services or sales effected by the salon. To obtain a fair balance, a method of apportionment of these charges to the 'point of sale' has to be determined. In salons where both a hairdressing service and a retail outlet are provided it is important to apportion the overheads to each of these two categories.

As in the previous two categories of cost, the theoretical method of apportionment would be to consider each and every item of overhead expenditure as a separate entity and to develop or maintain an individual basis of apportionment. The following examples show the variety of criteria used to apportion overheads between retail sales operations and salon service operations:

1. Employment Costs

It has been shown previously in this chapter and in Chapter V 'Work Study in the Salon' that employees' time that is not devoted to the provision of the direct hairdressing operations is either idle or lost time or may be spent on overhead activities. It is likely that there will be individuals whose total employment time is dedicated to overhead activities, i.e. receptionists, cleaners, storekeepers, accountants or managers. In addition, a certain amount of time may be spent on the performance of these duties by employees who are primarily engaged in the direct hairdressing operations. Consequently, it is important to establish from the work study records the proportion of total time spent on the overhead functions. It is then necessary to establish the proportion of the functional time that is devoted to both of the prime activities, i.e. retail sales and hairdressing services. The basis for such apportionment has to be appropriate to the function; e.g. if the storekeeper is responsible for the provisioning, purchase and issue of materials, then an appropriate method of apportionment may be the percentage of transactions conducted. To illustrate these principles in quantitative terms the following example is used:

It is established that 10 per cent of the total employment hours are devoted to the storekeeping function. In turn, 60 per cent of the stores transactions are related to retail sales, with the remaining 40 per cent of transactions being divided between direct material hairdressing services (30 per cent) and salon general overhead (10 per cent). It is further estimated that the total employment costs for the forthcoming year will be £40 000. Therefore:

Total Storekeeping Employment Cost = 10% of £40 000 = £4000
Retail Sales Storekeeping Employment Cost = 60% of £4000 = £2400
Salon Storekeeping Employment Cost = 40% of £4000 = £1600

2. Indirect Material Costs

The listing of *Indirect Material Costs* shows that with the exception of 'wastage material' all the other costs are 'salon service related'. It is accordingly possible to apportion or allocate the indirect material costs in a direct ratio to previous performance; e.g. 'It has been found that 5 per cent of the retail sales stock purchased was wasted; it is planned in the coming financial year to spend £20 000 on retail purchases.'

Retail Sales Indirect Overheads = 5% of £20 000 = £1000

3. General Overheads

The method of apportionment is dependent upon the nature of expense and, therefore, each item will require careful individual attention. A study of the items listed as general overheads on pp. 148–9 will show:

(a) Telephone, laundry, advertising, meals and refreshments, travelling expenses and association subscriptions are chargeable to salon overheads only.

(b) Rent, rates, heating and lighting may be apportioned according to the floor area occupied by each of the two business activities.

(c) Interest or mortgage repayments, bank charges and professional charges may be apportioned on the basis of monthly average capital employed.

(d) Repairs and renewals can be apportioned in proportion to the asset valuation of the fixtures, fittings and equipment employed.

(e) Insurance can be considered on an individual basis: e.g. Professional Indemnity Insurance as 100 per cent to salon services, Fire and Theft Insurance in proportion to the average value of stock holding plus asset value.

(f) Stationery apportionment on a factual basis will require considerable research for a relatively small sum and it is likely that a general apportionment basis such as the percentage of employment costs would be just as effective.

With the exception of the indirect material costs, the division of the remaining overhead expenditure into apportionable amounts requires considerable detailed calculation. For practical purposes a similar result may be obtained if the employment costs and general overheads are apportioned in total using as a base the effective hours apportioned between salon services and retail sales. To illustrate this apportionment, reference is made to the previous example of Histyles shown on pp. 132–9. The planned direct hours are 269.15. In addition, a further 35 effective hours are expended by Employee F on storekeeping/reception duties. A further 71.75 effective hours are planned to be expended by the owners/senior staff on administrative and general management duties. Further studies show that 37 hours are spent by senior staff on reception and stock tasks and the overall proportion of reception-related tasks to stock-related tasks is 1 : 2. It is also established that 60 per cent of the stock tasks and 25 per cent of the reception tasks are related to retail sales. The remaining 34.75 hours of senior management's time is proportional to the amount of personnel activity in each of the two functions (retail sales and salon services.) Thus:

1. Reception Hours   =   24
   Stock Hours   =   48

        TOTAL (1):   72   (35 in respect of F and 37 Senior Staff)

2. Retail Sales Time Reception   =   25% of 24   =   6
   Retail Sales Time Stock   =   60% of 48   =   28.8

        TOTAL (2):   34.8

3. Salon Related Overhead Time (1) − (2) = 37.2 hours
4. Total Services Time = 37.2 + 269.15 = 306.35 hours
5. Allocation of remaining Senior Management Time 71.75 − 37 = 34.75 hours is in the proportion of 34.80 : 306.35 and is:-
   Retail Sales   =   3.54
   Salon Services = 31.21
6. Effective Hours proportion is
   Retail Sales 3.54 + 34.80   =   38.34 hours (10.20%)
   Salon Services 31.21 + 306.35 =   337.56 hours (89.80%)

If the employment costs for the year December 19–7 to November 19–8 are estimated to be £35 000 of which £25 000 is in respect of direct hairdressing labour hours, general overheads are £14 000, retail purchases are £20 000 of which 5 per cent is wastage, and indirect material purchase salon are £1700, then the overheads to be apportioned are:

Employment Costs	Total £	Retail Sales £	Salon Services £
£35 000 – £25 000	10 000	1020 (10.2%)	8 980 (89.8%)
General Overheads	14 000	1428 (10.2%)	12 572 (89.8%)
5% Retail Purchases	1 000	1000	—
Indirect Mat. Salon	1 700	—	1 700
Overhead apportionment	£26 700	£3448	£23 252

From the above it can be seen that Histyles plan to expend £26 700 on overheads and, therefore, the 'sales price' charged to the customers, has to include a cost element for the recovery of this expenditure over and above the direct material and labour cost before a profit is made. In costing terms this is referred to as the *planned absorption* of overheads. Using the above example of

Histyles the planned absorption will have the following impact upon the price structure:

1. *Retail Sales* If Histyles plan to make a 20 per cent profit on all retail sales and maintain the current stock level then:

Cost of Sales (i.e. Retail Purchases)	=	£20 000
Apportioned Overheads	=	3 448
Profit 20% of Cost of Sales	=	4 000
Required Sales Receipts	=	27 448

From the above, the percentage to be added to the purchase price of each individual item to achieve the planned recovery of overheads and the required profit is calculated thus:

$$\text{Overhead Recovered} \quad \frac{3448}{20\ 000} \times 100 \quad = \quad 17.24\%$$

$$\text{Profit} \quad \frac{4000}{20\ 000} \times 100 \quad = \quad 20.00\%$$

$$\text{TOTAL \% Addition} \quad = \quad 37.24\%$$

The addition of 37.24 per cent to the standard purchase price for each and every retail item will produce the proposed retail sales price to achieve a 20 per cent profit. In practice, the proposed retail sales price may exceed or fall short of the manufacturer's recommended retail sales price. It will generally be uneconomic to establish an actual retail price above this recommended price. The management will, therefore, have to decide whether to:

(a) Accept a lower profit margin (if the recommended price is between 17.24 per cent and 37.24 per cent above the purchase price).
(b) Discontinue the sale of the item as being uneconomic (if the recommended price is 17.24 per cent or less above the purchase price).
(c) Continue with an unprofitable line if the overheads and accepted profit level can be 'balanced' by increasing proposed retail sales price of other items to the recommended sales price. For example, if the recommended retail sales price for the 100 ml and 300 ml containers of conditioner, referred to in the example of material standard setting on p. 142 were £0.45 and £0.90 respectively, the following data would be available to Histyles management:

100 ml containers
Standard Cost + Overhead and Profit = £0.378 + (37.24% of £0.378)
                                     = £0.52 approximately.
Unit Under-Recovery of Overhead and Profit if Recommended Price charged
= £0.52 − 0.45 = 0.07
Annual Under-Recovery = 800 (Planned Purchase Units) × 0.07
                       = £56

300 ml containers
Standard Cost + Overhead and Profit = £0.60 + (37.24% of £0.60)
                                     = £0.82 approximately.

Unit Over-Recovery of Overhead and Profit if Recommended Price charged
= £0.90 − 0.82 = 0.08

Annual Over-Recovery   = 2600 × 0.08
                         = £208.

Thus, the adoption of the recommended sales price for both these items would show an increase in profit of £208 − £56 = £152 per annum, and a sales price of £0.85 for the 300 ml containers would still produce the required level of overhead recovery plus anticipated profit.

2. *Hairdressing Service* In the quoted example above, it is necessary for Histyles to recover some £23 252 in respect of planned overhead expenditure in addition to the direct labour and material costs before a profit can be made. It is recommended that these overheads should be recovered in proportion to the *Chair Hours* that are planned for each service provided by the salon. The implementation of this principle involves the establishment of a *Standard Chair Hour Absorption Rate* which is arrived at by dividing the planned overhead expenditure by the total planned chair hours which are also the total planned standard hours.

In the case of Histyles we have previously quoted that the planned weekly standard/chair hours were 269.15. From this information:

$$\text{Standard Chair Hour Absorption Rate} = \frac{23\,252}{269.15 \times 52 \text{ weeks}}$$

$$= \underline{\underline{£1.66 \text{ per Standard Hour}}}$$

Given this information, together with details of the standard/chair hours and direct material content, the cost of the service can be obtained; e.g. Histyles has calculated that to provide Bleach Streaks, 2.00 standard/chair hours and £0.35 in materials are involved; the standard labour rate is £1.55 per hour.

Cost of Service is	Standard Labour (2 × 1.55)	=	£3.10
plus	Standard Material	=	0.35
plus	Overhead Recovery (2 × 1.66)	=	3.32
			6.77

If it is Histyles' intention to make 20 per cent profit on each hairdressing service, the price charged to the client for Bleach Streaks is:

£6.77 plus 20 per cent = £8.12.

Whether such a charge is a commercial proposition is a decision to be made by the salon's management.

At the commencement of this Section the principle of identifying an over- or under-recovery of overheads was explained. A more detailed description of this activity is outlined in the following chapter, which also consolidates the use of the other costing analysis in the overall control data required to maintain a viable salon.

CHAPTER X

Budgetary Control in the Salon

Budgetary Control was originally designed as a system of scientifically planning ahead which involved the formulation of a plan for each branch of the business activity in a fixed future period. In the case of the hairdressing salon this will involve the preparation of:

1. A *Sales Budget* for both hairdressing services and retail sales.
2. An *Employment* or *Labour Budget* which relates to the expenditure incurred in staff remuneration and associated costs.
3. A *Materials* or *Purchase Budget* in respect of both retail purchases and direct salon material purchases.
4. An *Expense Budget* which identifies the estimated expenditure on 'overhead' items.
5. A *Capital Expenditure Budget* showing the estimated costs and dates of any planned additions to capital equipment.
6. A *Financial* or *Cash Flow Budget* which links the balance of planned receipts and expenditure and identifies any periods of cash shortage so that management action may be taken to address this shortfall.

Enlightened managements recognise that no matter how conscientiously the budgets are prepared, the actual performance will be at variance to the planned activity. Owing to the omnibus nature of the deviations from planned performance it has usually been found that the preparation of a flexible budget, i.e. one that caters for varying levels of activity, has done little to improve the realism of the planned budget. It is, therefore, recommended that the budgets should be prepared in such a format as to allow the actual performance data to be 'entered' alongside the planned data so that a comparison can easily be made of significant changes. Management's attention is drawn to these factors and further investigation, possibly using the costing analysis techniques described in the previous chapter, will identify the cause of disadvantageous trends so that prompt corrective action may be initiated.

To enable such management action to be taken it is necessary to break down the time period of the budget (normally one year) into control periods – these may be weeks, calendar months or thirteen four-week periods per year. The former offers a high degree of control but the data collection and arrangement cost may be excessive so one of the latter two control periods is normally adopted. For illustration purposes in this chapter, the calendar monthly control periods are used.

To balance the time scale variations between planned and actual receipts and payments which can occur between consecutive control periods, both the budget and actual data should be presented as a monthly and year-to-date total. The preparation of the various budgets, the recording of the actual data and the major control features are shown in the following sections.

SALES BUDGET

The Sales Budget is arguably the most important of all the budgets since the value of receipts will usually reflect the amount of activity required from the salon staff, the amount of material to be purchased, the equipment and space required to meet the demands of clients and, ultimately, the profitability of the salon. The sales budget is also the most difficult to prepare because the factors which influence the extent of trade are often beyond the immediate control of the salon management or are intangible by nature. They include:

1. The style and fashion which is popularised during the budget period.
2. The ability of the salon to recognise and respond to the requirements of fashion.
3. The introduction of new products and new methods.
4. The prosperity or otherwise of the immediate community from which the salon draws its clientele.
5. The state of the national economy.
6. The prevailing climatic conditions can also be an important factor particularly to holiday resort salons.

A sales budget that includes both salon services and retail sales should be divided into two discrete sections so that the profitability of each activity can be established. In theory, the budgets should be developed on an item-by-item basis. Such a process is possible in the case of salon services where the number of individual items is limited. These items can be expressed in both quantitative terms (number of each service) and value terms. Such an itemised development will frequently be found impossible to operate in the case of retail sales where the number of items stocked may be excessive. However, due weighting should be given to fluctuations in the demand for popular items.

With the exception of 6. above, it is usual for the influence of the other variable factors mentioned to develop progressively over a period of time. A study of the historical performance data of the salon will often identify the cumulative influence of these factors, which is frequently referred to as the *Business Trend.* In contrast to the more commonly used gross volume or value data which is often presented in graph form, a trend graph gives an immediate indication as to whether the business is expanding or contracting and also the rate of the expansion or contraction. To illustrate the use of the trend graph and/or the trend calculation the following example is provided:

During 19–7 and 19–8 the numbers of Shampoo and Sets performed by Histyles were:

Month	19–7	19–8
January	220	200
February	280	260
March	340	380
April	420	360
May	240	300
June	260	220
July	200	260
August	180	320
September	300	340
October	220	220
November	200	280
December	340	460
TOTAL:	3200	3600

FIG. 10.1

VOLUME — SHAMPOO AND SET PROVIDED JAN 19–7 TO PRESENT

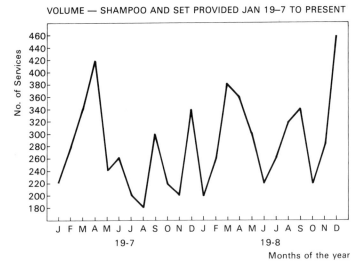

In Fig. 10.1 these data are plotted on a straight *volume of sales against periods* graph and in common with the data listed above give little indication of the popularity of the Shampoo and Set given by the salon compared to two years before. The use of the 'trend' principle, which involves plotting an average number of items over the last twelve months, shows the overall increase or decrease in business. Thus the average volume for December 19–7 is the sum of the Services provided in 19–7 divided by 12 months, i.e.

$$\frac{3200}{12} = 267 \text{ approx.}$$

To calculate the January level the January 19–8 volume is substituted for the January 19–7 volume, i.e.

$$\frac{3200 - 220 + 200}{12} = \frac{3180}{12} = 265$$

In a similar manner, the level is established for each subsequent month and the resultant trend graph is shown in Fig. 10.2.

FIG. 10.2

TREND — SHAMPOO AND SET PROVIDED JAN 19–7 TO PRESENT

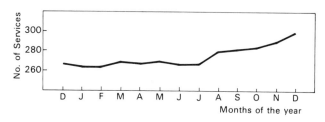

From the trend graph it can clearly be seen that in the last five months the salon has consistently provided more Shampoo and Sets than in the previous seven months, and since the trend is still showing an increase, for planning purposes their volume should be increased above the 19–8 level. The graph also shows the size of such an increase; i.e. from 268 to 300 in the period July 19–8 to December 19–8 which represents a 10.66 per cent increase. Thus it is logical to apply this percentage to the 19–8 total to give the 19–9 planned total, i.e. 3600 + 10.66 per cent of 3600 = 3984.

A similar exercise for each of the services will establish the total level of activity to be planned for completion during the coming financial year. It is suggested that at this stage attention should be given to the spread of this activity into the control periods (months of the year). This will largely be influenced by the seasonal factors which apply to the particular salon; e.g. a salon in a holiday resort may expect an increase in trade in July and August with 'low points' in October and November and from January to Easter, whereas the industrial city salon is likely to have a low point in July and August. Indeed, in the case of the latter salon the management may decide to close for a period to allow 'block' staff holidays to be taken.

The final stage in preparing the information required for the sales budget (salon service) is to obtain a *Receipt Value* and this is calculated by multiplying the planned volume by the sales price developed as a result of the pricing element of cost accounting described in Chapter IX.

The development of the retail sales budget is more broadly based and is usually strictly confined to value, whether this is value of purchased items sold or sales receipts. Again, a trend graph is most useful since the difference between the two trends shows the gross value available to offset overheads and provide a profit. In Fig. 10.3 the total sales receipts and value of purchased items sold are plotted on a trend graph. Close study of the graph will show that in December 19–7 goods purchased for £900 were sold for £1200, i.e. 25 per cent contribution to overheads, and profit amounting to £300. In December 19–8 £1700 was taken as receipts but the purchases cost was £1360, i.e. a 20 per cent contribution to overheads and profits amounting to £340. The graph also shows that over the preceding twelve month period the value of purchased items had increased by 51 per cent which indicates that this rise is attributable both to inflation in the national economy and an increase in retail sales activity within the salon. In such an instance it is suggested that for planning purposes the value of purchased items should be held at the latest value, i.e. £1360 per month, and the percentage increment to recover planned overheads and required profit should be added to this amount. For example, if in the above case the overhead recovery was planned to be £1800 in the complete year and the required profit was 20 per cent, then the total planned sales receipts would be $(12 \times 1360) + 1800 = £18\,120 + 20$ per cent profit $= £21\,744$ per annum or £1812 per average month.

FIG. 10.3

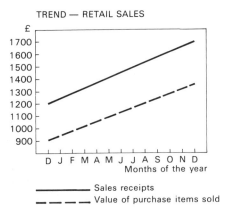

TREND — RETAIL SALES

——————— Sales receipts
— — — — Value of purchase items sold

If a seasonal factor were apparent from past records the distribution of the planned £21 744 would be spread according to the peaks and troughs shown in the previous control period's performance data.

For ease of comparison it is recommended that a separate schedule be prepared for each control period. A sample layout is shown in Fig. 10.4 which refers to December 19–8 in respect of Histyles. The charges for each of the eight services provided are as follows:

Service No.	Description	Charge £
01	Shampoo and Set	3
02	Cutting and Restyling	5
03	Permanent Waving Cold	7
04	Tinting	8
05	Cut and Blow-Dry	5
06	Oil Treatment and Massage	3
07	Comb-out and Dressing only	2
08	Bleach Streaks	8

FIG. 10.4

Histyles Salon
Sales Budget/Operating Statement — December 19–8

Service No./Description	Budget				Actual				Comparison			
	No. in month	Value (£) for month	No. year to date	Value (£) year to date	No. in month	Value (£) for month	No. year to date	Value (£) year to date	No. in month	Value (£) for month	No. year to date	Value (£) year to date
A Hairdressing Services												
01 Shampoo and Set	350	1050	350	1050	416	1248	416	1248	66	198	66	198
02 Cutting and Restyling	240	1200	240	1200	220	1100	220	1100	(20)	(100)	(20)	(100)
03 Permanent Waving Cold	150	1050	150	1050	140	980	140	980	(10)	(70)	(10)	(70)
04 Tinting	45	360	45	360	36	288	36	288	(9)	(72)	(9)	(72)
05 Cut and Blow-Dry	300	1500	300	1500	310	1550	310	1550	10	50	10	50
06 Oil Treatment Massage	30	90	30	90	48	144	48	144	18	54	18	54
07 Comb-out Dressing only	80	160	80	160	46	92	46	92	(34)	(68)	(34)	(68)
08 Bleach Streaks	50	400	50	400	64	512	64	512	14	112	14	112
TOTAL:	1245	5810	1245	5810	1280	5914	1280	5914	35	104	35	104
B Retail Sales		1500		1500		1450		1450		(50)		(50)
C TOTAL ALL SALES		7310		7310		7364		7364		54		54

Since the example is in respect of December, the first period of the fiscal year, the monthly totals agree with the year-to-date totals. The preparation of the schedules for each of the control periods in the budget year is performed prior to the start of the year. Thus the amounts shown in the Period 12 schedule – in the case of Histyles the November schedule – will show, in the 'Value Year To Date' column, the total planned receipts for the year. Fig. 10.4 also shows the completion of the schedule with the actual trading performance in December 19–8 and the subsequent comparison with the budget, the volume of hairdressing services being those quoted in the example on p. 137.

The overall total of actual receipts shows very little difference from the budget or planned total (less than 1 per cent increase) but the receipts for individual hairdressing services show considerable variations; e.g. Service 08 an increase of 28 per cent and Service 07 a decrease of 42.5 per cent. Critics of budget control maintain with some justification that comparison with a fixed budget is of little value when circumstances have compelled managements to change their original strategy. It is further contended that the existence of the detailed budget or plan can induce management to attempt to conform to that plan rather than to respond to the market or customer requirements. Ultimately, it is suggested that budgets should only be prepared one month in advance; in other words, only short-term planning is a feasible proposition. This conclusion is supported by the fact that as the year progresses, so the length of advance planning decreases so that at the end of the year, i.e. the start of Period 12, only one month's activity is planned unless, as in large organisations, financial resources are employed in the development of a continual series of budgets or financial plans.

It is suggested that these objections can largely be overcome by continually reviewing the progress of the business against the plan each month and extending the budget by one month. For example, in the case of Histyles, at the conclusion of December 19–8 the budget for December 19–9 should be outlined. Where significant changes are implemented the budget should be adjusted. To retain control, the adjustment should be shown as a separate item, either as an addition to the schedule or, if space does not permit, on a separate schedule. In Fig. 10.5 the final schedule for the year December 19–8 to November 19–9, in respect of Histyles, shows the final actual performance and also the budget adjustments made for:

1.   Service 04 – Tinting

At the end of February 19–9 it was found that the planned increase of Tinting from 45 per month to 75 per month by June 19–9 was not likely to be achieved, the actual number of services in December, January and February being 36, 31 and 31 respectively. It was considered that this short-fall was due to the charge of £8 being £0.50 above the average of neighbouring salons. Since Histyles had equipped a special tinting and bleaching area which was under utilised, and sufficient labour was available from March 19–9, the price charged would be £7.

2.   Retail Sales

After an initial period of two months when the retail sales total was £2425 as

FIG. 10.5

Histyles Salon
Sales Budget/Operating Statement – November 19-9

Service No./Description	Budget				Actual				Comparison			
	No. in month	Value (£) for month	No. year to date	Value (£) year date	No. in month	Value (£) for month	No. year to date	Value (£) year to date	No. in month	Value (£) for month	No. year to date	Value (£) year to date
A Hairdressing Services												
01 Shampoo and Set	250	750	3200	9 600	284	852	3564	10 692	34	102	364	1092
02 Cutting and Restyling	130	650	2080	10 400	120	600	1994	9 970	(10)	(50)	(86)	(430)
03 Permanent Waving Cold	100	700	1100	7 700	81	567	1172	8 204	(19)	(133)	72	504
04 Tinting	75	600	800	6 400	83	581	793	5 653	8	(19)	(7)	(747)
05 Cut and Blow-Dry	175	875	2400	12 000	189	945	2628	13 140	14	70	228	1140
06 Oil Treatment and Massage	20	60	360	1 080	33	99	430	1 290	13	39	70	210
07 Comb-out Dressing Only	40	80	520	1 040	17	34	210	420	(23)	(46)	(310)	(€20)
08 Bleach Streaks	10	80	300	2 400	14	112	290	2 320	4	32	(10)	(80)
TOTAL:	800	3795	10 760	50 620	821	3790	11 081	51 689	21	(5)	321	1069
B Retail Sales		1000		9 500		1250		12 800		250		3300
C TOTAL ALL SALES		4795		60 120		5040		64 489		245		4369
D Adjustments												
(i) March – reduction in Service Charge 04		75		650								
(ii) May – increase in Retail Price by 10%		100		450								
Net Adjustment		25		200								
Adjusted Sales Receipts		4820		59 920								

compared to a planned £2500 a significant increase in trade occurred, and by the end of April the actual total receipts were £5195 compared with the budgeted total of £5000. At the same time it was found that the cost of purchases was rising faster than the anticipated 1.5 per cent increase per month. It was therefore decided to increase the sales price of all items by 10 per cent from May 19–9 which would, in general, still mean that less than the manufacturer's current recommended retail sales price would be charged.

From Fig. 10.5 it can be seen that these adjustments resulted in the salon retaining its market position as regards salon services in total, and that an increase in receipts from retail sales was also obtained. The latter will only indicate improved results if the increase in receipts is greater than the increase in cost of purchases (see *Materials Budget* below). In view of these results it is unlikely that any radical adjustments will be required to the provisional budget for the year December 19–9 to November 19–9 as regards volume of trade, but if the costing process indicates that price changes are required, the value of receipts may have to be adjusted.

EMPLOYMENT OR LABOUR BUDGET

This budget will show the total cost of the gross remuneration to employees, plus any statutory employment-related expenditure, i.e. employer's National Insurance contributions. The total cost will include holiday pay, sickness pay, overtime payments (including overtime premiums) and bonus or incentive payments. An estimate has to be made in respect of any anticipated increments in base salaries, variations in contracted working hours, changes in paid holiday entitlement, non-statutory sickness payments and the need to employ additional labour to meet the required demand.

The calculation of employment budgets – by taking the total salaries plus a percentage for overtime, increments and insurance contributions and dividing by 12 to give the monthly budget spend – usually produces a large deviation from actual spend, and no indication of the reasons for such deviations. In addition, it assumes that the present staffing level of the salon is the optimum to service the future demands made upon the salon by the clients. The employment budget should be developed as a result of applying the anticipated trading volumes depicted in the sales budget to the known performance data contained in the work study and costing records. These will show that the total spend on employment costs is the sum of:

1.   Direct Standard Hairdressing Cost

The Standard Cost of the Direct Hairdressing operations performed at 100 per cent efficiency is given by multiplying the Standard Time for each planned hairdressing operation by the Standard Hourly Rate.

2.   Direct Hairdressing Efficiency

This is an adjustment, normally incremental, to the standard cost of direct hairdressing and reflects the fact that the actual performance achieved against the standard time is seldom 100 per cent. The time component of the actual Direct Standard and Direct Efficiency cost is equal to the Direct Hair-dressing hours recorded on the actual time records, and is only split into its component elements as part of the standard cost analysis.

3. Indirect Hairdressing and Overhead Labour Times

These are those hours recorded by salon staff when performing tasks essential to the operation of the salon which are other than direct hairdressing operations, e.g. reception, stock control and general management. The time records will identify the extent of this time, both as a percentage of the direct hairdressing hours and as a percentage of the total paid hours, whether they are performed by dedicated staff, e.g. a receptionist, or as part involvement by employees who normally perform direct hairdressing operations.

4. Employee Benefits

This is a general heading used to consolidate the payments made to employees for the periods when no effective work is performed, e.g. in-salon rest, absence of clientele, awaiting facilities, holidays, sickness, temporary absence etc. It is given in total by the Effective Rate; i.e. if the Effective Rate of a salon over a given period is 70 per cent, then 30 per cent of the payment made to employees is in Employee Benefits.

5. Off-Standard Variance

In Chapter IX it was shown that the *Standard Cost* included as a multiplicant the *Standard Rate* which is an estimate of the average hourly rate of pay for the complete year. In the calculation of the average rate, account was taken of known and anticipated changes to the individual rates of pay during the *Standard Year*. It was also identified that the difference between the standard rate and the planned period (one month) rate would produce variances in each individual period of the standard year which would cumulate to zero over the complete standard year. For control purposes, however, it is important to measure the actual difference against the planned or budget variance. Therefore, the off-standard variance is an important part of the budget or plan and is proportional to the hours and values of Sections 1–4 above.

6. Employer Contribution to Benefits

The sum of Sections 1-5 above is a budget of the total gross wages paid to the salon employees. This does not, however, reflect the total cost of employment since, under statutory law, employers are required to contribute to the employee's National Insurance and State Pension subscriptions. Additionally, if a private pension scheme is operated by the salon a contribution may be made directly to the scheme by the employer. Frequently, the extent of the employer's contribution will vary for each individual employee. But all will be expressible as a percentage of the employee's gross wage. For budget purposes it is expedient to calculate the contribution paid in previous periods as a percentage of the gross wages paid, and to apply this percentage plus or minus to the total anticipated gross wages in the coming year.

To illustrate the above principles, an Employment Budget/Operating Statement is shown in Fig. 10.6 for Histyles in respect of December 19–8. The budget details were prepared from the following data:

1. The sales activity planned in the sales budget (Fig. 10.4).
2. A direct hairdressing efficiency level of 95 per cent.
3. A standard labour cost of £1.55 per hour was set for the year December 19–8 to November 19–9.
4. An off-standard labour variance of £0.16 (Favourable) per hour for December 19–8.
5. The effective rate was 62 per cent, of which 43 per cent was attributable to direct hairdressing and 19 per cent to indirect and overhead tasks. The employer contribution to benefits was 8 per cent of gross wages.
6. The standard times for each of the eight services 01 to 08 are 0.583, 0.50, 1.75, 3.00, 1.25, 0.75, 0.50 and 2.00 hours respectively.

The calculations required to produce the budget are:

(a) Direct Hairdressing Hours and Direct Hairdressing Cost at Standard

No. of Services	× Standard Time		Direct Hours
350	0.583	=	204.05
240	0.50	=	120.00
150	1.75	=	262.50
45	3.00	=	135.00
300	1.25	=	375.00
30	0.75	=	22.50
80	0.50	=	40.00
50	2.00	=	100.00

Total Direct Hairdressing Hours: 1259.05

Cost of Direct Hairdressing Hours   = $1259.05 \times £1.55$
                                      =   £1952 (rounded to nearest £)

(b) Efficiency Supplement Hours and Value at Standard

Direct Efficiency Hours   = $\dfrac{1259.05 \times 5}{95}$

                            =   66 hours

Cost of Direct Efficiency Hours   = $66 \times £1.55$
                                    =   £102 (rounded)

FIG. 10.6

Histyles Salon
Employment Budget/Operating Statement – December 19-8

Expense	Budget Month Hours	Budget Month £	Budget Cumulative Hours	Budget Cumulative £	Actual Month Hours	Actual Month £	Actual Cumulative Hours	Actual Cumulative £	Comparison Month Hours	Comparison Month £	Comparison Cumulative Hours	Comparison Cumulative £
(a) Direct Hairdressing	1259	1952	1259	1952	1280	1984	1280	1984	21	32	21	32
(b) Efficiency Supplement	66	102	66	102	53	82	53	82	(13)	(20)	(13)	(20)
(c) Indirect and Overhead	585	907	585	907	560	868	560	868	(25)	(39)	(25)	(39)
(d) Employee Benefit	1171	1815	1171	1815	1384	2145	1384	2145	213	330	213	330
(e) Off-Standard Variance	—	(493)	—	(493)	—	(379)	—	(379)	—	114	—	114
Total Gross Pay	3081	4283	3081	4283	3277	4700	3277	4700	196	417	196	417
(f) Employer Benefit	—	343	—	343	—	343	—	343	—	—	—	—
Total Employment Cost	—	4626	—	4626	—	5043	—	5043	—	417	—	417

(c) Indirect Hairdressing and Overhead Hours and Value at Standard

Indirect and Overhead Hours $\qquad = \qquad \dfrac{(1259 + 66) \times 19}{43}$

$\qquad\qquad\qquad\qquad\qquad\qquad = \underline{585 \text{ hours}}$

Cost of Indirect and Overhead Hours $\qquad = \qquad 585 \times £1.55$

$\qquad\qquad\qquad\qquad\qquad\qquad = \underline{£907} \text{ (rounded)}$

(d) Employee Benefits Hours and Value at Standard

Employee Benefits Hours $\qquad = \qquad \dfrac{(1259 + 66 + 585) \times 38}{62}$

$\qquad\qquad\qquad\qquad\qquad\qquad = \underline{1171 \text{ hours}}$

Cost of Employee Benefit Hours $\qquad = \qquad 1171 \times £1.55$

$\qquad\qquad\qquad\qquad\qquad\qquad = \underline{£1815} \text{ (rounded)}$

(e) Off-Standard Variance
Number of Hours $(1325 + 585 + 1171) \times £0.16 = \underline{£493 \text{ Favourable}}$

(f) Employer Benefit Contribution
Is 8 per cent of $£(1952 + 102 + 907 + 1815 - 493) = \underline{£343}$ (rounded)
The total employment budget for December 19–9 is, therefore, £4626.

Control against Budget

For control purposes the actual spend incurred in respect of total employment expenditure has to be compared to the budget or planned expenditure.
In total this amount is readily available from the salon statutory wage records,
i.e. gross wages plus employer's contributions. It should be noted that if gross
wages include the reimbursement to the employee of any expenses, the sum of
these expenses should be deducted from the gross wages total. In general
terms, it is often sufficient to confine the analysis to such a 'bottom-line'
comparison particularly if the actual expenditure to budget is within plus or
minus 2 per cent, both for the month and cumulative for the year to date. Prior
to limiting the analysis it should be confirmed that the total employment cost
is also consistent with the percentage of activity which is reflected by the
planned receipts and the actual receipts, e.g. in the case of Histyles the
employment costs for December 19–8 are planned to be £4626 and the sales
receipts £7310 (see Figs. 10.6 and 10.4). Thus, employment costs are 63 per
cent of sales receipts. If the actual sales receipts are £7364 (see Fig. 10.4), then
for compatibility to the plan, the actual employment cost has to be in the range
of £4492 to £4786. If the actual employment cost is outside this range, it is
appropriate to conduct a detailed analysis as outlined below.

1. Employer Contribution to Benefits

The actual spend is normally readily available from the financial accounts and
can, therefore, be directly entered in the 'Actual' section of the employment
budget/operating statement. For illustration purposes it is assumed that
Histyles' contribution agreed with budget (see Fig. 10.6 – 'Actual' section (f)).

2. Direct Hairdressing

The cost attributable to Direct Hairdressing is obtained by multiplying the standard hours relating to the actual services provided, by the standard rate. Thus, in the case of Histyles, for the activity performed in December 19–8 (see Fig. 10.4) the calculation of employment expenditure attributable to direct hairdressing is as follows:

(a) Standard Hours of Direct Hairdressing

Service No.	No. of Services	Standard Time for Service	Total Time for Service
01	416	0.583	242.5
02	220	0.50	110.0
03	140	1.75	245.0
04	36	3.00	108.0
05	310	1.25	387.5
06	48	0.75	36.0
07	46	0.50	23.0
08	64	2.00	128.0

Total Standard Hours, Direct Hairdressing Dec. 19–8   1280

(b) Cost of Standard Direct Hairdressing Hours
$$= 1280 \times £1.55$$
$$= £1984$$

Both the standard hours and cost are entered in the 'Actual' section (a) in Fig. 10.6.

3. Direct Efficiency Supplement

In practice, the difference between the standard hours as calculated in 2. *(a)* above and the actual hours recorded on the time records immediately gives the value to be shown as the *Direct Efficiency Supplement*. It will normally be found that the actual time recorded is greater than the standard time and, therefore, reflects additional expenditure. Where, however, the actual time is less than the standard time not only is the efficiency rate above 100 per cent, but also, due to the above-normal performances by the hairdressers, the profitability of the salon is increased. This is shown in the budget as negative values. In the case of Histyles, for December 19–9 the actual hours recorded for direct hairdressing were 1333; thus 53 hours at £1.55 per hour were expended as a direct efficiency supplement and are recorded as shown in Fig. 10.6 in the 'Actual' section (b). For reference purposes this performance is 96 per cent efficient.

4. Indirect and Overhead

The salon time records will show the amount of time booked to indirect and overhead activities. As an illustration, it is assumed that Histyles staff and management recorded 560 hours in December 19–9 and this, together with the value at standard is shown in the 'Actual' section (c) of Fig. 10.6.

5.   Employee Benefits

The time classified as employee benefit should again be shown by the time records, but since omissions could have occurred it is important to check that the time recorded is equal to the total paid hours less the productive hours, whether these hours are direct hairdressing or indirect and overhead, i.e. the sum of 2. and 4. above. To continue the worked example of Histyles for December 19–9, the recorded time was consolidated at 1384 hours and this time is again evaluated at £1.55 per hour in Fig. 10.6, 'Actual' section line (d).

6.   Off-Standard Variance

The value to be shown as off-standard variance is the difference between the actual total employment and the allocation already in action. Thus, if in the case of Histyles the total employment cost for December 19–9 was £5043 then the off-standard variance is:

$$£5043 - (343 + 1984 + 82 + 868 + 2145) = \text{Minus } £379$$

this value being shown in the 'Actual' section of Fig. 10.6, line (e).

The completion of the 'Comparison' section of Fig. 10.6 shows that the increase in employment cost as compared to budget was caused by the increase in employee benefit and a decrease in the planned saving as compared to the standard rate for which an off-standard variance was identified. Further investigation is, therefore, required to identify the cause of the increase in employee benefit; e.g. did staff incur excess sickness or holidays, or was it caused by temporary absence? If the latter reason, the loss of the off-standard variance planned 'saving' is likely to have occurred due to the payment of overtime supplements as specified by Wages Council regulations to make up the lost time. The availability of this information will provide management with an ongoing indication of adverse and favourable business factors and also the impact upon the profitability of the salon.

MATERIALS OR PURCHASE BUDGET

In preparation of the sales budget the planned receipts from retail sales were treated as one complete item, and for the purposes of establishing a budget in respect of the purchase of the required materials, a similar treatment is recommended. In the case of Histyles, the retail sales receipts for the complete year were budgeted as £21 744 after an uplift was applied to the estimated total annual purchases of £16 320, for overhead recovery and a 20 per cent profit. Expressed in terms of a percentage of the budgeted sales value, the purchase value is:

$$\frac{16\ 320}{21\ 744} \times 100 = 75\%$$

Thus for December 19–9, when the sales receipts are planned to be £1500 (see Fig. 10.4), the budget material value is:

$$\frac{1500 \times 75}{100} = £1125 \text{ (see Fig. 10.7)}$$

In the majority of hairdressing salons which are also retail outlets, a large proportion of the procurement of materials is from wholesalers or 'Cash and Carries' which allows almost immediate replenishment of materials sold and consequently reduces the amount of stock needing to be held in the salon. It is important to management to hold as low a stock value as possible without damaging the volume of retail business conducted. It is, therefore, necessary to include in the budget, for subsequent comparison with the actual volume, a valuation of stock held at the beginning and end of each period. Use should therefore be made of past performance data, the most important of which is the *Stock Turnover* which is given by the formula:

$$\frac{\text{Total Cost of Material Sold}}{\text{Average Stock Holding}}$$

For example, if in the records of Histyles it was recorded that the cost of materials sold in the twelve months ending 30 November 19–8 was £12 600, and the average stock holding was £525, the stock turnover was, therefore $\frac{12\,600}{525} = 24$ times per year, or twice per monthly period. For planning purposes, if the purchases for the following year are estimated at £16 320 then the planned stock holding is $\frac{16\,320}{24} = £680$ (see Fig. 10.7).

It follows that for planning purposes the opening and closing stock in a given period is always the same. In the case of Histyles' £680, the cost of sales must equal the cost of purchases in the same period. The subsequent comparison with the actual performance data for an individual period may, therefore, show large discrepancies. But in an environment of rapid stock turnover these discrepancies will level out and, therefore, the cumulative year-to-date figures are of greater significance to management than those of the individual periods' comparative performance. Reference has already been made to the important process of comparing the actual performances against the budget or plan. It is shown below that such a comparison can be effected where a standard costing system does not exist, but difficulties will be experienced not only in arranging the actual performance data but also in interpreting the reasons for the variances which may be identified. The actual performance data required are:

1. Cost of Additions to Stock

The major proportion of this cost is shown in the financial accounts as the sum of all suppliers' invoices paid, but adjustment has to be made to this value for:

(a) Material received but not actually paid for.
(b) Material received with no invoice from the supplier.
(c) Material rejected and returned to the supplier, credit for which is not reflected in the financial records.
(d) Payments made during the period for stock received in previous periods.
(e) The receipt of stock for which a prepayment was made in a previous period.

FIG. 10.7

Histyles Salon Material Statement – December 19–8						
	Budget (£)		**Actual (£)**		**Comparison (£)**	
A RETAIL STOCK	*Month*	*Cumul-ative*	*Month*	*Cumul-ative*	*Month*	*Cumul-ative*
1. Stock at Standard Opening Inventory Value	680	680	668	668	(12)	(12)
Plus – Purchases	850	850	875	875	25	25
Transfers In	17	17	5	5	(12)	(12)
Less – Cost of Sales	1125	1125	1088	1088	(37)	(37)
Transfers Out	15	15	22	22	7	7
Scrap	17	17	36	36	19	19
Inventory Value at Close	390	390	402	402	12	12
2. Variances Volume	—	—	F2	F2	2	2
Price	F70	F70	F59	F59	(11)	(11)
TOTAL:	F70	F70	F61	F61	(9)	(9)

	Budget (£)		**Actual (£)**		**Comparison (£)**	
B SALON STOCK	*Month*	*Cumul-ative*	*Month*	*Cumul-ative*	*Month*	*Cumul-ative*
1. Stock at Standard Opening Inventory Value	150	150	162	162	12	12
Plus – Purchases	298	298	287	287	(11)	(11)
Transfers In	15	15	22	22	7	7
Less – Std. Usage	291	291	296	296	5	5
Transfers Out	17	17	5	5	(12)	(12)
Scrap	7	7	4	4	(3)	(3)
Inventory Value at Close	148	148	166	166	18	18
2. Variances Volume	—	—	F1	F1	1	1
Price	F25	F25	F24	F24	(1)	(1)
TOTAL:	25	25	25	25	—	—

The necessary calculation is shown below for Histyles in December 19–9, where at the close of the period the payments made to suppliers amounted to £840, invoices to the value of £10 were awaiting payment and goods with an order value of £15 were awaiting the suppliers' invoices. During the period goods valued at £8 had been returned to the suppliers, and credit was awaited. In addition, payment had been made for the unpaid receipts to the value of £12 from the previous period, and the £5 item for which cash with order was required had been received.

Cost of Additions to Stock	£
Payments made to Suppliers	840
Plus: Unpaid invoices	10
Order value of goods received not invoiced	15
Value of prepaid goods received	5
	870
Less: Goods returned awaiting credit	8
Value of stock received in previous periods	12
	850

2. Cost of Sales

Particularly in times of rapidly fluctuating prices, the establishment of the purchase value of the goods sold can present management with a considerable problem. The nature of the problem can best be shown by considering the example of one item 'A' and the relevant transactions during a monthly period which were as follows:

(a) Stock at commencement of period quantity 40 – value   £20.00

(b) Purchase quantity 100 – value   45.00

(c) Purchase quantity 25 – value   15.00

(d) Purchase quantity 100 – value   48.00

(e) Purchase quantity 50 – value   27.00

(f) Sales in period – 257 at £0.75 each, i.e. £192.75

If standard costing is not used it is probable that one of the following methods of costing the material sold and also the remaining stock value will be used:

(a) F.I.F.O. (First In First Out) to avoid the 'shop-soiled' appearance of material sold which does not deteriorate with the passage of time, it is prudent to sell the stock in the order of receipt. F.I.F.O. assumes that this stock-keeping rule has been rigidly adhered to. Thus the cost of sales and remaining stock value in the example above is:

Cost of Sales

No. of Items	Unit Cost £	Total Cost £
40	0.50	20
100	0.45	45
25	0.60	15
92	0.48	44.16
257 Items – Total Cost of Sales		124.16

Inventory Value

No. of Items	Unit Cost £	Total Cost £
8	0.48	3.84
50	0.54	27.00
58 Items – Total Inventory Value		30.84 or £0.53 each

(b) Weighted Average. Under this method the cost of each item either sold or held in stock is the average price for each item held or received during the period. In the example above the total cost of 315 items was £155, i.e. £0.49 each. Therefore:

Cost of Sales	=	257 × 0.49	=	£125.93
Inventory Value	=	58 × 0.49	=	£ 28.42

It will be observed from the above that a variance attributable to the method of costing is obtained both to the cost of sales and the residual stock value. The former variance will affect the calculation of contribution to overheads and profits; i.e. if F.I.F.O. is used this contribution would be £192.75 − £124.16 = £68.59 and if weighted average is used it would be £192.75 − £125.93 = £66.82. In addition, the inventory value will tend to become unrepresentative of the market value.

The most important feature of adopting either method of obtaining the cost of sales is that an individual calculation has to be performed from the stock records for each and every item on which there has been a stock movement. Such an action is impractical for the normal salon to perform on a monthly basis as an additional administrative task.

3.   Inventory Value

Reference has already been made in Sections 1 and 2 above to the importance of inventory value and its relationship with each of these sections. This relationship is shown below.

Current Inventory Value = Inventory Value at end of previous period plus Cost of Additions to Stock minus Cost of Items Sold.

It should, therefore, be appreciated that if a stock check was physically performed and evaluated at the close of each period, and accurate data was available regarding stock additions, the cost of sales could be calculated. Such an exercise, though important on an annual basis for the confirmation of the recording system, is again impractical for the normal operating salon. It should be noted that the results of such an exercise would require adjustment for the contingencies described in Section 4 below.

4. Stock Transfers including Scrap

During the course of an operating period, instances will occur when retail stock is used in the salon, i.e. transferred to salon stock, or alternatively salon stock is sold direct to a client or another salon. Instances where stock is damaged or deteriorates are also likely to occur and, in common with stock transfers, usually result in the loss of the anticipated contribution to overheads and profit in addition to the direct loss of the cost of the material. Management, therefore, needs information regarding the extent of such activities and consequently they are included in the 'Material Budget' and 'Comparison with Actual Sheet' as a separate item or items.

For budgetary purposes, a percentage of the annual material cost as indicated by the previous year's actual results is normally used. Unless standard costing is used, difficulties in evaluation of actual stock losses, inventory value and the cost of sales will be experienced.

It is, therefore, strongly recommended that the budgetary control system should be used in conjunction with standard costing, an outline of the use, advantages and integration with the salon control records is given below.

Integrated Budget Control and Standard Costing System for Retail Sales Operating Principles

A standard is set for a complete financial year for each individual item of material, and each movement of stock is evaluated at this value whenever it is recorded in the financial or stock records. For the purpose of subsequent illustration, the standard set for item 'A' referred to in 2. (a) above was £0.50.

Upon receipt of material a difference may be found between the actual price charged and the standard cost. The standard cost is debited to the Stock Account in the financial accounts, the actual value being credited to the relevant creditor's (supplier's) account (or, in the case of a cash payment, a credit entry being made in the cash book), and the difference is either debited or credited to the variance account. For example, in the case of transaction (b) (p. 171) concerning item 'A', the accounting entries, assuming direct cash payment, are:

Debit	Stock Account	—	£50	(see Fig. 10.9)
Credit	Cash Account	—	£45	(see Fig. 10.8)
	Variance Account	—	£ 5	(see Fig. 10.10)

In the case of transaction (c) the accounting entries are:

Debit	Stock Account	—	£12.50
	Variance Account	—	£ 2.50
Credit	Cash	—	£15.00

FIG. 10.8

| DR. | | | | | | ACCOUNT _Cash_ | | | | | | CR. |

DATE	REF	AMOUNT	ANALYSIS			DATE	REF	AMOUNT	ANALYSIS		
	Narrative vi)	192 . 75					Narrative i)	20 . 00			
							" ii)	45 . 00			
							" iii)	15 . 00			
							" iv)	48 . 00			
							" v)	27 . 00			
							Balance C/D	37 . 75			
	Balance B/D	37 . 75									

FIG. 10.9

| DR. | | | | | | ACCOUNT _Stock_ | | | | | | CR. |

DATE	REF	AMOUNT	ANALYSIS			DATE	REF	AMOUNT	ANALYSIS		
	Narrative i)	20 . 00					Narrative vi)	128 . 50			
	" ii)	50 . 00									
	" iii)	12 . 50									
	" iv)	50 . 00									
	" v)	25 . 00					Balance C/D	29 . 00			
	Balance B/D	29 . 00									

FIG. 10.10

| DR. | | | | | | ACCOUNT _Variance_ | | | | | | CR. |

DATE	REF	AMOUNT	ANALYSIS			DATE	REF	AMOUNT	ANALYSIS		
	Narrative iii)	2 . 50					Narrative ii)	5 . 00			
	" v)	2 . 00					" iv)	2 . 00			
	Balance C/D	2 . 50									
							Balance B/D	2 . 50			

FIG. 10.11

DR. _____Sales_____ ACCOUNT   CR.

DATE	REF	AMOUNT	ANALYSIS			DATE	REF	AMOUNT	ANALYSIS		
	Cost of Sales	128 . 50					Sales Receipts	192 . 75			
	(Narrative vi)						(Narrative vi)				
	Balance c/D	64 . 25									
							Balance B/D	64 . 25			

In practice, it is unnecessary to record separately each item on an invoice, indeed if many invoices are cash paid, they may be combined into one series of financial entries. Entries for credit purchases should have an individual series of bookings per invoice.

Material 'transferred' between retail stock and salon stock is always valued at standard value, i.e.: debit 'Receiving Stock' and credit 'Issuing Stock'. Material that has been scrapped or lost, or that has deteriorated etc. is 'written-off' at standard cost, i.e.: debit Scrap Account and credit Stock Account.

At the end of the period the standard cost of the material sold (cost of sales) is debited to the Sales Account and credited to the Stock Account. In turn, the Sales Account is credited with the value of sales receipts which have been recorded as debits to the cash book during the period. For example, in the case of Item A – 257 items were sold and yielded £192.75, the bookings were:

Debit	Sales Account	—	£128.50	(see Fig. 10.11)
Credit	Stock Account	—	£128.50	(see Fig. 10.9)
Debit	Cash Account	—	£192.75	(see Fig. 10.8)
Credit	Sales Account	—	£192.75	(see Fig. 10.11)

Preparation of Budgets

As an alternative to the method of establishing the budget for retail purchases described on p. 168 it is possible to 'build-up' the budget on an item-by-item basis using the standard cost as the means of evaluation. Such a method is theoretically correct but very time-consuming and its effectiveness is dependent upon a very accurate estimate of the turnover.

Where there are large variations between the volume of sales planned in successive periods, dependent upon the ability to effect procurement of materials, a certain amount of stockpiling may be planned. For example, Salon B, which is situated in a seaside town, has an average turnover of retail stock 24 times per year, the sales and, therefore, the cost of sales, vary on a seasonal basis given the following estimated 'Cost of Sales' per month:

January	— £200
February	— £200
March	— £240
April	— £300
May	— £260
June	— £320
July	— £400
August	— £600
September	— £350
October	— £200
November	— £200
December	— £200

The planned cost of material purchases and inventory values were as follows:

	(a) *Opening Stock £*	(b) *Purchases £*	(c) *Closing Stock £*	(a) + (b) − (c) *Cost of Sales £*
Jan.	100	200	100	200
Feb.	100	220	120	200
Mar.	120	270	150	240
Apr.	150	280	130	300
May	130	290	160	260
June	160	360	200	320
July	200	500	300	400
Aug.	300	475	175	600
Sept.	175	275	100	350
Oct.	100	200	100	200
Nov.	100	200	100	200
Dec.	100	200	100	200

In the above, the closing stock is half the cost of sales for the following period, i.e. the cost of sales for March, being £240, produces a required closing stock for February of £120 which is also the opening stock for March. At the end of March the stock has to be half of April's estimated cost of sales (£150). Thus the purchases in March are: Required Closing Stock (£150) plus Cost of Sales (£240) minus Opening Stock (£120) = £270. It has already been shown that the standard cost of materials set for the future standard year is a weighted average of the 'estimated' cost of purchase during the course of the year. The cost of purchases in times of inflation can be planned to increase during the course of the year. Thus, as in our previous example, if the rate of inflation was 18 per cent per annum then an item costing £2 at the beginning of the year would cost £2.36 at the end of the year. In simple terms, if only these two items were purchased, the average price would be £2.18 and this would be the standard cost set for the item. To continue the example, when the first item is purchased the book-keeping entries will be:

Debit	Stock Account	—	£2.18	(the standard value)
Credit	Cash Account	—	£2.00	(the actual cost)
	Variance Account	—	£0.18	(the planned difference)

And when the second item is purchased at the end of the year, the book-keeping entries will be:

Debit	Stock Account	—	£2.18	(the standard value)
	Variance Account	—	£0.18	(the planned difference)
Credit	Cash Account	—	£2.36	(the actual cost)

In costing terminology, it is *planned* to have a favourable variance at the beginning of the year and an adverse variance at the end of the year. In budget terms, a comparison between actual cost of purchases and standard cost of purchases shown in the budget would show an apparent gain at the beginning of the year and loss at the end of the year – if the price conformed to plan. To avoid this, a value has to be included in the budget as off-standard variance, either plus or minus cost of purchases, as appropriate.

If the planned purchases are consistent for each month of the year when valued at standard, e.g. £850 per month as in the case of Histyles, and an inflation rate of 18 per cent for the standard year has been incorporated into the standard then:

Month	Planned Standard Value £	Plus or Minus Off-Standard Variance £	=	Net Budget Value £
Dec.	850	− 70.21	=	779.79
Jan.	850	− 58.48	=	791.52
Feb.	850	− 46.75	=	803.25
Mar.	850	− 35.02	=	814.98
Apr.	850	− 23.29	=	826.71
May	850	− 11.56	=	838.44
June	850	+ 11.56	=	861.56
July	850	+ 23.29	=	873.29
Aug.	850	+ 35.02	=	885.02
Sept.	850	+ 46.75	=	896.75
Oct.	850	+ 58.48	=	908.48
Nov.	850	+ 70.21	=	920.21
TOTALS:	10 200	NIL		10 200

It should be appreciated that the above is purely an estimated division between standard value, off-standard value and actual planned value, and that little significance can be drawn if differences are identified in a single period. The general principle when developing such budgets is that the sum of the off-standard variance must equal zero over the complete year and be proportional to the time scale rather than to the value purchased. Thus, if in the above example Histyles planned to purchase £800 of goods in each of the first six months and £900 of goods in each month of the second half-year and the off-standard variance for each month was as above, then the budget would show:

Month	Planned Standard Value £	Plus or Minus Off-Standard Variance £	=	Net Budget Value
Dec.	800	− 70.21	=	729.79
Jan.	800	− 58.48	=	741.52
Feb.	800	− 46.75	=	753.25
Mar.	800	− 35.02	=	764.98
Apr.	800	− 23.29	=	776.71
May	800	− 11.56	=	788.44
June	900	+ 11.56	=	911.56
July	900	+ 23.29	=	923.29
Aug.	900	+ 35.02	=	935.02
Sept.	900	+ 46.75	=	946.75
Oct.	900	+ 58.48	=	958.48
Nov.	900	+ 70.21	=	970.21
TOTALS:	10 200	NIL		10 200

It must be stressed that the comprehensive coverage given above of the preparation of a budget where standard costing is used in the salon is intended to show that this system can be employed in all business environments. In practice, all the above circumstances are unlikely to apply in a particular salon, and where they are appropriate, in the interests of expediency a 'flexible interpretation' may be made. This approach is shown below in respect of Histyles and the development of its budget for the first 2 periods of 19–8/19–9. Using the data already available:

(a) Normal stock holding value £680.

(b) Standard value of purchases to be £850 per month.

(c) Cost of sales at standard value represents 75 per cent of the sales receipts.

(d) Planned off-standard variance to be compatible with the 18 per cent per annum 'inflation' factor used in establishing the standard material value.

The records also show that in previous years' operations:

(a) 2 per cent of the material purchased was 'scrapped'.

(b) 1 per cent of the retail stock turnover was transferred to salon stock.

(c) 1.5 per cent of the retail sales were in respect of salon stock.

If the planned sales receipts for Periods 1 and 2 above were £1500 and £1000 respectively then the retail sales budgets would be:

	Budget Period 1 (Dec.)		Budget Period 2 (Jan.)
	£		£
Inventory value at start of period	680		390
Plus:			
Purchases at Standard	850		850
'Transfers In' at Standard			
(1.5% of £1125)	17	(1.5% of 733)	11
Less:			
Cost of Sales at Standard			
(75% of Sales Value)	1125		750
'Transfers Out' at Standard			
(1% of 680 + 850)	15	(1% of 390 + 850)	12
Scrap/Wastage			
(2% of £850)	17	(2% of 850)	17
Inventory Value at close of period	390		472
Planned Off-Standard Variance			
Debit Profit/Loss Account	Nil		Nil
Credit Profit/Loss Account	70	(Favourable (F) variance)	58

The above details for Periods 1 and 2 are used in the Budget Sections of the material statements shown in Figs. 10.7 and 10.12.

Recording of Actual Performance Data and its Comparison with Budget

It has already been shown that the details of actual performance can be obtained, with very little rearrangement, from the ongoing salon financial and stock records. These data are entered onto the material statement for the appropriate period and a comparison with the budget made. In Figs. 10.7 and 10.12 we have included the hypothetical performance data achieved by Histyles and below give some indication of the possible managerial action required as a result of the comparison exercises conducted.

The points to be noted from Fig. 10.7 are:

(a)   Opening inventory value.   Since the budget is developed in advance of the availability of the actual stock value at the beginning of the month, a difference will always occur. In the example shown this is so small that no management action is needed, but if a large difference was found, management would have to increase or decrease the planned volume of purchases as appropriate. It should be noted that the differences between budget and actual opening inventory values are carried forward until a stock check or a revision of Standards exercise is conducted.

FIG. 10.12

Histyles Salon Material Statement – January 19–9						
A RETAIL STOCK	**Budget (£)**		**Actual (£)**		**Comparison (£)**	
	Month	*Cumul- ative*	*Month*	*Cumul- ative*	*Month*	*Cumul- ative*
1. Stock at Standard Opening Inventory Value	390	680	402	668	(12)	(12)
Plus – Purchases	850	1700	860	1735	10	35
Transfers In	11	28	14	19	3	(9)
Less – Cost of Sales	750	1875	731	1819	(19)	(56)
Transfers Out	12	27	18	40	6	13
Scrap	17	34	3	39	(14)	5
Inventory Value at Close	472	472	524	524	52	52
2. Variances Volume	—	—	1	3	1	3
Price	F58	F128	F42	F101	16	27
TOTAL:	**F58**	**F128**	**F43**	**F104**	**15**	**24**

B SALON STOCK	**Budget (£)**		**Actual (£)**		**Comparison (£)**	
	Month	*Cumul- ative*	*Month*	*Cumul- ative*	*Month*	*Cumul- ative*
1. Stock at Standard Opening Inventory Value	148	150	166	162	12	12
Plus – Purchases	205	503	205	492	—	(11)
Transfers In	12	27	18	40	6	13
Less – Std. Usage	200	491	190	486	(10)	(5)
Transfers Out	11	28	14	19	3	(9)
Scrap	5	12	6	10	1	(2)
Inventory Value at Close	149	149	179	179	30	30
2. Variances Volume	—	—	3	4	3	4
Price	F14	F39	F11	F35	3	4
TOTAL:	**F14**	**F39**	**F14**	**F39**	**—**	**—**

(b)   Inventory value at close.   The net value of the inventory held is £12 higher than anticipated, and whilst this can be regarded as insignificant, it is important to note that the 'Cost of Sales' was £37 less than budget, this being in line with the actual £50 short-fall in sales receipts (see Fig. 10.4). The differences in Purchases and Transfers In and Out, could be regarded as insignificant but the increase in Scrap of 112 per cent to the estimated or budgeted value requires investigation to identify the reason.

(c)   Variances.   The basic variance data available are:
(i)   A planned off-standard variance of £70 favourable due to the 'inflation factor' contained in the standard cost of purchases; i.e. if £850 of stock was purchased in this period only £780 would actually be paid.
(ii)   The variance (favourable) actually achieved was £61 in respect of material with a standard value of £875.

It is, therefore, apparent that the actual variance comprises both a volume and price element. The volume element is in respect of the £25 additional stock at standard value purchased and is calculated as follows:

$$\frac{\text{Planned Off-Standard Variance} \times \text{Difference in Value of Standard Purchases}}{\text{Budgeted Value of Standard Purchase}}$$

i.e. In the quoted example $\dfrac{-70 \times (875 - 850)}{850} = 2$ Favourable.

Thus, by deduction from the total actual variance, price variance = 59 Favourable. The result is that due to price increases, £11 of the anticipated 'profit' on the purchase of £875 of material at standard value at this time of the year has been 'lost', and a continuation of this trend over the complete year would result in a loss of £132 of profit at planned volumes.

From Fig. 10.12 it can be seen that the 'Scrap' level has largely balanced out, possibly as a result of management action in the previous period, and that transfers out and in have tended to 'balance out'. The important trends are the continuance of a drop in the cost of sales due to reduced sales and a continuance of the adverse trend of cost of purchases. These latter factors have resulted in an increase in the stock holding to that planned but as yet it has not reached the normal holding, i.e. £680. The problems of lower sales volume and higher purchase price are not at present critical to the profitability of the salon, but management are aware of the adverse trend and should be considering the corrective options open to them. We have previously shown, in the adjustment to sales budget, the action taken at a later date to correct the remaining adverse purchase price trend. No adjustment is necessary to the material budget since the differences will be clearly shown in the 'Variance' section of the retail stock statement.

Salon Stock i.e. Material Used in Performing the Hairdressing Service

The material statement in respect of salon stock is similar to that for retail stock: the use of standard costing is not essential to the setting of a budget and the subsequent comparison with actual performance, but its advantages are equally great. The conceptual differences are outlined below:

(a)   Budgeted purchases.   Assuming that the intention is to retain a fairly constant stock level, and that, as is normally the case, the availability of storage space is a restricting factor which precludes stockpiling, the material purchased will be made to replace the material consumed. The amount of material consumed is in turn directly related to the volume and type of services. For budget purposes, if standard costing is employed, the required purchase value is given by the sum of the standard material cost of each service planned in a particular period, plus an allowance for 'wastage'. For ease of reference, in the examples pertaining to Histyles shown in Figs. 10.7 and 10.12, it is assumed that in all services the material cost of each service is 5 per cent of the sales value and that the 'wastage' is 2.5 per cent of the purchase value.

(b)   Actual cost of issues.   The equivalent of 'cost of sales' for salon material is the cost of issues to the salon. For practical control purposes it may be appropriate to return all 'floor stock' to the stores at the end of the period. Thus the cost of issues, when adjusted for the standard value of the returns, will give the cost of material used. The material used is proportional to the actual activity performed, and is therefore for comparison purposes entered as the standard value of the material content of the actual activity performed; i.e. in the case of Histyles in December 19–8 the actual sales value was £5914. Therefore, standard value of material used at 5 per cent of sales value is £296. The difference identified between the budgeted standard usage and actual standard usage is effectively a *Volume Variance*. The difference between the actual material used and the actual standard material is a *Usage Variance* and may be recorded as such, provided any scrap or wastage materials is reported to the stores, who formally raise a scrap note which, when accumulated, gives a separate *Scrap Value*. In general, however, true scrap is in practice not reported to stores and therefore, as in our example of Histyles, is shown as one value, together with the usage variance.

In the example shown in Fig. 10.7 both the budget and the actual data are consistent with the performance data used in Fig. 10.4. For Fig. 10.12 (January 19–9) the budgeted value of salon services is £4000 and the actual is £3800.

It can be seen that in the examples shown the variations to budget are minimal, but if great differences were shown salon management would be aware at an early date of an adverse trend and have an opportunity to implement corrective measures to achieve the planned profitability.

EXPENSE BUDGET

The *Expense Budget* may be regarded as the overhead budget since it is con-cerned with all the items of expenditure which are of a revenue nature that have not already been included in either the employment or material budgets. The majority of the expense categories will be incurred no matter what the level of salon business, e.g. rent and rates. But in most cases the amount of expense will in part depend upon the level of activity; e.g. in the case of electricity, a proportion of the charge will be a 'fixed charge' for the connection to the mains electricity system, a proportion will be in respect of heating and lighting, and the remainder will be for the electricity consumed by the equipment used in the provision of the hairdressing services. In this example the first two proportions are incurred whether or not any business is conducted, but the final proportion is directly related to the business activity level.

The preparation of the expense budget consequently involves the application of a large amount of managerial judgement to the historical data contained in the salon records. It is recommended that the expense budget should be developed category by category, and that a record should be made of the data used and assumptions made. For example:

Electricity

Expenditure in previous 12 months	£500
Plus: Estimated tariff increase of 20%	100
Plus: Increased utilisation of equipment to meet anticipated business volume 10%	60
TOTAL FOR YEAR:	660

As a result of the above records, comparisons with actual performance will identify the validity or otherwise of the budget assumptions, as well as providing an indication of the profitability trend. So that these processes may be ongoing throughout the year, the total budget spend has to be 'phased' over the course of the year. In general terms, the phasing of the budget should be consistent with the time that the expenditure is incurred, provided that actual data over the same time-scale will be available for comparison purposes. If the stationery budget is estimated to be £120 per annum and the usage is estimated to be evenly spread, with stock replenishment occurring at each period-end, then it would be evenly set as £10 for each period within the standard year.

Certain expenses, e.g. rent or hire of equipment, will usually be expressed as a weekly or monthly rate or value but the terms of payment expressed in such contracts or agreements stipulate payment in advance and at less frequent intervals. For example, the rent of Salon B is £21 per week, to be paid quarterly in advance. In such a case the budget would be set at 3 times the number of days in the calendar month (the reporting period) so that the January value is £93 and the February value in a non-leap year is £84.

It will also be found that charges will be received in arrears covering a longer time-span than the reporting period, e.g. the quarterly accounts of gas and electricity. In such instances, if the budget was spread over all 12 periods, on 8 of the periods an apparent saving would be shown. It is accordingly suggested that this item should be included only in the periods when the bills are due to be received. It should be noted that if the salon management is prepared to read the meters on a monthly basis and calculate the cost of the units of power used, the normal periodic budget may be prepared for comparison with a 'salon calculated actual'.

The details of actual expenditure incurred against the various categories of expense or overhead expenditure can, in the main, be obtained from the financial records. It is, however, important to include all the charges incurred during the period. The financial accounts will normally show amounts paid during the period and such values will include:

1. Payment for goods or services received in previous periods.
2. Prepayments or payments in advance, e.g. the example above of Histyles' rent.
3. Goods received for which bills are awaited.
4. Bills or accounts not paid.

It is therefore necessary to adjust the financial account value for these factors before completing the 'Actual' section of the monthly expense statement. This statement is structured in a similar manner to the employment and material statements; i.e. it shows for each category of expense: the budget (for both the period and cumulative year to date values); the actual performance; and the comparison, either plus or minus budget. As in the case of the other budgets discussed above, this information directs management attention to adverse performances.

CAPITAL EXPENDITURE BUDGET

The previous four budgets and their subsequent comparison with actual performance enable management to control the profitability of the salon operations. We have already shown in Chapter II that, before a salon can commence business, capital has to be provided to finance the provision of the necessary facilities and the initial operating expenses. It has also been shown that the pricing structure allows for recovery of the operating expenses and a surplus, or profit, which may be taken out of the business in the form of interest on the capital investment, or even to 'repay' the capital value invested, particularly if it is 'loan capital'. In practice, however, it is found that at least the same total value of capital investment is required to maintain the business as a 'going concern' for not only is 'working capital' required, but also, the facilities provided in the form of fixed assets need replacement, improvement or addition and extension. For these purposes a percentage of the profits is retained by the proprietors within the business to finance such projects as will occur in the future financial year. Frequently, the extent of such projects exceeds the finance available from within the business with the result that additional capital input to the business has to be obtained if the required developments are to be actioned.

The above simplified summary shows that the extent of the capital available which forms the total value of the capital expenditure budget is established at 'proprietorship level'. The formal stages required in the budget development are as follows:

(a) Capital Requirement.   The range of projects which require capital is great, and can vary considerably in value. Even in a small concern, it is likely that in the same year it could be proposed to open a new salon, and to purchase a new cash register. For each project, the responsible manager should develop a *Capital Requirement Statement* which not only includes the reason for the expenditure, but also an estimate of the cost involved, the financial benefits to be obtained and the 'payback period' of the project. Each proposal is submitted for 'approval in principle' to the subsequent levels of management.

(b) Budget Approval.   Normally on an annual basis, the projects which have received approval in principle are reviewed by the originator, revised in detail if necessary and submitted for budget approval to the proprietorship. A decision is then made as to which projects may be implemented during the coming year. The extent of the approvals given will be dependent on the amount of available capital anticipated, as well as the relative importance or viability of the various projects.

In addition, the time of the project within the financial year is determined, thus enabling a capital expenditure budget to be prepared. It should, however, be noted that no firm commitment to the expenditure has been made, but failure to implement the project may produce great variance in the actual operating performance to the budgeted performance. For example, if the additional chair for the anticipated increase in clients was not provided, either the anticipated sales receipts would not be achieved, or the salon costs would increase as a result of extended working hours and increased idle time awaiting facilities.

(c) Capital Approval.   On an individual project basis, a record is maintained of all procurement requisitions raised and approved (usually at proprietorship level), orders subsequently placed and charges received upon completion of the work. The comparison of actual to budget is, therefore, an ongoing activity and, accordingly, a standardised capital statement on a periodic basis is seldom appropriate.

It is usual, however, to include within the monthly reporting package a summary of the status of the capital budget as a whole and the outline of such a statement is shown in Fig. 10.13.

FINANCIAL OR CASH FLOW BUDGET

In addition to providing management with information as to when a cash shortage may restrict the operation of the salon, this budget shows the overall profitability of the planned activities. For purposes of comparison it is only the bottom-line or total value of working capital that is important, the individual reasons for variations having been shown in more detail in the budgets detailed previously in this chapter. The financial budget, being a summary of the other budgets, will, when compared to the actual performance data, reflect the total difference which has occurred during the budget year to date. If the cumulative effect of these differences is great, the budget for the rest of the year will give little indication of the future 'business position' of the salon and does not provide management with the necessary information to make correct decisions or plans. It is, therefore, normal to prepare for subsequent periods

FIG. 10.13   Capital Summary – Period 7

Project Narrative	Budget Value	Completion Period	Value Requested	Value Approved	Order Value	Invoiced Value	Capital Payment	Remarks	Reset Number
A – 1	60	1	59	59	59	61	61		F8/001
A – 2	20		21	21	21	21	21		
Total	80		80	80	80	82	82	Agreed Supplement to Order Price	
B – 1	140	3	NIL	NIL	NIL	NIL	NIL		
C – 1	312	6	312	312	312			Delivery Overdue	
C – 2	67		67	67	67	67		Delivery Overdue	
C – 3	42		42	42	42				
Total	421		421	421	421	67			
D – 1	180	7	240					Project under review – Supplier's Price Increase	
E – 1	94	8	94	94				In progress as planned	
E – 2	135		135	135	135				
Total	229		229	229					
F – 1	475	11							
Totals	1525		970	730	636	149	82		

an *Outlook Budget* which in simple terms is an accumulation of the budget data in respect of future periods additional to the actual performance data to date. In addition, the outlook budgets will take account of any changes to the original plan or budget which will have an impact on future trading operations.

Before considering the development of financial budgets, it is important to understand clearly what *Working Capital* is, since it is the subject of the major part of the financial budget. 'Working Capital' is an accounting term used to describe the excess of the current assets of a business over its current liabilities. For example, the working capital for Histyles at 3 December 19–8, extracted from the balance sheet shown on p. 127 is:

			£
Current Assets – Stock (Retail)	£1064.10		
Stock (Salon)	347.68		
Cash at Bank	1887.35		
Cash Float	5.00		
Prepayments	187.00		3491.13
Less: Liabilities			372.87
		Working Capital	3118.26

In addition to the proprietors investing additional money into the business, working capital is increased by the profit made on trading operations. Seldom will this profit be in the form of cash only; stock holdings may have increased, debtors may have been increased, liabilities may have been decreased etc. The liquidity or availability of the working capital is often as important to management as is its amount; e.g. in the above example only £1892.35 (61 per cent of the working capital) is immediately available to Histyles' management. Therefore, any expenditure above this amount could not be made without producing a 'cash deficiency'.

Working capital is reduced when a trading loss has been made, although this may not have affected the amount of 'cash holdings'; e.g. the trading loss may be balanced by a reduction in stock holdings and an increase in liabilities in the form of creditors. In addition, working capital may be reduced as a result of the withdrawal of money by the proprietors in the form of drawings, dividends etc., or by the purchase of fixed assets, i.e. capital expenditure as shown in the capital budget.

To complete a financial budget, an outlook budget or the actual performance report it is necessary to:

1. Apply the trading results to the outstanding balance of working capital from the previous period to give the gross working capital at the end of the review period.

2. From the gross working capital deduct any capital disbursements, whether these are in the form of expenditure on fixed assets or dividends or drawings paid to the proprietors to give the net working capital available to commence the next period.

The above may be summarised as:

Net Working Capital at Close of Previous Period
+ (or −) Trading Profit (or Loss)

= Gross Working Capital

+ Additional Capital Input
− Expenditure on Fixed Assets
− Dividends and Drawings

= Net Working Capital

For control purposes each aspect should be divided into its major constituent items which are to be found in the other budgets or which would appear in a balance sheet if one were prepared at each period's end. The following sections which consider in greater depth the individual budgets, reports and outlooks are purely for illustration and should not be taken to be the recommended itemised contents of such documents. The extent of itemisation should be determined by each management to suit the particular business.

1. Budgets or Plans

In view of the fact that considerable itemised changes are likely to occur between the budget (or plan) and actual performance, which will produce the need to adjust the budget for future periods, it is inappropriate to develop detailed budgets for each of the 12 periods which constitute the financial year. Unless there is a specific intention to expend a significant amount of working capital on a particular project in an intervening period, it is often sufficient to prepare a financial budget for the next period (the first period of the financial year) and a cumulative financial budget for the complete year.

In Fig. 10.14 we have developed the financial budgets for Histyles for Period 1 of the budget year, and the cumulative budget for the year. The following notes refer both to the amounts shown and the methodology employed in the construction of these budgets.

(a) Net working capital at commencement of period. Since both budgets start at the same time this section is identical. The cash values of £5 in hand and £500 in the bank are the agreed balances to be retained at the commencement of the year, whether this result is obtained by H. and I. Styles (the proprietors) withdrawing or inputting cash at the close of the previous year. Although, in common with most businesses, every effort is made to clear all liabilities incurred at the end of a particular year, some will always remain; e.g. payment of the balance of VAT charged to VAT claimed, charges for credit purchases due to be delivered on the last day of the financial year etc. The extent of such charges is normally easily identified, and in the case of Histyles they accumulated to £200. Similarly, whilst every effort is made to avoid any debts being outstanding awaiting payment, there will usually be some, even if they are prepayments; e.g. in the case of Histyles the insurance premium of £252 per annum is payable in advance from 1 August of each year. Therefore, at 1 December a prepayment exists of $\dfrac{252 \times 8}{12} = £168$. The stock value of £830 is the planned stockholding shown in the material budget Fig. 10.7 as £680 retail stock and £150 salon stock.

(b) Trading results. The amounts are taken directly from the Sales, Employment, Material (Purchases and Variance values only) and Expense budgets. In our example (Fig. 10.14), to the information already used in respect of Histyles, we have added the expense budget (Period 1) of £610, and the total budget values for the complete year as shown.

(c) Additional capital input. No additional capital input is planned and, therefore, NIL is shown in Fig. 10.14.

(d) Capital expenditure. The values shown correspond to those shown in Fig. 10.13.

(e) Drawings. These are the anticipated amounts to be withdrawn by H. and I. Styles additional to their planned salaries.

FIG. 10.14

Description	Budget Period 1 (£)	Budget Annual (£)
A) *Current Assets*		
Cash in hand	5	5
Cash in bank	500	500
Stock	830	830
Debtors and Prepayments	168	168
Liabilities – Sundry Creditors	(200)	(200)
B) Net Working Capital – Brought Forward	1303	1303
C) *Plus or minus Trading Results*		
Sales Receipts	7310	(60120)
Employment Costs	(4626)	(36072)
Material Purchases	(1148)	(9825)
Material Variance	95F	NIL
Expenses	(610)	(6710)
D) Gross Working Capital	2324	8413
E) Additional Capital Input	NIL	NIL
F) Capital Expenditure	80	1525
G) Drawings	300	1400
H) Net Working Capital – Carried Forward	1944	5488

2. Actual Results

It is highly probable that not only will the trading results be at variance with the budget but also the opening balances which form the current assets and the adjustments to gross working capital will differ from the budgeted amounts. It should be noted that the amount of net working capital should be the sum of the balances on the Current Asset Accounts. In practice these can be reconciled within the financial accounts, i.e. physical cash in hand, cash book balance after bank reconciliation, Outstanding Debtors and Creditors Accounts, Prepayment Account etc. A stock value may not, however, be available unless an integrated cost accounting system was in use, but a valuation can be determined by subtracting the known current assets at the end of the period from the net working capital. Below we show the 'Actual' financial statement for Histyles at the end of Period 1, i.e. December 19–9. Where appropriate, the values used are as in previous examples quoted in this Chapter:

Current Assets

Cash in hand	£5	
Cash in Bank	484	
Stock	668	
Debtors and Prepayment	168	
Less: Liabilities – Various	214	
Net Working Capital brought forward	1111	

Trading Results

Sales Receipts – Total	£7364	
Less: Employment Costs	5043	
Less: Material Purchases	1162	
Plus: Material Variance	86	
Less: Expense	596	649
Gross Working Capital		1760
Additional Capital Input		NIL
Capital Expenditure		82
Drawings		350
Net Working Capital		1328

3. Outlooks

The actual financial return for Period 1 above, in respect of Histyles, shows that the net working capital is £616 below that which was budgeted (see Fig. 10.14), i.e. £1328 actual as compared to £1944 budgeted.

If the planned trading performance was achieved for subsequent periods, the actual financial position of the salon would remain £616 adverse. For management decision-making it is, therefore, important to adjust the budget in the light of actual achievement. In the immediate future this will entail the budget for Period 2, and provided no management action is planned for trading activities, this requirement can be achieved by replacing the budgeted current asset data with the actual amount shown in the financial records, which in the case of Histyles is £1328. The outlook budget for Period 2 would be:

Current Assets

	Cash in Hand	£5
	Cash in Bank	733
	Stock	568
	Debtors and Prepayment	147
Less: Liabilities – Various		125
Net Working Capital brought forward		1328

Plus or Minus *Trading Results*

Sales Receipts – Total	£4800	
Less: Employment Costs	3900	
Less: Material Purchased	1055	
Plus: Material – Variance	72	
Less: Expense	400	483
Gross Working Capital		845
Additional Capital Input		NIL
Capital Expenditure		NIL
Drawings		NIL
Net Working Capital		845

Finalisation of the coming month's financial budget is therefore deferred until the trading results of the present month are known, thus enabling management to make responsible short-term decisions, e.g. to delay capital acquisitions or to reduce the 'build-up' of stock etc. However, it is likely that management will require an outlook over a longer period of time; in such instances the outlook budget is based on the 'cumulative' budgets, i.e. if after three periods, outlook budgets are required after 6, 9 and 12 periods in that year, then the actual trading amounts reflected as the net working capital brought forward after three periods are added to the budget amounts for the following 3, 6 and 9 periods respectively. In addition, if any known changes implemented by management – e.g. in Histyles' case the uplifting of retail prices – have occurred, then the trading budgets variations are also included in the outlook. For example, the year-end outlook budget for Histyles after the Period 1 actuals had been prepared would be:

Actual Current Assets – brought forward from previous year   £1 111
Plus: Sales Receipts – 60 120 plus (7364 − 7310)   60 174
Less: Employment Costs – 36 072 plus (5043 − 4626)   36 489
Less: Material Costs – 8925 plus (1162 − 1148)   8 939
Less: Material Variance – 95 minus 86   9
Less: Expense 6710 minus (610 − 596)   6 696
                                                                 ──────
                          Gross Working Capital   9 152
                                                                 ══════

Additional Capital Input   NIL
Capital Expenditure – 1525 plus (82 − 80)   1527
Drawings – 1400 plus (350 − 300)   1450
                                                                 ──────
                          Net Working Capital   6175
                                                                 ══════

Thus, the use of budgetary control, which is really a rearrangement of the financial Profit and Loss Account and balance sheet enables management on an ongoing basis to monitor the performance of the salon and also provides an indication of the future business position of the enterprise. More importantly, it provides the management with data upon which decisions can be made to improve the viability of the business.

The specimen Hairdressing Apprenticeship Indenture on pp. 193–8 is reproduced by kind permission of the Joint Training Council for the Hairdressing Industry.

Apprentice Name ....

Serial No. ....

British Hairdressing Apprenticeship Council

indenture
of apprenticeship
for
hairdressing
apprentices

SPECIMEN

APPROVED BY THE JOINT TRAINING COUNCIL
FOR THE HAIRDRESSING INDUSTRY

Published by
British Hairdressing Apprenticeship Council

CROSSROADS HOUSE 165 THE PARADE WATFORD HERTS

BRITISH HAIRDRESSING APPRENTICESHIP COUNCIL

deed of apprenticeship

(All entries to be in block letters)

This Agreement between

Name of
Apprentice   .... of

Address of
Apprentice   ....

a minor of (age).......... years (hereinafter called the "Appren-

Name of
Parent/Guardian   tice") of the first part and............................. of

Address of
Parent/Guardian   ....

Parent/Guardian of the Apprentice (hereinafter called the "Parent/

Name of
Employer   Guardian") of the second part and .... of

Address of
Employer   ....

(hereinafter called the "Employer") of the third part, and the British
Hairdressing Apprenticeship Council of Crossroads House, 165 The
Parade, Watford, Herts., (hereinafter called "the Council") of the
fourth part.

Whereas the Apprentice has continuously served the Employer since

Date of
commencement
of employment   ....

Insert Ladies'   as a prospective Apprentice with a view to his/her employment as an
or Gentlemen's
or Ladies' and
Gentlemen's   Apprentice by the Employer in.................. Hairdressing
as applicable   for a term of three years from that date.

Now it is hereby agreed between the parties hereto as follows:—

1. (a) The Apprentice of his/her own free will and with the consent
of his/her Parent/Guardian hereby binds himself/herself to serve the
Employer as his/her Apprentice in hairdressing for the remainder of
the said term of three years.

2.   In consideration of the covenants and agreements entered
into by the Parent/Guardian and the Apprentice the Employer hereby
covenants with the Parent/Guardian and the Apprentice and with
each of them severally as follows:—

(a) The Employer will employ the Apprentice during the said term and to the best of his/her power, skill and knowledge instruct the Apprentice or cause him/her to be instructed in either, ladies' or gentlemen's hairdressing, or both, in accordance with the syllabus laid down by the Council.

(b) That the Apprentice will during the said term serve the Employer at

Address
of Salon

. . . .

or any other place or places mutually agreed between Employer, Parent/Guardian, and Apprentice, any extra travel costs to be met by the Employer, and due compensation in the form of time off in lieu or overtime payments be made for extra travel time incurred.

(c) That he/she will keep the Apprentice under his/her supervision or place him/her under the supervision of one or more operative hairdressers, who shall also accept the obligation to instruct the Apprentice as set out in clause 2 (a).

(d) That he/she will pay the Apprentice during the said term of his/her service not less than the appropriate statutory remuneration operative from time to time under the Wages Council Act 1959, or any statutory modification or re-enactment thereof for the time being in force of such extra provisions arrived at by voluntary agreement between the Employer and Apprentice, and shall allow the Apprentice the statutory meal breaks.

(e) The Employer will allow the Apprentice leave of absence on one day or two half days each week, or for an equivalent continuous period each year of the Apprenticeship period to enable him/her to attend day classes for Technical and Further Education as provided by the local Authority. Where no Technical and Further Education classes exist locally, the attendance will be at classes operated by other local Education Authorities provided they are within reasonable and convenient travelling distances of the Employers' business or the Apprentice's home address.

(f) The Employer undertakes that leave of absence to attend Technical and Further Education classes in accordance with 3 (e) shall be deemed to be during the normal working hours of the Apprentice.

(g) At the expiry of the said term of Apprenticeship the Employer will sign the Apprentice's discharge, providing that the Apprentice shall have faithfully served the Employer during the said term, and will register such discharge with the Council.

3.   In consideration of the foregoing the Parent/Guardian and the Apprentice respectively and severally covenant with the Employers as follows:—

(a) That the Apprentice shall faithfully and diligently serve the Employer as his/her Apprentice, and observe the general salon rules;

(b) That the Apprentice shall keep the Employer's secrets and obey his/her lawful commands;

(c) That the Apprentice shall not absent himself/herself from the Employer's services without leave;

(d) That the Apprentice shall not do any wilful damage or knowingly suffer any damage to be done to the goods or other property of the Employer;

(e) That the Apprentice shall attend Technical and Further Education classes without loss of wages by such attendance;

(f) Not at any time during or after the said determination of the said employment and either on his/her own account or for any other person or for any other firm or company to solicit interfere with or endeavour to entice away from the said employer any person who at any time during the continuance of the said employment shall have been a customer in the said place of employment.

(g) That in the case of any dispute or grievance relating to the carrying out of the terms of this agreement such dispute difference or grievance shall be referred in writing to the Council which shall if the matter cannot within six weeks from the date of reference to the Council be settled to the satisfaction of the parties hereto by mutual agreement refer the matter to a single arbitrator to be appointed by the Council and this shall be a submission to arbitration, under the provisions of the Arbitration Act 1950 or any statutory re-enactment, modification or extension thereof for the time being in force.

(h) An Arbitrator appointed pursuant to sub-clause (f) hereof shall have power to make any award he shall think fit. Such power shall include power to cancel this agreement upon whatever terms he shall think fit if in the opinion of the Arbitrator:

> (i) Any of the parties hereto shall have committed any serious or persistent breach of any term hereof,
>
> or
>
> (ii) the Apprentice shall in his opinion be unfitted for hairdressing as a career or if the Apprentice will be unable satisfactorily to complete the Apprenticeship.

4.   In the event of the Employer disposing of his/her interest in the business or ceasing to trade as a result of bankruptcy, liquidation or for any other reason, the Employer shall exercise his/her best endeavours in ensuring that the Apprentice shall find a new Employer willing to employ the Apprentice for the unexpired period of this agreement, and the Employer shall by an endorsement on this agreement transfer his/her rights and liabilities under this agreement to the new Employer who shall also execute the endorsement.

5.   Provided that the Apprentice shall have satisfactorily completed his/her Apprenticeship the Council shall issue to the Apprentice a certificate certifying that the Apprentice has completed his/her period of Apprenticeship provided he/she has taken and passed an examination approved by the Joint Training Council for the Hairdressing Industry.

6.   At the signing hereof the apprentice receives and does hereby acknowledge receipt of an identical copy of the Indenture subject to its registration with this Council.

As witness the hands of the parties this . . . . day of **(Month)**

. . . . one thousand nine hundred and. . . . .

Signed. . . . .(Apprentice)

Witnessed by . . . .   Witnessed by . . . .

Address. . . . .   Address. . . . .

. . . .

(Occupation) . . . .   (Occupation) . . . .

Signed . . . .(Parent/Guardian)

Witnessed by . . . .   Witnessed by . . . .

Address. . . . .   Address. . . . .

. . . .

(Occupation) . . . .   (Occupation) . . . .

Signed . . . .(Employer)

Witnessed by . . . .   Witnessed by . . . .

Address. . . . .   Address. . . . .

. . . .

(Occupation) . . . .   (Occupation) . . . .

Signed for and on behalf of the British Hairdressing Apprenticeship Council, Crossroads House, 165 The Parade, Watford, Herts., and entered in the Register.

. . . . Date . . . .

N.B. (a) In Scotland each signature must have two witnesses.
     (b) Sick Pay shall be the subject of a separate agreement between Employer, Parent/Guardian and Apprentice.

GUIDANCE NOTES

1.   These Indentures must be signed by all parties to the Contract and duly witnessed within three months of the Apprentice commencing employment. This is proved by the date of the actual commencement of employment which must be indicated on page 2, and the date of the signing of the Indenture by all parties, being no longer than three months apart. This is in line with the legal requirements as laid down by the Hairdressing Undertakings Wages Council. It is not lawful to back-date Indentures.

2.   Upon signature completion of the Indenture, both copies should be sent to the British Hairdressing Apprenticeship Council (address shown on front page) for registration. The Indentures will then be sent back to the employer who must hand the copy Indenture to the Apprentice. BOTH SHOULD THEN BE KEPT IN A SAFE PLACE.

3.   Upon the completion of the Apprenticeship, the EMPLOYER should secure the copy Indenture from the Apprentice and then post both the master and the copy Indentures to this address for final certification. They will then be so endorsed and the copy Indenture returned to the employer for the record, and the master Indenture to the apprentice for future use and evidence of serving an apprenticeship.

4.   Subsequent to this the Apprentice will also receive a final Certificate for retention and display, for which a nominal fee is payable. This should be read in conjunction with clause 5 of the indenture and both employer and employee should attempt to ensure that an approved examination takes place.

5.   Special attention is drawn to Clause 3(g) of the Indenture concerning disputes procedures. Its use in the event of disputes can save heartsearching afterwards.

To be completed by the Employer at the end of the Apprenticeship period.

This endorsement is to certify that the Apprentice named in this Indenture has completed the period laid down in accordance with the prescribed conditions and is now free of any further obligations in respect of this agreement.

Signed by Employer. . . . .

Date . . . .

Signed for and on behalf of the British Hairdressing Apprenticeship

. . . .

Date . . . .

Index

Absence   60, 61, 69
Access, salon   27
Accounts, appropriation   106
   capital   105
   cost   129, 130
   credit   106
   current   106
   financial   89, 93, 99
   ledger   59
   nominal   107
   profit and loss   99, 107–10
   real   106
Activity percentage   70
Acts, Contracts of Employment, 1963,
   1972   3
   Employers' Liability   2
   Employment Protection, 1975   3
   Equal Pay, 1970   3
   Finance   88
   Health and Safety at Work   2, 24, 30
   Limited Partnership, 1907   11
   Offices Shops and Railway Premises,
      1963   24, 27, 28, 30
   Partnership, 1890   11
   Redundancy Payments, 1969   3
   Registration of Business Names   4
   Sex Discrimination, 1975   3
   Trade Description   2
Administration   87
Administrative responsibilities   4
Agency labour   109
Appointment making   94
Apprenticeship   15, 47
   indentures   15, 193–8
Articles of Association   13
Attendance hours   61, 68
Authorised absence   69

Balance sheet   4, 99, 112, 127
Bank reconciliations   59
Bequests   9
Book-keeping, double-entry   99
Budget approval   185
   cash flow   185
   capital expenditure   184
   control   166, 173
   employment   162, 165
   expense   154, 182
   financial   185
   labour   154, 162
   plans   188
   preparation   154, 168, 179
   purchase   154, 168, 179
   sales   154, 155, 159
Budgetary control   129, 154
Budgeting   4

Business plans   18, 19
Buyer   76–9

Capital accounts   105
   additional input   189
   adjustments   23
   approach   185
   balance   113
   budget   184
   equipment   71, 73
   expenditure   22, 113, 184, 189
   net working   188
   outlay   9
   summary   185
Cash   100
   and carry   74, 100
   book   59
   financial records   91
   floats   4
   receipts   97
   reconciliation   90
   records   90
   register   90
      journal   101
   security   90
Cashier   79
Chair hours   131
City salon   6
Cleanliness   29
Clientele   6
Clients' receipts   21
   record cards   94
   requirements   2
College training   48
Contracts of Employment Act, 1963   3
   1972   3
Communication   95
Consumable items   72
Consumption   74
   maximum   74
   minimum   74
   normal   74
Corporation tax   112
Cost accounting   129, 130
Costs, employment   100, 149, 153
   indirect material   148
   of addition to stock   169, 170, 171
   purchase   100
   sales   100, 171
   wages   99
Credit purchases   104
Credit sales   102
Current account   116
Current accounting   129, 130
Current assets   190

Data recording   64
Deduction, statutory   92
        voluntary   92
Defective goods   82
Depreciation   106, 107
Dispensary   26
Direct efficient supplement   167
        labour costs   131
        labour time   59
        operations   62, 133, 167
        service   167
        standard cost   162
        standard efficiency   162
Discount   140
        annual turnover   140
        cash   140
        quantity   74, 140
        trade   78, 140
Diversification   4
Drawings   189

Economic factor   141
Effective hours   69, 133
Effective labour rate   69
Efficiency rate   69, 162
Electricity   25
Employees' benefits   163, 168
        rights   2
Employer's contributions   163, 166
Employment budget   165
        costs   149, 153
        market   37
Employment Protection Act, 1975   3
Environment   28
Environmental controls   3
Equal Pay Act   2
Equipment   29, 71, 110
        electrical   30
Expansion   17
Expenditure, capital   22
        fixed costs   22
        initial   20
        revenue   22
        variable costs   23
Expense budget   154, 182
Expense items   71

F.I.F.O.   171
Finance   9
Finance Acts   87
Financial accounting   89, 93, 99
        budget   185
        examples   114–28
        records   91
First-aid   30–1
Fittings   13–15, 20, 25, 71, 110
Fixed assets   20, 21, 71
        costs   22
        overheads   131
Fixtures   13–15, 20, 25, 29, 71, 110

Franchise agreement   9, 10
Freehold   14–20

Gas   25
General staff training   50
Goodwill   11, 13–16
Gross payments   92

Hairdressing Undertakings Wages
        Council   2, 43, 132
Health and Safety at Work Act   2, 24, 30
Heating   28
Histyles   5, 20, 67, 90, 103, 105
H.M. Customs and Excise   4, 87, 132
Holidays   60
        annual   69
        statutory   69
Home hairdressing   8
Hospital salon   8
Hotel salon   7

Idle time   64, 91, 112
Income   147
Income tax   147
Income tax traders   5, 112
Increments, inflation   131
        merit   132
        time served   132
Indentures   15, 193–8
Indirect hairdressing tasks   62
        activities   167
        overhead labour time   163
Ineffective time   64
Initial expenditure   20
Inland Revenue deductions   4, 93, 99
        payments   93
Interest   9
Interview rating   40, 41
Interviews   37
Inventory, perpetual   86
        value   172, 180, 181
Issuing   4

Job description   36, 59
Journal   99

Labour budget   154, 162
        costs   130, 131
        mix of grades   132
Lease   13, 14
Leasehold   13, 14, 20
Ledger accounts   59
Lighting   28
Limited companies, private   12
        public   12
        partners   11
Living expenses   23
Loans   9
Local Authorities   3, 16
Locations, fixed   84
        random   84

Management, control data   63
   definition   1, 33
   objectives   1
   office   26
   staff relationships   41
Material cost, direct   139
   receipt   81
   requisition   73
   statement   170
Materials   71, 130, 139
   or purchase budget   154, 168, 179
Memorandum of Association   13
Method study   53–7
   element   56
Merit increments   132
Mobile salon   8
Mortgages   9

National Insurance   3, 4
   deductions   99, 100
National Joint Industrial Council for
   Hairdressing   2
Negligence   31
Net working capital   188, 191, 192
Nominal accounts   107
Normal consumption   74

Office records   96
   accessibility   96
   files   97
   storage   97
Offices Shops and Railway Premises Act,
   1963   24, 27, 28, 30
Off-standard variance   163, 168
Organisation and method study   53, 54
Outlooks   190
Overhead expenditure   4, 30, 146, 147,
   150, 167
   absorption rate   153
   apportionment   149
   classification   147
   fixed or variable   130
   general   148
Overtime   23
Overstaffing   35
Ownership   15

Paid hours   60, 68
Paid rest   69
Partnership   10, 11
   Act, 1890   10, 11
   Agreement   11
PAYE   4, 91, 92
   deductions   91, 99, 100
   payment to Inland Revenue   93, 101,
   102
Payroll preparation   91
Personal facilities   29
   files   97
   finance   9
   loans   9

Personnel management   33
   planning   34
Piece work   43
Planned hours   133
Premises, alterations to   16
Preparation of budgets   175
   wages   59
Private School Training   48
Profit and Loss account   99, 107–10, 113
   appropriation account   111
   salon stock   110
Prospective owner   9
Protective clothing   30, 72
Provisioning   4
Publicity   16
Purchase budget   154, 168, 179
   cash   100
   contract   77
   defective   82
   discrepancy   82
   non-receipt   82
   orders   77, 97
   receipt   81
   requisition   76
   retail stock   110
   salon stock   110
   variance unit   144
Purchased unit   140

Quantity discrepancy   82

Rate of interest   11
   pay   131
Rates   5
Record cards, clients'   94
Real accounts   106
Receipt value   157
Receipts   21, 101
Reception   25, 62, 93
Redress   2
Redundancy Payments Act, 1969   3
Registrar of Companies   13
Registration of Business Names Act   10
Registration of companies   11
Relationships, general   46
   staff   41, 45
   staff and clients   41, 45
Rent   109
Reorder level   74
   period   74
   quantity   74
Rest allowance   61, 133
Rest periods   62
Retail sales   160
Retailing   4
Revenue expenditure   22
Rights, employees'   2

Safety facilities   30

Sales, analysis   101
    budget   154, 155, 159, 161
    cards   97
    cash   100
    cost of   171
    receipts   97, 101
    retail   109
Salon siting, city   6
    country   7
    home   8
    hospital   8
    hotel   7
    mobile   8
    seaside   7
    store   7
Salon stock   181
Seaside salon   7
Secondary tasks   62
Service charge   146
Services   4, 153
Sex Discrimination Act, 1975   3
Shareholder   12
Sickness   60, 69
Social relationships   33
Sole traders   9, 10
Solicitors   14
Specialised functions   59
Staff advancement   44
    relationships   45
    remuneration   43
    selection   36, 37
    training   47–51, 62
    turnover   36–7
Staffing, economic   35
Staffroom   26
Standard, labour   141
    variance   135
    material   141
Standard costing system   173
    hourly rate   133
    time   63
    year   134
State pension   4
Stationery   110
Statutory requirements, deductions   92
    H.M. Customs and Excise   4
    holidays   69
    income tax   5
    laws   60
    National Insurance   4
    PAYE   4
    Rates   4
    regulations   12, 24
    State pension   4
    VAT   4
Stock, cost of additions   169, 171
    levels   75, 75
    record cards   74, 84–6, 97
    retail   62, 72, 73, 110
    salon   62, 72, 73, 109, 110, 181
    transfers   173

Stock-keeping   4, 83–6
Stockroom   26
Store salon   7, 9

Tasks   58
    abnormal   59
    indirect   62
    normal   59
    secondary   62
    stock   62, 63
Tax adjustment statement   113
    invoice   88
    returns   89
Testing   31, 32
Time payment   43
    -served increments   132
    variance   136
Tools   72
Trade Boards Act, 1909   2
Trade Description Act   2
Trade Council   67
Training Schemes   49, 51, 52
Trend graph   157
Trial balance   108
Turnover   4

Understaffing   35
Usage   4
Utilities   25

Valuation   14
Value Added Tax   4, 87, 101, 102, 104
    input   109
    output   109
    rates   88
    records   101
    registration   88
    returns   104
Variable costs   22
    overheads   131
Variance, labour   138
        utilisation   139
    off-standard   135, 145, 163, 168
    purchase price   144–5
        volume   145
    rate   136, 138, 139
    time   136, 138
Vendor   14
Ventilation   28

Wages book   93, 99
Water   25
Weighted average   172
Work analysis   66
    daily time sheet   65
    example   67
    interpretation   66
    measurement   53, 57
    payment   43
    piece   43
    study   53–70
    returns   68